*for Emily*

"The world breaks everyone, and afterward,
many are strong at the broken places."

— Ernest Hemingway

"We never know how high we are
Till we are called to rise
And then if we are true to plan
Our statures touch the skies."

— Emily Dickinson

# OUT CAME THE SUN

# OUT CAME THE SUN

One Family's Triumph Over
a Rare Genetic Syndrome

Judith Scott

Academy Chicago Publishers

Published in 2008 by
Academy Chicago Publishers
363 West Erie Street
Chicago, Illinois 60654

Printed and bound in the U.S.A.

**Library of Congress Cataloging-in-Publication Data**

Scott, Judith, 1967–
  Out came the sun : one family's triumph over a rare genetic syndrome /
by Judith Scott.
    p. cm.
  ISBN 978-0-89733-582-9 (pbk.)
  1. Scott, Emily Katharine—Health. 2. Trisomy—Patients—United
States—Biography. I. Title.
  RJ506.T75.S36 2008
  362.198'920042—dc22
  [B]
                          2008037440

# ACKNOWLEDGEMENTS

It took an amazing group of people to bring this experience to fruition as a book. I owe them all the deepest debt of gratitude. First, to Greg, my steadfast love who makes it all possible, every moment—man, husband and father utmost. To the Big F and the littles, my heart walks around outside my body with you every day. To Heather, my first reader, editor, and my "oldest" friend, for your never ending support and love. To Mom, who planted the seed years ago that I needed to write this all down when I was ready. Your constant encouragement will never be forgotten. And to Dad, who gave me the love of language and the confidence to accomplish anything. To my sister Rachel, who is the glorious poet of our childhood and my life-saving sounding board. To Bun and Bean, who have held my hand when I needed it most.

To the Millers at Academy Chicago, who read a love story about a little girl and took a chance, my thanks.

To Martie Hill, Rachel Roark Morey, Mindy Torres, Renee Castell, Julia DeMino, and Heather Dvoskin, teachers extraordinaire.

To Drs. Khurana, Bhasin, Cameron, Tuchman, Buck, Zuckerberg, Voigt and Gratz, all of whom held Emily's life in their hands.

To Sue and Soo, who share both a name and a strength of spirit and traverse the same road with me.

To Wendy, Kathy, Lauren C., Jill, and Chris—thank you for running, reading, laughing, and sharing life with me.

To Debbie Flynn, who said I could and should. And so I did.

But most of all to Emily, whose smile lightens up the day, whose perseverance makes me stand in awe, and whose joyful spirit teaches me all I ever need to know about love.

JS

# PROLOGUE: DIAGNOSIS

The geneticist takes off his glasses, rubs the bridge of his nose with two pinched fingers, repositions the glasses, clears his throat, and begins. "Your daughter has a very rare chromosomal syndrome called Partial Trisomy 13. She has numerous physical abnormalities and will have severe learning impairments. . . ."

After this I only hear phrases: mentally retarded, won't walk, won't talk, little quality of life. My head spins and my ears roar. I try to hold the tears back but they come anyway. There is no Kleenex in this office, so the assistant runs out to get a gritty paper towel from the bathroom. While my world is destroyed, this sandpaper wipes my face.

The geneticist drones on, "Only 50 documented cases, chromosomes are duplicated and inverted . . . extra genetic material in every cell. . . ."

He begins to talk about chromosomes and then passes a diagram around. I hear his words and I get the message loud and clear. Something is terribly wrong with my daughter. I have known it, on some level, since her birth, only now it has a name and I must face it. I look for anything positive, search the doctor's face for hope, but I see just professional reserve and scientific curiosity. I need to make sure there is no mistake.

"Are you telling me she will never read?" I say, because this seems to me the worst of all the limits he has listed.

"Absolutely not," he replies, so certain, so dispassionate. I crumple and need to leave. Somehow we are out in the hall, then in the hospital stairwell together, holding each other. I cry into Greg's coat, "What will we do?"

The floor tips and I cannot see or breathe.

# CHAPTER 1

Our marriage is in its 6th year before we talk about kids. Greg and I jump through all the right hoops first—the jobs, the cute starter home, the nice furniture—and now it is time for the next step. I never thought I wanted children, but after many years of teaching and watching friends with their children, I know something will be missing if we don't do this.

I stop taking the pill in April 1995 and begin counting the days of my cycle. By August, we are expecting. As each day passes, we grow more and more thrilled with the little life we have created. We tell everyone we know and start thinking of names. At a routine exam, however, my OB looks concerned. She sends me in for an ultrasound and there is no heartbeat. Four endless days elapse before I get in for a D&C, and I watch the blood trickle from my body for those days. I mourn a child who never had a chance. When I wake up from the sedative in the hospital, I think there is nothing sadder in the world than going into a hospital pregnant and leaving, empty.

We agree to wait three months before trying again. On February 14, 1996, I go to the local grocery store to buy a pregnancy test. The clerk in the pharmacy touches her own rounded belly and says, "Good luck to you!" It is then that I know how much I want this baby. When Greg gets home from work, I try to keep my face impassive, but he knows I took the test and his first words are,

"Well?" We hug and kiss and tell each other that this time it will be all right. This time we will not tell anyone until we are sure. This time we will not be let down.

At ten weeks, we have the ultrasound and this time the heartbeat flickers away, strong as can be. Greg is at the foot of the examination table and he squeezes my toes, so I know he is relieved as well. Now I go public, telling my coworkers at school, putting the due date on the calendar, planning the next few months. We buy yellow paint for the baby's room, repaint the crib, and buy toys. I become a devotee of the *What to Expect* books and line up all the must-haves for baby care. I glory in my pregnant body, for once in my life not caring about what I eat or how much I exercise. We test out names and decide on Emily for a girl and Evan for a boy.

At sixteen weeks, my doctor offers the AFP blood test to check for fetal abnormalities, but I sign a piece of paper, declining. I am only twenty-eight years old, and the idea of the baby having any problems is preposterous. At twenty-two weeks, I finally feel the baby move and that's late, but I am a first time mom and am not inclined to worry. Other women say, isn't it amazing when the baby kicks so hard and rolls and does little flips? I say yes, but really my baby is only nudging me. This little child doesn't keep me up at night with his or her antics, and for this I feel grateful.

I lounge through the summer days, taking naps when I feel fatigued, going on long walks with my mom. My family's reunion is in Kiawah, South Carolina, so Greg and I drive down for a week of sun. The ride is uncomfortable, and I shift around all day, trying to find a position where the weight of the baby doesn't bother my hips. Kiawah is brutal—hot like an oven blast, even at six in the morning. But I am a trooper, brave enough to put on a maternity bathing suit to join my sisters as they read on the beach.

Greg and I ride bikes down the long stretch of sand to look for dolphins, sometimes visible from isolated spots. The market in town is called the Piggly Wiggly, and we amuse ourselves by taking pictures of me clasping my growing belly in a Piggly Wiggly T-shirt. This vacation is all lightness—marathon tennis matches, naps in the afternoon, seaside meals, and movies at night. Our respite in the sun feels like suspended animation—a magic spell of salt air and seashells that inevitably must come to an end. I do not know it now, but this is the last gasp of carefree life I will have for a long while.

Back at home, Greg's brother is ill, dying in fact, so Greg heads up to New York on the train. Brian is in the AIDS wing of the hospital and tuberculosis is rampant, so I am safest at home. We speak on the phone every night, and there's less of Brian every time. When he dies, it's expected, but a shock all the same. The funeral is in Indiana, so we're back on the road, this time heading to the Midwest. My belly is burgeoning in the church pew, and I hold the hard mound protectively. The air is suffused with the strains of "Ave Maria," and I think it is the most breathtaking music I have ever heard. Greg cries for Brian and rubs my belly. This baby coming takes a bit of sharpness out of the pain.

I return to teach for six weeks in the fall, and everyone says how well I look. My high school students are amazed when I say that the due date is so close. They seem to fear that the delivery will take place in the classroom. I get a bad cold and begin my maternity leave three days early so I can recover before the baby is born. On my due date, I see my O.B., who says my cervix is completely closed and I will be induced in ten days if nothing happens. I am frustrated, but resolved to be patient. The library is nearby, so I load up on books and videos to watch while I wait for the birth.

That afternoon, my mom comes over and we walk for ninety minutes. After I get home, my water breaks with a gush in the bathroom. I try to lie down on the couch and hold my belly. Greg is on his way home and I can hardly wait. The pain has not hit yet and I can't stop pacing, checking my hospital bag, making a small dinner for Greg. I know life is about to change and I am ready, but nervous all the same.

At the hospital, my contractions begin with a vengeance, made worse because the baby's spine is pressing on mine. I have heard of back labor before, but had no idea it would be this bad. Greg tries to stick to our game plan of no medications, but I scream at him to find the doctor and get me some relief.

After the epidural, I can finally sleep. Greg watches the monitors all night, and my mom sleeps in an exam room. At 6:30 in the morning, it is time to push. This baby has a big head and I am numb from the epidural, so it's a real struggle to make progress. After three hours of pushing, our little girl, Emily Katharine, emerges into the world. Her cheeky face is bruised from my pelvic bones and she's all covered with vernix, but she looks perfect to me.

# CHAPTER 2

"We have a baby problem," is how she puts it, the lactation consultant who has been called to help little Emily latch on. The baby is hungry, and I am frustrated with our attempts to master breast-feeding. I hear her comment and feel hurt, slighted that someone finds fault with my baby. I think the lactation consultant is pushy and aggressive with me, molding and mashing my breasts, but I keep quiet because I need to figure this out.

When the consultant looks at Emily's mouth, she is the one who solves the problem. Emily has a very high palate, she says, and her tongue is tied, making it impossible to grasp the breast tissue. She shows me that in Emily's mouth, a small band of tissue cements her tongue to the floor of her mouth. Her tongue is literally "tied" into her mouth. Breast-feeding may still be possible, I am told, but it will be a real challenge. I feel a first twinge of disappointment, but consider this a minor hitch. I will keep trying and make this work.

When I was eight months pregnant, I interviewed pediatricians, visited their offices, wanting to get the right fit for our baby. I settled on Dr. Khurana, a slightly built Indian woman who has a practice with her sister. Selecting the person who will figure so prominently in our child's life is a stab in the dark, and I am hoping for the best. The pediatrician is the first doctor to evaluate a newborn, and we are anxious to see what she has to say about Emily.

Dr. Khurana comes in to my hospital room mid-morning to tell us she has given Emily her first exam. She is concerned about a slight heart murmur she hears. She wants us to get it checked out as soon as we leave the hospital, and she refers us to a cardiology team at the University of Maryland. We are not alarmed because the doctor seems matter-of-fact, but this is not the homecoming we envisioned.

Greg and I leave the county hospital on Monday morning and drive up to Baltimore. We have the first appointment of the day. I am sore from the delivery and anxious because the nursing is still not going well. I worry that my baby will starve. I refuse to focus on our two-day-old baby who already has a cardiologist.

An intern sees us before the doctor comes in and takes a listen to Emily's chest with his stethoscope. He pronounces the murmur nothing to worry about, at the most a tiny hole in the wall of her heart that will close on its own in time. Then the doctor comes in to do an echocardiogram, an ultrasound of the heart, running the transducer over Emily's tiny chest as she screams in indignation. We know something is wrong when they stop, start again, and whisper. They are taking too long for a regular heart, and we are afraid.

Emily wails with hunger, and I attempt to nurse her while the doctor delivers the news. She has Tetralogy of Fallot, a rare heart condition where her pulmonary valve is constricted and a large hole exists between two chambers of the heart wall. She may have "tet spells" where she turns blue because her heart is not getting enough oxygen. She will need surgery when she's about 7 months old. Greg and I are stunned—we simply reel with all this information.

The doctor draws us a picture of Emily's heart because we seem so confused. I clasp the drawing all the way home, hoping I will somehow understand. I keep saying, "I wanted her to be perfect!" and Greg tells me that we are lucky to have such wonderful doctors who can fix her heart. I know that's true, but I also know this is not what I signed up for. I feel sad and deflated.

Emily cries all the way home, gnawing on my finger as I try in vain to calm her. We arrive home and show the drawing to Greg's parents. I hold the diagram in front of me like a shield, then I present their granddaughter. I sit in a chair with bags of frozen peas pressed to my chest, trying to ease the painful engorgement. I overflow with milk that Emily cannot get to, and I hold a picture of her broken heart.

# CHAPTER 3

Life at home with baby Emily is miserable. Try as I might, I cannot make this baby happy. The crying is constant, and the nursing is still not going well. We are up at all hours, feeding, bouncing, rocking. Breast milk from a bottle seems better than formula, makes me feel as if I am doing something to help, so I rent a hospital-grade breast pump. Every three hours I use a double pump on my breasts, which grow sore and bloody. Storage bags in the freezer fill with all my milk, thick cream on the top. Greg defrosts the milk, heats it in the bottles, while I pump a fresh supply. Emily seems ravenous, then instantly uncomfortable after she eats. She is hard to burp and spits up a lot. We grow tired and snappish with each other, not talking much, just trying to manage.

Dr. Khurana says Emily may have jaundice and takes blood from her heel to test. Before the results are back, we figure out she has jaundice all on our own. The orange color of her skin blooms seemingly overnight. So she is back in the hospital, under the "bili" lights, wearing protective sunglasses. I try to find humor in this naked baby under a sun lamp, wearing shades, but it is just not funny.

I sit in the rocking chair next to the sunlamp, using the breast pump, feeling like a failure. Nothing has gone right. I think of the plush blue terrycloth robe I ordered from Land's End last month and the visions I had of wearing the robe, cooing to my baby, lounging in the first few glowing days of motherhood. The robe and the dreams of our baby mock me now.

Emily comes home after three days and we begin again. In mid-October the days get markedly shorter. Greg leaves for work in the dark, and when I hear the latch click on the door, I cringe. How will I make it for twelve hours with a baby who cries nonstop? I call the pediatrician every day and she says, probably colic, try changing your diet. So I eliminate all dairy, chocolate, spicy foods, vegetables, until I eat very little at all.

Still, Emily arches her back after feedings, struggles to release all the trapped gas in her body, and spits up large puddles on my shoulders. I find myself boiling all her bottles daily, just in case bacteria might be lurking. I am desperate to help Emily. She is not comfortable anywhere and only naps for brief periods after hours of crying. A pacifier seems to help, and she sucks on it with wild abandon. It muffles her cries and soothes her distress a bit. Some days, I hold the pacifier in her mouth for hours.

Once in a while, I take Emily over to my mom's and come home to my bed, burrow under the covers, and emerge after four hours from a dreamless sleep, feeling drugged. We call the pediatrician two times a day. Surely there is something we can do. She suggests a series of expensive formulas instead of breast milk. Maybe these will be easier to digest. We are galvanized by the thought of anything easing Emily's discomfort. We buy soy formulas, one brand after another, so costly that it is like liquid gold, but there is no change except for thicker spit-up. We decide that Emily is just a fussy baby and the colic will disappear after three months, like all the books say. We hunker down and wait for January, when the crying will surely stop and we can enjoy this child.

Somehow, I manage to get up to Baltimore again, this time on my own, for a second cardiology appointment. I wonder at how routine it suddenly seems to view my infant's leaky heart on the monitor. While I am here, the staff sends a geneticist up to the cardiac floor. This new doctor explains that sometimes a child's heart condition is a random occurrence and sometimes the anomaly is part of a larger syndrome. I cannot process what this means, but I let the geneticist examine Emily anyway. He pays special attention to her ears, her fingers, her toes, and intimately scrutinizes her face and her skull. Emily fusses while the doctor takes copious notes, scritch-scratching on a small tablet. I am so tired that I don't ask any questions, just hand her over and watch silently. Lastly, the doctor takes blood for genetic testing and I am suddenly afraid.

At home, we begin to notice Emily's eyes. That first smile doesn't come at five weeks or at eight weeks, and in fact she will not look at us at all. Emily stares out the window when she is not crying or sleeping a tortured sleep. She favors her left side, turning that way to avoid our anxious smiles. She doesn't stare at us or other people, doesn't chortle or babble or coo. I feel that pit of fear again, but try to write it off. After all, we are first-time parents and what do we know? Besides, I am not reading the *What to Expect* chapters right now, I am just trying to get through the days until this colic ends.

I call Mom to say I have tried everything and I just cannot make her be quiet. Mom says put her somewhere safe, go sit in the bathroom, turn on the fan, and try to have a minute of peace. She hears how frazzled I am and knows I need permission to give myself this break. I come out of the bathroom, tears crusted on my cheeks, to find Emily in her swing, asleep. Her eyes have dark circles under them, her face is mottled from her screaming, and she is as far from cherubic as can be. Our little girl is two months old.

It turns out that, during the birth, all that pushing took a toll on Emily's neck. The pediatrician says there must be a pulled muscle. This explains why she cranes over to the left. So now every evening, Greg turns her head slowly to the right as we count twenty repetitions. We look at each other in disbelief—it is a cruel irony that our days are filled with calming maneuvers, anything to get the crying to stop, yet at night we torture Emily, ratcheting her outbursts to a new level.

We decide to drive out to the Midwest over the holidays to see both of our families. Emily sleeps for the entire ten-hour journey. The motion of the car and the tight fit of the car seat seems to calm her, and we are grateful for the respite. Greg's parents are overjoyed to see us and we put on a happy face, but we have been through the mill and it shows. We don't talk about the heart surgery, scheduled for May, or about the fact that Emily doesn't look at us or smile. Everyone is just content to hold her. Anyone who can soothe her spends the day carting her around, smiling in victory. They seem to say, see? This baby isn't so bad. If you hold her just so, she's fine.

But they don't know what it's like all day and night, every day and night, and our resentment simmers below the surface. We feel cheated out of the newborn experience by this shrieking bundle. My milk has dried up, I cannot even pump a drop out, so Emily gets bottles and formula all the time. Watching other people feed my baby hurts and I am inadequate all over again.

Christmas morning, 1996, dawns bleak and silent. For the first time, Emily sleeps through the night. We race into her room, overcome with fear, but there she is. This is the best gift of all, and we are shell-shocked after getting up every three hours for the last ten weeks. Her long slumber feels like turning a corner.

At my folks' house, this first grandchild receives a boisterous welcome. My brothers and sisters take turns, grappling with Emily's flailing limbs, proclaiming her cute and sweet. Pictures show a bald little girl, staring off into the distance. The pit of fear is still there, but now the nights are better and I push the fear aside. We travel home to finish the holidays as our little family of three, glad to have almost made it through these early months.

On New Year's Eve, something from Emily's room wakes us. She is screaming, but it is more than that. Emily's bedroom wall is splattered with reddish-black curds, and these curds are in Emily's bed, in her hair, in her diaper. We think she has spit up, but how did it get across the room? We call the pediatrician who is on call, not the one who usually sees Emily, and she is clearly at a New Year's gathering. Bring her in first thing in the morning, she counsels. Her prediction is a tummy bug, so we try not to worry.

Dr. Khurana is in the office waiting for us at 9 a.m. We report what has happened and show her the diaper, which looks like a coffee filter stained with grounds. Something is very wrong and we all know it. The doctor makes some calls and we are on the road to Sinai Hospital up in Baltimore. A renowned pediatric gastroenterologist practices there whom we like right away. Dr. Tuchman takes Emily's history while we bounce her and worry. He asks about feedings, bowel movements, and spit-up, yet he remains perplexed. He orders several tests.

Emily requires an endoscopy, a tube investigating her stomach, then a colonoscopy, to check out her lower intestines and rectum. She must be sedated for these tests, and so we meet an anesthesiologist who will soon count as a friend. Dr. Zuckerberg is a bear of a man with a yarmulke haphazardly perched on his head. His gentle words and confident manner make us feel this is not a crisis, but a mystery that will soon be solved. We are indebted to him for putting Emily into the most peaceful sleep of her short life.

During another test, an abdominal ultrasound, the tech performing the exam blurts, "Do we know she has hydro?" I turn to my mom, who is a sonographer herself, and she translates: "hydro" is short for hydronephrosis, a backup of urine in the kidney caused by a blockage or narrowing of the ureter. On the ultrasound screen, this "hydro" looks like a small hose with a kink in it. "Hydro" is something else wrong with our daughter, something we weren't even looking for, another abnormality. But this is not what we are here for, so we push this complication aside to deal with later. No one acts like it is an emergency, so as far as we're concerned, the "hydro" can wait.

The lab takes time to tally all the results of the tests, but in the meantime a pediatric surgeon stops in, pushes on Emily's belly, and then has us take a feel. A hard little pea sits in her lower belly, an olive pit of a structure. He explains that Emily has pyloric stenosis, a crimping in the lower muscular part of the stomach that prevents digested food from leaving the stomach and traveling through the intestine. Only a hairs-breath of space remains for the food to pass, so the food backs up into her stomach, stews in the digestive juices, foams, and boils, until it is ejected in a bout of projectile vomiting. Emily is distended and gassy because all the formula stays in one place instead of passing down. The liquid literally burns a hole in her stomach. Those curds on her bedroom wall and in her diaper were the blood-tinged remains of formula combined with her stomach lining, which her digestive acids shear off like paint thinner.

So she's been telling us with all the screaming and the arching and the spitting up that something is wrong with her belly. We feel remiss for waiting this long to get serious, for not insisting that she has more than colic. The surgeon remains a bit puzzled—he explains that pyloric stenosis usually "presents" differently—it is primarily seen in boys and in much younger babies. Emily will have corrective surgery in the morning.

# CHAPTER 4

A holiday air clings to the pediatric wing of the hospital—sparkling lights and tabletop Christmas trees and ornaments. The nurses decorate to make the atmosphere less frightening for the parents and the children, but they cannot mask the smells of adhesive and alcohol and fear. We prepare for our infant daughter's surgery on the second day of the new year.

Emily is taken in for surgery at eight in the morning, groggy from an anesthesia "cocktail." We are strangely relieved to see her wheeled down the hall, sure that she will return a changed baby once the stomach anomaly is fixed. Dr. Zuckerberg says he will treat her as his own in the operating room, and that is just what we need to hear. She is in good hands, and all we can do is wait.

She emerges two hours later, and I am not prepared for all the tubes and wires and gauze. An IV line presses into a vein on the top of her hand, held in place with a rigid contraption of boards and surgical tape. Wire "leads" snake across her chest to track her heart rhythms and tubes are taped to her sides. Babies like to fiddle with their lines, and the pediatric staff knows just how to thwart them. Emily's face is slack, and her legs are splayed open. The hospital gown rides up, revealing her incision, right above the waistband of her diaper. Holding her is impossible right now, so we settle for squeezing her fingers and nuzzling her cheeks. The anesthesiologist tells us that Emily was harder to intubate than he had expected. He has discovered she has "tracheomalasia," or a floppy windpipe. This oddity requires a sleight of hand to insert a breathing tube. He adds that it is a strange anomaly, one that we'll need to alert future doctors about.

The surgeon comes to consult with us and says everything went well. He and the anesthesiologist seem to be old friends and are jocular with each other. Dr. Zuckerberg says that while they were "in there," they snipped Emily's tongue, in effect fixing her tied tongue. Now she will be able to lick an ice cream cone, he says.

I am momentarily shocked that something else was done to Emily, without our knowledge or consent, but very quickly I am thankful. One more procedure is out of the way, one more thing made right. I am trying to stay in the here and now, to forget about the "hydro" in her kidney that we must pursue or about the heart surgery looming. For this moment, we are happy that the stomach issue is resolved. I look forward to giving her the first post-surgical bottle, both to see how her new tongue operates and to see how her stomach tolerates food that doesn't fester and give her pain. The nursing staff encourages us to go home for the night. My mom agrees to come by in the early morning hours, so Greg and I head home for our first night alone together since before Emily was born.

That night we get the call from the geneticist's office. His assistant needs to see us to discuss the results of Emily's blood test from a couple of weeks back. I can tell the call is serious because Greg's shoulders hunch up and his voice is grave. The assistant will not tell us the nature of the things they need to discuss, but Greg presses on for a few details. Emily is currently in the hospital, we are already stressed beyond belief, please don't keep us hanging. Tonight is Friday and we just can't wait until Monday for this meeting.

The assistant relents, and I hear Greg repeating "extra genetic material" and "13th chromosome," words that remind me of a science textbook and cannot have anything to do with my daughter. Greg hangs up and tells me what he little he knows, that Emily's

13th chromosome has extra material on it, affecting every cell of her body. The assistant has told him it's like Down Syndrome, only much more rare and serious.

I run into Emily's room, not even aware of my legs moving, but suddenly they give way under me and I am clutching the bars of her crib, screaming, "NO NO NO NO!!!!!" I am angrier than I have ever been in my life. The empty crib is just an added insult. This little baby of ours cannot be fixed by surgery after all. What she has is permanent and very, very bad. We have been fooling ourselves that everything will get better when, in fact, it won't. For almost three months, we have been ignoring all the signs that something serious is wrong, and now we can't ignore it anymore.

I am pounding anything in Emily's room I can get my hands on, the changing table, the dresser, the nursing chair. Greg comes in and restrains me, holds me tight. He is frightened by my rage, but it must be all he can do to contain his own. He tells me Emily is the same little girl we had this morning, yesterday, last month. Nothing about her has changed. That is true, I know, but I feel a hardening in my core and a deep knowledge that, no matter what we say, our lives will be different from this moment onward.

We spend the weekend at the hospital, waiting as Emily is moved from the PICU to the regular floor. She is pretty difficult now that the anesthesia has worn off. She doesn't like being in the crib all day, doesn't like all the tape on her body, and will not calm down enough to sleep. At one point, we come back from lunch to find a pacifier actually affixed to her mouth with surgical tape. One of the nurses gives her the most thorough bath of her life, and I envy her expertise and confidence.

As we get final discharge instructions, Dr. Zuckerberg stops by for a quick visit. We tell him we are on our way to another hospital to see the geneticist. Greg informs Dr. Zuckerberg of Emily's diagnosis, what little we know. The doctor startles us by saying he thought he noticed a little something, that the "architecture of her chest is a little different." His manner is cavalier, almost casual. Perhaps he sees abnormalities all the time and has grown immune. I feel the fool again for not acknowledging to myself what everyone else seems to have noticed already—that Emily has a myriad of problems which transcend the physical. Whatever the definition of "normal" is, it will not be part of our lexicon for our daughter.

My mom and sister, Maureen, who is nineteen, stay home with Emily while we head off to the other hospital for our meeting with the geneticist. We have been here for cardiology and find ourselves old pros at navigating the labyrinth of sterile hallways. The geneticist must know he is destroying us with the diagnosis, but he remains stoic and remote throughout the meeting. He is impressed that Emily has made it even this far and is curious about her overall prognosis. Her syndrome is so rare that he has few predictions. Those he offers are grim.

Every cell in Emily's body contains extra genetic material, a mistake that occurred at the moment of conception. Her physical problems are only part of the story. She will be disabled across the board—developmentally, cognitively, neurologically, psychologically. Testing a three-month-old baby is nearly impossible, the geneticist says, but the microscope under which he examined Emily's chromosomes presents the basic idea. She will not walk or talk or read. He encourages us to get our own blood tested to see whether either of us is a carrier of a chromosomal translocation that might have led to Emily's condition. But we cannot wrap our minds around that step right now.

Our meeting ends, and as we stumble for the door, the geneticist tries to soften the blow. Just like any child, he says, Emily will give you joy as well as heartbreak. So far, all we know is the heartbreak part, and now we cling to each other to keep from falling apart.

Mom and Maureen are bouncing Emily in the family room. They have been for a walk, and Emily seems calmer than usual, almost asleep. I look down at my daughter, drowsy in my mother's arms, and cannot bring myself to touch her as I speak. "She's going to be retarded," I say. I have never uttered this ugly word out loud before, and it hurts more than anything. I feel bottomless grief for this tiny little girl, coupled with pity for myself and then anger, rising, swelling anger, at the unfairness of a world where something like this can happen to my little family.

I get a letter from Maureen the next day, festooned with stickers, magic marker stars, and hearts. In it she says, "Your lives will be different than you had ever imagined. But, different is NOT worse, just different. You and Emily will find joy in unexpected ways and you will be happy again, I promise. . . . I have all the confidence you will be a wonderful mother to Emily."

These words swim through my dripping eyes. I am touched and moved, yet doubtful. I cannot share Maureen's hope or confidence, I am that destroyed. My reservoir of strength is gone, and I am just crushed.

# CHAPTER 5

The next day, Emily's pediatrician calls to check on Emily's progress after the surgery. It is up to me to give her the diagnosis from the geneticist. Dr. Khurana does not seem shocked, but does pause and relates a personal story to me about her own second pregnancy. She had amniocentesis since she was older than thirty-five at the time, and the wait for the results, about two weeks, made her wonder what she would do if the results were abnormal. Her baby was fine, but she feels compelled to tell me that she can in some way sympathize with us.

I try to understand that this doctor is attempting to comfort us, but all I can do is feel insulted that anyone imagines they have any clue how we feel. We don't even fully grasp what we are dealing with. From now on, our lives are divided into two parts, Before We Knew and After We Knew. We are woefully unprepared to be the parents of this child who needs so much.

Luckily, we will not have to do it alone. Seemingly, out of the woodwork, a phalanx of experts arrives at our doorstep to help. Once a child has an official disability diagnosis in the state of Maryland, she is eligible for a host of services, most of them free and easy to receive. This is something of which I was not aware until now, even as an educator myself. We obtain Early Intervention Services for Emily without even making a phone call. The idea is that children can make the most progress and reach their best potential if their work begins early.

A team of professionals arrive at the house on a bleak day in mid-January to do an initial evaluation so they can set up a plan for Emily's services. Emily has been fussing off and on all morning and can't get comfortable. I shower quickly and try to put on a brave front, but it is clear that I am sleep-deprived and stressed. A bevy of smartly dressed women arrive the door, here to help my daughter, and I cannot seem to put together a coherent sentence.

The case manager, a curvy young woman named Theresa, does the "intake interview" while the other women put Emily on the floor to see what she can do. I do my best to provide information about my pregnancy, the birth, and the subsequent physical problems that emerged. Teresa has never heard of Partial Trisomy 13, so I try to explain. The syndrome is not cerebral palsy, although it does share some components of that disability. Emily's condition is not autism either, although we will certainly see some autistic traits in the future. Neither is it Down Syndrome, so no tell-tale features appear on Emily's face.

Teresa seems perplexed that this diagnosis doesn't fit nicely into any of the boxes provided by the state forms. She opts for "Other Health Impaired" and explains that being in this category means Emily is entitled to special education services from infancy until she is twenty-one years old. I gulp to hear the words "special education," then check myself. I have vowed to be more realistic, and I am already falling down on the job. For some reason, all the bad news about Emily is taking an awfully long time to sink in.

On the floor, the physical therapist and the occupational therapist are "working" with Emily, but they're not getting much done. They have a checklist of what a typical three-and-a-half-month-old baby should be able to do. Emily can't calm down long enough for these specialists to go down the list. They try to see if she will roll from side to side, prop her head up in the tummy position, and track a moving object with her eyes. Emily shuts down and averts her gaze, and her whimpers of protest turn to wails. I explain about the feeding issues, the gassiness, how she gets easily overwhelmed and over-stimulated. The looks on their faces say they don't know how to proceed. They decide to scrap the checklist and try to teach me some calming techniques.

The occupational therapist, a quiet Indian woman named Jayshree, shows me how to rock Emily vigorously, then how to swaddle her tightly. This maneuver does seem to help, and the crying subsides a bit. The minute I stop swaying side to side, the shrieking intensifies. I learn that Emily is a vestibular baby, meaning the rocking motions organize her sensory system so she can calm down and process the world better. The physical therapist, a friendly woman named Barbara, pulls out the infant swing we use sporadically and suggests we put it into use every day as a way to stabilize Emily's system.

We try to get Emily back onto the floor, but she won't have it. She does a log roll from side to side, which is not a voluntary movement, merely a reaction to being on her back. She is clearly tired, so I put her in the swing and she immediately falls asleep. The only sound is the scratching of pens as everyone takes notes on the session. My initiation into the world of therapies and intervention for my child is overwhelming. The services Emily seems to need and the number of specialists who are ready to help us boggles my mind. The therapists are preparing a file on Emily that will include her diagnosis and medical history, her current skills, her emerging skills, and future goals. Their job is to make a plan for Emily's growth and potential, and it is my job to learn from them. I know very little about early childhood development in the first place and even less about the hurdles a child with special needs must overcome. I feel hopelessly naive and inadequate, but I pretend to take all this in stride. Paperwork awaits my signature and I have appointments to arrange for the next few weeks. It is January, Emily is three months old, and already she has a team whose purpose is to help her learn what most newborns learn on their own.

Life settles into a routine of sorts. I decide to establish a schedule for myself and for Emily—something to make me feel more

in control. Two naps will take place each day with feedings sand-
wiched in between, then time for short walks, errands, or therapies. I put Emily down for her naps at exactly the same time every
day and listen to her struggle to fall asleep. Some days she cries for
the whole naptime and other days she sleeps. The crying is tough
to hear, but I soldier on, convinced she will learn, and within two
weeks, she is like clockwork. She starts to sleep through the night
on a regular basis and even dozes in her swing while Greg and I
eat supper at night. She seems to be making up for the months of
never sleeping at all.

When awake, she still fusses and pulls her legs up. She won't
really attend to any activity or reach for toys yet, but we try. I surround her with rattles and colorful chewy toys, but after one glance,
she looks away. The new schedule and more sleep make it easier to
cope when Emily is awake, but I am disappointed when she still
won't look at me or interact at all. That bonding feeling I expected
to have with my child has not happened yet, and I feel guilty for
that. We are managing, but we don't feel much like a family.

The case manager, Theresa, comes back alone to review Emily's paperwork. The forms look intimidating, but they are actually
simple. A page is devoted to each of Emily's therapists, accompanied by a list of milestones she needs to work toward. These milestones are as simple as rolling from front to back, but I know that
each one represents a huge struggle for Emily. She is already so far
behind other infants her age. Theresa asks me what I think Emily's strengths are, and all I can think of is "sweet," which doesn't
even feel true. When Theresa asks what I would like to see Emily
achieve, I try to say, "I'd like for her to establish eye contact," but
I cannot even make it through the sentence before I am crying,
just weeping at my kitchen table with this stranger. My daughter
doesn't look at me, her own mother, and I am sad and strangely
ashamed.

Theresa looks at me with sympathy and quietly explains that
kids with disabilities and cognitive impairments have a great deal
of trouble focusing on the human face because of its complexity.

A face is too difficult to process, consisting of such discrete parts and a variety of expressions. She continues to explain that Emily appears to be overly stimulated by most things right now, including noises, lights, and people. It is just too hard for her to look at people. Turning away and staring out the window is her way of shutting down. We have to slowly get her attention without overwhelming her delicate sensory system. She needs to become part of our world, instead of tuning it out.

Despite my feeling of urgency to "check off" items on Emily's milestone agenda, I am faced with reality early on: This won't be easy. My child struggles mightily now and will continue to struggle with the smallest things. In order to learn the simplest tasks, it takes many repetitions. On most days when she actually does achieve something from The List, as I now think of it, she forgets it by the next day and has to be re-taught. Her struggle to do things that other infants learn on their own is frustrating to watch.

But I learn with Emily and feel empowered with the immense responsibility of helping this child. I receive a crash course in early childhood education, physical therapy, occupational therapy, and speech therapy, all rolled into one. We work on self-calming for weeks. Unless Emily can settle down and stop fussing, we will not be able to reach her. I spend hours each day rubbing her belly to work the gas down. Greg does what we dub the "Daddy dance" to get out difficult burps.

Even when physically comfortable, Emily is so overly stimulated that she whines and writhes. We design a repertoire of songs to sing while we bounce her around the house. She does best in semidarkness, so we keep the lights low. Even trips to the grocery store are too much right now, so we stay at home and sing to this little girl in the dark. Her infant swing works wonders, and we crank it up several times a day. Some days feel successful, like we are handling this well, and other days we're just managing until the next nap, when we can get a break.

One day, I go to Emily's crib to pick her up and discover her sucking on the first two fingers of her right hand. I call the occupational therapist and report with glee that Emily has figured out a way to calm herself. We find a soft pink blanket, name it "Teeny," and give it to Emily. Now she sucks her fingers and holds her Teeny, and this allows her to gaze around the room and, yes, even at me without looking away. Maybe she has finally decided to join us after all.

# CHAPTER 6

February opens bitterly cold. Emily is four months old, and Greg and I are automatons, moving through each day, but not really existing. Pictures show me holding Emily against my chest and I look so tired. Winter is merely a countdown until the major cardiac surgery in the spring. The heart surgery is a dreaded event, but also one that will fix at least one of the things wrong with our daughter. We are eager to put it behind us.

Despite the stomach surgery, Emily is still uncomfortable after every feeding. She arches, winces, and screams. She copes a bit better if we can get her to burp, but not by much. She seems more than just gassy, she seems in pain, so we go back to the pediatrician, who wastes no time. We return to the hospital where the stomach surgery was performed and see the gastroenterologist, Dr. Tuchman. He performs a repeat endoscopy and a colonoscopy, inserting a tube down Emily's throat and one into her rectum that takes tissue samples. They explain to us that it is common for children with special needs to have digestive issues; the doctors just need to determine what is going on.

We are powerless as we watch Emily, yet again immobile on a tiny pediatric bed, being prodded and monitored. The verdict comes back swiftly—our old friend the anesthesiologist delivers the news: Emily has reflux and "rip-roaring esophagitis." Basically, her esophageal sphincter, which should remain closed after a meal, is underdeveloped. The sphincter flaps up and down like a flag in the wind, washing stomach acids back into her esophagus and throat. Emily's esophagus is decorated with ulcerated sores. Once down in her stomach, the formula she eats does fine, but when sloshing back up, it rips holes in her throat. Eating simply hurts Emily.

High doses of reflux medications are prescribed, along with basic antacids, so now part of the routine becomes administering syringes of medicine before and after the feedings. We are learning what some of the limited literature already told us—kids with chromosomal syndromes usually have "midline" issues; their physical impairments occur down the center of the body in a bisecting line. Emily has a long list already: the tied tongue, her heart, kidneys, stomach, and now the esophagus. For a little girl with such a short life, it is far too many things.

Greg's parents surprise us with a check for $500 and orders to get away for the weekend. They will take care of Emily while we regroup. They tell Greg privately that they are worried about what will happen to us, to our marriage, if we don't get a break. So we book two nights at the Bethesda Embassy Suites and head away from home.

Greg is so nervous about being separated from Emily that he is sick to his stomach the entire trip to the hotel. We settle into our luxurious suite and by unspoken pact do not talk about our daughter or what has happened to our life. Dinner that night is at the Cheesecake Factory, more food than we can possibly eat, but we try anyway. It has been so long since we sat for this long at a table and didn't have to do the dishes afterward. We see "Jerry Maguire" and go window shopping. The suite has a big marble tub and I sit in it for a half hour, shaving my legs for the first time in a week. We sleep until ten in the morning, and I read a Cosmopolitan magazine cover to cover, rubbing the perfume inserts on my wrists. For a while I actually forget that I am a mom and I feel like a wife again, a woman who can laugh and enjoy herself.

When we return home, Greg's folks appear to have lost five pounds each. It's hard to bounce Emily around the house all day, singing and chanting. But they are overjoyed to have spent so much time with her and are full of praise for all her little expressions and her cute face. It occurs to me that instead of focusing on all the things Emily can't do, or may never do, I should relish those things she does accomplish. I resolve to be more positive and use all my energy toward making Emily the best she can be. I have been wallowing in self-pity and enough is enough. It feels good to have been alone with Greg. I privately promise to reach out to him more, instead of being so quiet within myself.

Emily's therapies take off full force. She is a client of the Early Intervention Team now, and they have a regular schedule for seeing her, as well as meetings to discuss her progress. For now, all the therapies will be "home visits," and for this I am grateful. I find it too hard to get Emily out the door and into a different environment. She copes better at home and seems to relax better as well. It means the therapists have to transport huge bags and tubs of toys and developmental devices with them, but they don't seem to mind.

Now that Emily is a bit calmer, we ratchet up the physical therapy. There are so many things she should be learning right now, but none of it comes naturally. Greg and I think Emily is so strong because she can stand on our laps and her body seems so tight. Barbara informs us that this tightness is actually rigidity, a "high tone," that is working against her. Babies need a certain amount of flexibility and floppiness to get mobile, and Emily has none. She is as stiff as a board, like a soldier always at attention. We learn that it is common for children with disabilities to have low tone (excessive floppiness), or high tone, like Emily.

Relaxing Emily's body becomes a high priority. Although she can hold her head upright with no trouble, looking around the room is difficult because her neck, like the rest of her, is rigid. Greg and I continue the horrid neck twists every night and eventually notice a change. She sometimes turns her head to peer around the room instead of just following things with her eyes. Her arms and legs are rigid as well, and we begin an exercise routine to loosen her up. It reminds me of footage I have seen of paralysis victims, where the caregiver massages and bicycles the legs and arms to maintain mobility. We do these same sorts of motions for Emily. Her knees and elbows are always locked, so we push and pull and even tickle her to get the joints to relax.

Greg is a master at setting words to music, so he makes up silly songs to accompany our routine. It amuses us and makes it seem like less of a chore. We roll her from front to back, dangling bells and noisy toys above her head to encourage neck rotation. We circle her legs until they unlock and continue the motion in a more fluid fashion. I remember during my pregnancy, when this baby only nudged me, never rolled luxuriously. I know now that I should have somehow perceived this as a red flag.

Other babies are easily rolling over by the five-month mark, picking up toys, chewing everything in sight, but not Emily. She is noticeably calmer and can absorb her environment for longer periods of time before getting overwhelmed, but she is falling behind already. Our daughter is getting more pleasant to be around, yet we feel panicky as time passes and she is not doing much. The therapists say that every milestone will likely come late, and we know this already, but to see the confirmation is incredibly wrenching. Pushing her along is not a real option because she, like all children, is pre-wired to achieve at certain times, but we are in her face anyway, dangling toys, rolling her body around, trying to ward off the fear that continues to blossom.

One day Emily is in her swing while we eat dinner. When it is time to come out, I pick her up and notice her toenails are decidedly blue. Fearing a "tet spell" from her heart condition, we are at the pediatrician's in a matter of minutes. Dr. Khurana checks her oxygen saturation levels to see how oxygenated her blood is, and it is very low. Normal is 98 to 100, but normal for Emily, considering her heart, is 85 to 90. Today it is in the 70s. We are stumped as to what might have caused this drastic change, until the doctor listens to Emily's lungs. She reports that they are almost completely filled with fluid and that Emily has serious pneumonia. I wrack my brain trying to remember if she has been coughing or feverish, but no. I remember previous doctors stating that Emily "presents" or demonstrates a medical problem in a different manner. Her symptoms for serious maladies are not textbook, and sometimes she is entirely asymptomatic.

If we thought we were floundering before, now we are drowning in doubt. How will we tell if she's violently ill when her different little body doesn't give us the normal clues? This child, already such a puzzle to us and to her doctors, turns out to keep some things to herself, secrets we have to figure out all on our own. Chastened, we put Emily on powerful antibiotics and resolve to have an eagle eye about her health from now on.

# CHAPTER 7

My father and stepmom have not seen Emily since Christmas (Before We Knew), so we decide to make another trip to the Midwest during their spring break from the University. We have shared Emily's diagnosis with them, of course, but it is harder than I expect to come back. I try to be strong and resolute, but I feel myself crumbling at the edges. I have come prepared with the paperwork from the geneticist, the run-down of her syndrome and its repercussions. I hold this paper in front of me like a shield, my script in case I can't get through this on my own. Dad holds Emily as I repeat: the syndrome is really rare, she's mentally retarded, she may never walk or talk or read or have a normal life.

All of a sudden, Dad is gone and my stepmom is holding me, pain pooling in her eyes. It's all right, Jude, she's such a sweet little girl. I ask her, where's Dad? She tells me he took Emily to the basement. He cannot bear to see me in this much pain, and now it hits me. I am his little girl, just like Emily is mine, and it kills him to see me suffer. I need him here to tell me everything will be fine, but I know he can't say those words when it is not true. I envy his ability to walk away from the pain and to shield Emily, even temporarily, from the truth about herself.

Back in Maryland, it is time to check out Emily's kidneys before the heart surgery approaches in May. She needs a voiding cystourethrogram (VCUG) to see what actually happens when urine trickles through her ureter to the bladder and urethra. A thin catheter tube filled with dye will be inserted in her urethra and then her kidney and bladder will be scanned while the fluid runs out.

First, though, she will need an IV so she can be sedated for the procedure, and that poses a problem. When she was in the hospital before, we heard the nurses and doctors comment on what a "hard stick" Emily was, but now we get to see it firsthand. She has tiny veins that snake away from the needle, and the doctors aren't having any luck this time. They try to start the IV six times, and the bed is speckled with blood before I beg them to stop. Emily is hysterical, and I am numb from seeing her used as a pincushion. The doctor says they will reschedule the test, and next time there will be a pediatric specialist on board to start the IV. I worry about the trauma that all these tests and hospitalizations are having on my baby, but it's not like we have a choice.

We return a week later, and this time there's no problem with the "stick." I file away this piece of information with everything else I am learning: Don't let just anyone try to start an IV on Emily, insist on a pediatric person who is accustomed to little bodies. Instead of blindly turning ourselves over to the doctors, we must be advocates for this child who cannot speak for herself.

The VCUG indeed shows that Emily's right ureter has a significant kink in it, similar to a crimped garden hose. The urine barely trickles through, making her kidney enlarged and increasing the chances of infection as the urine sits for too long in one spot. This reminds us of her abdominal problem, where the tube was similarly too narrow, and again her heart, with its miniscule arteries.

The mechanics of Emily's innards are all slightly out of whack— not enough to malfunction, but enough to pose problems. The doctors decide to put Emily on antibiotics to ward off urinary tract infections and then to do kidney surgery later. Her doctor says, with the heart surgery coming up, it is unwise to stress her body too much. So we place yet another surgery on the horizon, but we can't think much past one thing at a time.

Spring blooms beautiful this year, our first with our daughter. Greg plants impatiens in the front mulch bed, and they flourish with all the rain. I take Emily out on stroller rides, where she promptly falls asleep. I look around the neighborhood, amazed to see how much the same everything is, while our entire landscape has changed over the winter. It seems an affront that life has gone on so blithely without us.

We have been hibernating with our child and our shattered dreams, but now it is time to come out and make the best of it. I try the baby front pack sometimes, and I walk for hours with a long stride and swinging arms, gulping air and hope.

Emily's hair is coming in, a pure white-blonde, and her eyes are a smoky green. She is a beautiful child, rosy-cheeked and plump. While we're out on our walks, people stop to comment on what an angel she is. I feel like a fraud for pretending everything is fine.

I have not developed the party line for invasive questions about Emily, so I am always stammering. Usually I choose to deflect the questions or to outright lie. People are trying to be nice when they ask what she's up to now, I know that, but I feel threatened and protective of Emily. I feel shame for being dishonest in the face of curiosity, but I can't bring myself to reveal Emily's deficiencies to the world. I know I should glory in what she can do, but in her short life, that's not too much. An irony invades the spring this year, a façade of sunshine and warm breezes, with an enormous cloud overhanging, tormenting us with the huge ordeal ahead.

# CHAPTER 8

The spring soldiers on, as we do, waiting for the Big Heart Surgery. I am looking for a way to pass the time, and my sister Maureen comes up with the idea to visit Grandma. I haven't seen Grandma for years, and she doesn't live that far away, so it is high time. But it is an ordeal to think of traveling again with Emily, so I balk. But when Dad calls to say he can take a long weekend from the University and will fly out to make the trip as well, I am on board. It will be my first trip with Emily, without Greg.

Grandma lives in the Adirondacks, in Upstate New York, a six-hour drive away. The mountainous landscape is worlds apart from the drive westward to Indiana, and it seems I've forgotten what beautiful scenery can be. The mountains unfold as soon as we leave Maryland, loaded into our green Ford Explorer. Maureen is in the rear next to Emily, with Dad and me taking turns at the wheel. We travel northward, leaving the urban freeways behind for the lure of the countryside.

Emily is fussy, as usual, and I keep reminding Maureen to press the pacifier into her mouth or give Emily her Teeny blanket. My nerves are on edge, wondering how this child of mine will be received once we reach Grandma's house. She is nowhere near those placid, lumpy babies who lie on blankets, cooing, the so-called "good babies." This child is as high maintenance as they come, all day long. As a packing afterthought, I dissemble the magic baby swing and force it into the truck. It seems that may have been a good idea.

Dad suggests we stop for lunch at Friendly's, clearly excited to get out of the car for a sit-down meal. I try to tell him it is too much for Emily, how this just won't work, but we're being shown into a booth before I can get the words out.

Just as I predicted, Emily can't tolerate the stimulation of the restaurant, the bright lights, the constant hum of noise, the smell. The cornucopia of sensory input sends Emily into overload. She begins to whine, then thrashes about in her car seat. When I remove her, it is clear my touch is anathema as well. She wants out of this place, now.

I look at Dad beseechingly, begging him to figure it out before I have to say it out loud. I'm embarrassed to take this simple plea-sure, this meal, away from my father, but we just can't stay. I hoist the car seat over my forearm and struggle back out to the car with Maureen and Dad trailing me. They say it doesn't matter. We can just get McDonald's, no big deal. I'm stewing in disappointment, though, over my inability to attempt the most mundane of things with my daughter.

Back on the road with our Big Macs in hand, Emily zonks out and we're free to let the miles tick away in silence. Near Grandma's house, the roads become twisty, the towns smaller. Grandma's speck of a village is as rural as can be, remote even, a peaceful change from the commuting sprawl of Maryland.

Grandma's house is partway up a substantial mountain, a steep gravel driveway leading the way. Like a hovering bumblebee, her yellow Dutch Colonial, topped with a black roof, squats on a patch of green lawn. When the house comes into view, my chest opens. As a child, I spent many summer vacations here, and there's a festive quality to those memories: lavish meals, long afternoons exploring the mountain and the spring house, days that stretched forever. Coming back as an adult with a child seems unreal.

Grandma greets us with open arms, her cap of grey hair fluffy and her embrace warm and soft. Grandma is German through and through, with a love of good food and family. She welcomes me, takes Emily out of the carrier, and fawns over her. She's all praise for Emily's pudgy cheeks and wisps of blonde hair, tells me I look good for someone who just had a baby. I watch her intently, scrutinizing her introduction to this first great-grandchild. If there is any letdown there, I can't see it.

Grandma shows me to my room, the universal "kid's camp" room for all visiting grandkids. This room under the eaves is chock-a-block with twin beds, pillows galore, and piles of scratchy wool blankets for cold winter nights. A crib is in the corner, with a mattress so old that there's actually an indentation in the foam padding. This hollow is the approximate size of a six-month-old baby, so Emily will do just fine nestled there. I can't help but think of all the children, then grandchildren, who have slept in this crib, wearing the groove deeper with each night's sleep.

I have never slept in the same room with Emily, except for her hospitalization in January, and that doesn't count. A real night, in real beds, will be different. I actually look forward to the sweetness of being able to see and hear Emily throughout the night.

But the novelty of that idea wears off right away. It turns out that Emily snores, gurgles, snorts, and wheezes in her sleep. No sooner do I drift off than she cranks it up a notch, watery mucus reverberating through her sinus passages. How such a tiny baby can generate that much noise, I'll never know. I sleep that night with a pillow over my head, muffled.

After an oatmeal and omelet breakfast, homemade, Maureen and I want to walk up the mountain. The family tradition is to survey the property and then report back on the wildlife sightings or the neighbor's current crops. Grandma and Aunt Michele volunteer to watch Emily while we're gone, and I'm off in a flash, arms pumping, gulping in the fresh pine air.

It's the same, yet different, to be up there. The vegetation is slightly bushier than I remember, the climb more arduous. I can see my childhood self scampering about with my other sister, Rachel, and I ache for that innocent time, before hospitals and heart surgeries. I tell myself to buck up, get a grip, and stop feeling sorry for myself.

Back at the house, Grandma and Michele are having a time of it with Emily. They have discovered she is hard to soothe. Even with the swing I brought, Emily is still wailing and writhing. They tried bouncing her, swaddling her, and singing, all to no avail. Grandma looks tired, and Michele seems perplexed. Any surcease I gained on the mountaintop hike fades as I take Emily from them. I explain that sometimes she just needs a quiet, dark room.

I sit on one of the beds in the camp room, bouncing up and down on my rear end. I hum a nonsense tune and pat Emily rhythmically on the back, willing her to quiet down. She is sweaty from the exertion of crying, her face streaked with tears. In a matter of minutes, she is limply asleep, and I place her down in the crib, curling her body to fit the hollow. I am triumphant to have calmed her so quickly, but apprehensive about going downstairs.

I fear the Family Lore, the endless storytelling that becomes legend, the tales that are repeated through the years. When I was a child, these tales decorated the dinner table, sometimes stretching far into the night. Family feuds, hilarious anecdotes, children's adventures—all fodder for a tale. I just don't want one of those tales to focus on Judith with the Damaged Child.

But my fears are unfounded. Grandma, Dad, Michele, and Maureen are in the dining room playing rummy, soda glasses strewn across the table, empty beer bottles accruing at the end. Laughter and lightness reign, not judgment. I sit next to Grandma, watch her capable hands shuffle the deck, her wedding ring clinking on the table. My Grandpa is almost twenty years gone, but he is still here at the table, in our minds. I think of those lonely years and recognize that there are many sad things to bear.

Grandma deals the hand and then puts an arm around me. She squeezes my shoulders once, twice. I feel how tense I am, how guarded. It takes a monumental act of will to lower my shoulders, to relax, to let Grandma tell me everything will be all right. Even if I don't believe it, I hear her words of solace, smile at her New Jersey accent, and let her in.

# CHAPTER 9

Dr. Duke Cameron will perform Emily's open-heart surgery at Johns Hopkins Hospital in Baltimore. He is the best in the field and has done numerous Tetrology of Fallot repairs. Emily is six months old and weighs fifteen pounds, which is the benchmark we have been waiting for. We go in to meet Dr. Cameron for a pre-operative discussion. On Greg's 31st birthday, we drive up to Hopkins and are ushered into the cardiac center. Emily fusses while we wait, so we bounce her in the waiting room and sneak gazes at other parents and their children.

Dr. Cameron turns out to be a balding, rosy-cheeked man with a reassuring smile and a calm manner. He understands that the parents are just as much the patients as are the children. His office is all degrees and certifications, medical texts, and family pictures. He puts us at ease right away, explaining Emily's particular condition and how he will fix it. He plans to insert a Gore-Tex patch into her heart to stop the leaking blood. We are amazed at what the surgery entails and how calmly the doctor speaks of it. Maybe it's less of a crisis than we feared.

He mentions that Emily will need a transfusion, and I leap to attention. We share the same blood type, and I am desperate to help my baby. Surely she can receive my blood during the operation, I propose. The doctor agrees, although he cautions that it will take multiple trips to the blood bank to get an adequate supply.

The insurance company won't pay this expense because there is blood already stockpiled for surgical purposes. It would cost $1,000 to bank my blood for Emily, a cost we can't absorb.

My head swims with my own impotence. I still feel the loss of not being able to breast-feed my little girl, and now my blood won't be used either. If I could rip my own heart out of my body to give to her, I would. My own health and vitality mocks me, as I can do nothing for Emily but be a bystander.

Before the surgery, Emily needs a full cardiac workup to ascertain the exact position of all the chambers, valves, and arteries. She is sedated for an echocardiogram and a catheterization, and we are right back in that dark room, watching her heart pulse on the screen as she lies motionless on the table. The last time we saw her heart, she was a much littler person. Now that she has grown a bit, the details are clearer, and we can actually see the hole in the chamber of her heart and hear the waterfall of the leaking blood. This image is fascinating and macabre all at the same time. The doctors do not see too many cases like this, and they are pretty interested. We ply them with questions about the surgery and the recovery. All of this begins to seem more real.

Surgery day arrives, and it is still dark when we reach the hospital. Emily is fussy because she can't eat or drink anything, so we take turns holding her and distracting her with songs. The pre-op ritual involves a cocktail of an anesthetic called chloral hydrate. This orange syrup tastes bitter, and Emily gags as we use a syringe to get it down her throat. Minutes later, she is limp. Now she gets prepped for the ordeal. Her identification bracelet is attached to her wrist, she is given a fresh diaper, and her tiny body is wrapped in a hospital gown.

The nurse hands me a gown, surgical shoes, and a mask and then it dawns on me: I will transport Emily to the operating room. My mother grips my shoulders and whispers, through tears: "You are just the best mother in the world." I feel anything but this. I am scared, numb, and almost detached as the nurse leads us down the corridor. The hospital gown crinkles between my legs, and Emily is slack in my arms. Her mouth hangs open and her breathing is slow.

The operating room swings open, and I'm startled by how light it is. The room features overhead illumination, and multiple spotlights are trained on the table. The room is filled with rolling carts covered with surgical tools and supplies. Everyone is wearing green, and all I can see are eyes above the masks. The room feels brisk and smells of gauze and rubbing alcohol.

I place Emily on the table as the nurses begin to take her gown off, exposing the surgical site. One of the attending physicians asks for my name, Emily's name, and the purpose of this surgery. At first I think he must be joking, but then I realize the questions are for security purposes—a way to make sure I have been given the correct information and am in my right mind.

Somehow I make my way out of the room and walk unsteadily down the hall. My ears ring and I am lightheaded. I have left my daughter on the table to have her heart taken out of her body and repaired. My own heart feels as if it is in there, too, and I would believe that except I can feel a sickening pounding within my own chest as I fall into a chair to wait.

The waiting room is all comfortable chairs, generic hospital art work, and a center desk manned by staff members who give periodic updates on the status of surgeries. Most cardiac cases take all day, and the families would go crazy without some news. My mom is here, sitting right next to my stepmom, Margy. I am pleased to see them chatting and at ease with each other. I relax somewhat, and let their conversation wash over me. I page idly through a magazine and reach over once in a while to hold Greg's hand. We have no words, but we know each other pretty well. Greg's hand is sweaty and he's edgy. He hops up and down to pace, and when sitting he shifts nervously. He is never still. We have to be convinced to visit the cafeteria for some lunch, and even then we do not taste the food.

Time is simply suspended while we wait. After seven hours, the phone at the center desk rings for us and we receive good news.

The surgery went well, and now they are "warming her up." Emily's body temperature had to be lowered to 65 degrees to prevent excessive bleeding. Now that they are finished, they can begin to reheat all her systems.

Another two hours go by. We are twitchy and nervous, but finally Dr. Cameron rounds the corner, pulls up a chair, and faces us. He pulls down his mask so we can see his kind eyes and the beads of sweat peppering his chin. I am mesmerized by his hands, the hands that have been inside my daughter's chest, have repaired her heart, have sewn her up. They are ordinary hands, fleshy and a bit wrinkled, but I want to clasp them and kiss them. I am so grateful and relieved, I can't speak. The whole family releases a collective sigh of relief as we prepare to go see Emily.

There's an old-fashioned phone booth in the operating wing, and I stop to call my friend, Heather. She saw me through the whole pregnancy and was my first non-relative phone call after Emily was born, so it seems fitting to call her now. I pull the Plexi-glass accordion doors closed around me and choke into the phone that Emily is fine, she made it through. I can hear background noises at Heather's house, normal-life sounds of kids playing and a dog barking. I am in a different world.

Emily is taken to the Pediatric Intensive Care Unit (PICU) for the initial stage of her recovery. Our first sight of her is shocking. She's swaddled in gauze and her face is bloated, almost unrecognizable, from fluid retention. Wires are everywhere, machines are whirring, and there is a persistent beeping to monitor her vital signs. Her little fingers are barely visible for all the bandaging around the IV needles. We can touch the very tips, but that is about the only skin we can see. Even her cheeks are covered in tape to hold the oxygen tubes in her nose. She is still intubated, so her lips are taped to a flexible tube.

My hands flutter like a bird, itching to touch her somewhere, anywhere, and I settle for her eyelids. We bend down to whisper to her, but we are scared to pat her. She is not even the size of the pillow on the bed, practically lost amidst all the machinery. After all these hours, it is wonderful to see her, and we are weak with relief.

The surgeon hovers, wanting to check the incision. We have seen an incision on Emily's body before, from her stomach surgery, so we think we are prepared. A single vertical incision is what we expect, but it is more than that, and frightening. A jagged scar runs from her throat to her belly. The scar is partially covered with light gauze to absorb the blood. Two horizontal incisions lie at the base of the first one, like feet on a stick figure. They have thick tubes running out of them, draining fluid and blood into plastic receptacles. Dr. Cameron explains that these are chest tubes, designed to siphon off the blood that has accumulated during the surgery. The PICU is all beeps, whooshing oxygen tanks, and hushed voices. It is easy to forget that there are babies in here and that one of them is ours.

One bed over, partially cordoned off by a curtain, lies a little boy surrounded by his parents. He had heart surgery a few days before, and Dr. Cameron looks solemn. We sense things are not going well for that little boy, and Greg and I clasp hands in a silent prayer that things will go better for us. The nurses urge us to head home, get some sleep, and come back after the night has passed. There is nothing for us to do here.

At home, we fall into bed exhausted, but I can't sleep. I dial the number they have given me and I reach a nurse on night duty. Emily was extubated at 2 a.m., I am told, and she is breathing well on her own. Her oxygen saturation is 97%, which is higher than it has ever been before. Her heart is pumping the oxygenated blood more effectively, and she is "pinking up."

We arrive at the hospital by morning rounds, and the whole medical team seems pleased with Emily's surgery and recovery. If all continues to go well, Emily will go to the general floor for a few days to finish her recovery before she is discharged.

One nice thing about the Intensive Care Unit is just that: it is intensive. Once on the "floor," it is every man for himself. Nurses are hard to find, and there is no one hovering over our daughter.

That is left to us, and we do not feel up to the task. Greg and I are detached, like this is happening to someone else, and we struggle to be in the moment. When the doctors stop by to give us periodic updates, we quiz each other as soon as they leave to make sure we have both heard the same information.

Emily's crib has high metal bars and can be rolled around the room. With several beds to a room, it is reminiscent of the monkey house at the zoo, especially with the mewling and screeching of the recovering babies. In our room alone, there are three infants; along with parents, relatives, and doctors, it can be a tight fit.

We take turns poking our fingers through the bars, stroking Emily's face or adjusting a bandage. The doctors are cutting down on the medicines now, so Emily is not nearly so groggy. A fussy, postoperative baby is no fun, but we pull out the old standbys, lots of songs and silly faces. She has her little Teeny blanket, but can't suck her fingers for comfort because the IV is strapped onto that hand.

In this room, just like in the PICU, we observe other parents. Here there is a little guy with Down Syndrome. He looks a bit older than Emily, and he too has had cardiac surgery. His parents are an unmarried couple in their late teens or early 20s. They are so angry at each other they hardly speak, and, when they do, it is with bitterness and revulsion. They fling about words filled with blame and hate and frustration, but there is also love for their son. I cringe when the vitriolic words cross their son's crib. We are more tender with Emily now and more aware of our own effect on her world.

After a week, Emily is drinking formula and eating baby food with abandon. She is anxious to get out of here, and so are we. We receive instructions for changing the dressing on her incision and warning signs to watch for at home. Dr. Cameron writes the discharge orders, schedules a postoperative checkup appointment for us in two weeks, and waves us down the hall. It is great to put the hospital behind us, but I am reminded of the way I felt right after Emily was born: How can they let us bring her home? We haven't a clue what to do.

At home, my dad has come to help. He totes Emily around the yard, admiring the flowers and talking animatedly to her. Emily is so pale in the spring sunlight and still has adhesive glue stuck to her cheeks, but she is smiling and safe and finally here.

# CHAPTER 10

With the heart surgery behind us, I am curiously deflated. I poured so much emotional energy into the anticipation and the aftermath that the energy now has nowhere to go. Before Emily's therapies start up again in the fall, I vow to take this child out into the world. We have been holed up all winter and spring like caterpillars in cocoons, and it is time to come out.

We take walks every day, sometimes to the store, other times just meandering around. I drive Emily to the local pool and perch her on my hip as we head out into the water. She loves to kick and splash. I turn her from front to back, trying to develop her strength as she enjoys the water. She has to wear a t-shirt over her swimsuit to keep all sun off her scar, but she is pale anyway and the extra sun protection can't hurt. Here in the water, it is impossible to tell that she's eight months old and not sitting or crawling or playing with toys. She's just a baby having fun.

Some days, I put her in the gym nursery so I can have an hour to myself. The ladies in the nursery have been briefed about Emily: They know she has to be held like an infant and can't be left alone. They adore her and treat her like a doll. It doesn't seem to matter to them that this baby stares into space and isn't active. I count these hours as a true blessing and feel almost normal again as I ride an exercise bike or take an aerobics class. The detachment I have worn like a cloak for most of the last year is slipping off, and I can be around people now and think about things besides my child.

But we are not out of the woods, not by a long shot. Emily still takes antibiotics every day for her kidneys, as well as two medications for her reflux. She's a voracious eater, yet suffers mightily with her stomach. She is growing well and looks healthy. In fact, she never gets a cold, but she still feels medically fragile to us. We watch her every minute, unable to just let her set the pace as she develops.

The truth of the matter is that she's not developing, not really. Every day going by brings that home to us. The second half of a baby's first year is typically a time of tremendous achievement, but Emily has little to show for it. She can regulate her system better and can tolerate stimulation for longer periods of time, but that's about it. It is time to get the intervention team activated and see what can be accomplished.

The Early Beginnings Program runs with the school calendar, so Emily will get a new team every year. An enormous amount of paperwork passes from team to team each year. Emily is a pretty complicated case, so she needs to be handed off with care and many meetings. We are lucky this year—because Emily was diagnosed partway through last year, she technically only received half of a year with the Intervention Team. So she will be with the same folks this year, an unexpected blessing as Emily does best with familiar faces and little change to her routine.

We have Barbara for physical therapy, Jayshree for occupational therapy, and, instead of Theresa (who has left to get married), Martie as the case manager. This soft-spoken, delicate, white-haired woman comes into the house full of love for Emily and changes our lives. Miss Martie has a tender spot for all children, but she is not too touchy-feely, so she and I get along great. Her goal is to see Emily reach her full potential, and she will pull out all the stops to reach her. Martie is attentive and serious about doing whatever she can to help Emily achieve the important milestones. She surprises us by noticing how closely Emily listens when we speak. She believes that Emily's receptive language skills, the degree to which she can understand spoken language, are not too impaired. Expressively, Emily doesn't babble, blow raspberries, or utter a single vowel-consonant blend. Using emerging infant language skills as a judgment of cognitive ability, this is pretty grim. But Martie has an idea for me.

I register with the local parks and recreation department to take sign language classes. Now, every Tuesday night, I sit with a group of retirees learning basic sign. I read a supplementary text on signing, and now I think I know where Miss Martie is going with all this. After a few weeks, I perch across from Emily as she sits propped for lunch. I spoon mashed sweet potatoes into her mouth, bite by bite, and then stop. I sign "more," tapping the fingers of my right and left hands together, saying, "Do you want more, Emily? More?" Emily just stares at me quizzically, then begins to whine, clearly hungry and frustrated with me. I continue to spoon food into her mouth, stopping to sign "more" before each bite. Nothing but staring at me and opening her little mouth like a bird.

We finish and I wipe down her messy face, rubbing the wet cloth from ear to ear. I turn to take the dishes to the sink when, out of the corner of my eye, I see Emily's hands come together, once, twice, three times tapping her fingers together. For the first time in almost one year of life, Emily is attempting to communicate something to me. There are kisses and hugs and praise, and now I am crying. She can learn, she just did learn, and now she definitely gets more sweet potatoes.

I build on this quickly, using "more" for everything: more Baby Einstein videos, more splashing in the tub, more food, more drink, more swinging in the baby swing. Emily is thrilled with the power of cause and effect, smiling delightedly whenever she signs and then gets what she asks for. I pore through the signing textbook, looking for other easy, functional signs. Soon we add "milk," "eat," "drink," "please," "thank you," and "yes" to our repertoire. Every week that Martie comes for a home visit, we have more signs to show her and she is thrilled. Developmentally, children have a brief, furiously fast window for language acquisition, and we need to use every minute. Traditional speech therapy, which involves manipulating Emily's mouth, enticing her to imitate sounds, is going nowhere fast. Whether structural or cognitive, making intelligible sounds seems beyond Emily just yet.

We decide to use sign language in conjunction with the regular therapy as another language tool. Everyone who works with Emily is shown the basic signs, and soon we are making headway. Well before her typically developing peers are saying "mama" and "dada," Emily is signing to us, at us, and reveling in the praise she receives.

But Emily is nearing her first birthday and it is impossible to ignore the obvious. She is leagues behind in every way, and the gap just gets more pronounced every day. She has just learned to sit up unassisted but often topples, so she needs a nest of pillows to surround her. Most of her time is spent rolling from side to side, attempting to reach toys. She is awkward on her belly, struggling to lift her head and shoulders up, but mostly crashing her head into the carpet. She is far from crawling because her elbows and knees remain locked most of the time. Walking independently, a feat most one-year-olds are close to mastering, is not even on our radar.

The pictures I take at Emily's birthday party show a mostly bald little girl wearing a plaid dress. She is adrift in scores of presents and reams of paper and ribbons. In fact, a ribbon seizes her attention; a bright red ribbon appears in almost every shot. Emily is chewing on it with abandon, ignoring all the toys. She looks overwhelmed and infantile, not engaged with what is happening around her. When it is cupcake time, she lunges awkwardly at her cupcake before we are done singing the birthday song. So imperfect in her aim, she usually swings in a wide arc and misses. But this time she connects and burns her hand on the candle. I feel distressed about the burn, of course, but also bizarrely pleased. That desire to reach out and get what she wants will carry her far, I hope.

# CHAPTER 11

Fall arrives, and the leaves are spectacular. Emily dresses as a pumpkin for Halloween, and I take her from house to house in the front pack. The fabric pumpkin lid perches on her head, complete with a green stem. We mark the changing season with a bit of sadness. After all, one year ago, I was pregnant with Emily and unaware of the pain lying ahead, of the ordeal we would face. But we are cautiously joyful as well, triumphant that the heart surgery went so well and that Emily is progressing, albeit at a glacial pace.

Besides the weekly home visits for therapies, Emily has now graduated to a group session, coordinated by Miss Martie and held at a local elementary school. There she will be one of three special needs children participating in games and songs and finger plays. The program is super early preschool for these kids, with the goal being to bring them out of their shells a bit, to develop their sense of others. Emily is clearly the worst off of the bunch, a real blow to my parental self-esteem.

This class is my first real experience with measuring my child against others, and I take everything she can or cannot do personally. There is Kathi, who is visually impaired, but otherwise fine. She will never drive a car, but will go to college and marry and have a normal life, and that hurts. Vickie is also visually impaired and much the same as Kathi. They will have hurdles, of this I am sure, and I know their moms are struggling with loss, but in comparison to Emily, they seem pretty normal to me. The ease with which an almost-blind child can walk around the room and man-uever through a play tunnel better than my Emily may ever do is crushing. I hurt for Emily, and I am ashamed of myself for catego-rizing these little children and trying to pigeonhole people's pain. But facts are facts, and when these children are placed together in this school setting, Emily suffers by comparison.

I soldier on, gamely putting Emily through the motions, doing most of the work for her. An old refrigerator box looms in the class-room, outfitted like a school bus, complete with cutout windows and painted bright yellow. The kids are to crawl or scoot through the makeshift bus, exploring it and each other. I hold Emily under her armpits and haul her through the box, no mean feat for a grown woman. We pause here and there to peek out the windows at the other girls or just to sit in the box experiencing the dim light and cardboard smell. I praise Emily for the slightest thing, even just remaining calm, and I am rewarded with a beaming smile. Maybe there is something to this group stuff after all. All I know is that it gets us out of the house and allows me a chance to talk with other moms, which is a bonus. Emily and I have been in our house all day, every day, most all the time, and this little branching out in our routine is welcome.

The tire swing, mounted in the ceiling with a huge bolt, is a favorite with Emily. She sits stiffly on a board in the middle of the tire and swings to and fro. She seems to learn best here, when calmed by the rocking motion. Miss Martie encourages Emily to imitate actions such as patting her head or clapping. After three sessions of no response and a general feeling that she cannot or will not imitate, Emily surprises us by assuming her perch in the swing and actually initiating a clap before she is even shown the motion. Her clap is a little thing, something a 6-month-old baby can easily do, but I glow with pride the entire day. Proof that she is "in there," that Emily can think and learn, comes in tiny bits and pieces, and I treasure every morsel.

We have circle time, too, an old standby of most infant or preschool learning programs. We sing our names and point to each other. We sing "Wheels on the Bus" and "Itsy Bitsy Spider" until we are blue in the face. There are bells to shake and beanbags to pat, an assortment of musical and sensory items to stimulate learning in a myriad of ways. Emily adores all the music and I take this tip home with me. I can relate to my daughter through song. Although it doesn't come naturally to me, as it seems to for Greg, I incorporate silly rhymes and jingles into our daily routine. The songs seem to work, tempering Emily's fussiness a bit, and I feel I am doing something to help.

Our geneticist, the stoic man who diagnosed Emily, keeps calling. He is curious about Emily's progress, how the heart repair went, and her general health. I am monosyllabic with him, even rude. I have things to report, because by all measures Emily is doing well, despite her syndrome, but somehow I cannot bring myself to speak with this man. That morning in his office is seared in my memory. Without being consciously aware of it, I have placed some blame with this man. He was the messenger of terrible pain and disappointment, and I won't give him the satisfaction of how we are coping or how Emily is faring. After a while, he stops calling.

# CHAPTER 12

By Emily's second Christmas, she looks like any other fifteen-month-old, at least when confined in a stroller or car seat. Once placed on the floor, however, her total lack of gross motor skills tells a different story. She behaves like an infant, rolling around stiffly, struggling to get anywhere. Physical therapy is accelerated to twice a week in the home and a site visit once a week to the therapist's home school. I am rapt with attention during all these sessions, picking up skills of my own so I too can help Emily.

"Motor planning" is the act of knowing instinctively where to place a leg or an arm in order to move. Emily doesn't have this instinctive planning, so we have to teach it to her. Lying on her back or belly, she can't figure out how to get to a sitting position (or "coming to sit," in the physical therapy jargon). We bend her legs for her, roll her to the side, and push her hand against the floor for support until she is upright. Then we do it again and again. Once Barbara is sure I know the motions, I go it alone: legs, roll to the side, hand, sit up. We repeat this routine at every session, and I show Greg the drill so he can practice with Emily as well.

Months later she finally makes headway. Rolling on the floor clutching her teeny, she pikes her leg up, rolls to one side, places her hand on the floor, and comes right up to sit. The look on her face is one of confusion, then of pleasure. She knows she did this by herself. Her motion is not smooth or natural, but it gets her where she wants to be.

Some days this new trick is all Emily wants to do, rolling and sitting from place to place. But some days, she forgets how, whining in frustration on her back, kicking impotently, her arms flailing. I begin to see that a skill, once learned, isn't learned forever. Emily needs repetition to preserve her "motor memory," so we roll up our sleeves and show her again.

Next up is pivoting, the act of turning around in a sitting position to get a different view or reach a new toy. We take the same approach, bending first one leg and then sliding it closer to the other, time and time again. When Emily so much as moves a leg a fraction of an inch on her own, I am all praise and claps. She will do it again for such an appreciative audience, so that is how I motivate her. She would rather let me do all the work, and I want to help her, but she has to do it independently. The Early Intervention Team is forever scolding me for helping Emily too much, so I try to pull back and watch her struggle, but it's hard.

We begin to use Cheerios as treats when Emily does an action on her own, and I feel like a dog trainer rewarding an obedient puppy. But it works, and I can't argue with that. Greg jokes that Emily will work for food, and he's right. We need to stimulate both sides of her body, so we hold the snack just out of reach to her right side, hold her right hand down (the easy one), and make her reach across her body with her left hand. Known as "crossing midline," this process tortures her. It tends to throw her off balance, but she wants that Cheerio. We applaud her efforts and do it again.

Emily will never be fluid in her actions, but all this exercise has made a difference, and her world starts to grow a bit. She can reach toys on her own, roll across the room to get things, and sit up to see who is watching. She is officially mobile now, although not in the standard fashion. Emily's movement is not pretty to watch, but I'm proud anyway.

We live near Kennedy Krieger, a world-renowned hospital which studies children with all sorts of special needs. I put Emily's name on the waiting list right after she was diagnosed, and now, eighteen months later, it is time for her evaluation. The study is an expensive, time-consuming undertaking, but we hope to get some answers, some definitive ideas about what Emily will be able to do in the future. The uncertainty is killing me.

We head up to Baltimore for a full day of testing, packed to the gills with the diaper bag, food, books, toys, the all-important teeny for cuddling, and a change of clothes. There is no telling what the day holds, and I want to feel ready for any eventuality. We are greeted at the front desk and asked to fill out medical history forms. I have started a list of all Emily's surgeries and medications, so I write quickly.

We walk to the first testing room, which is basically an office with a desk and chair. Emily will undergo a developmental exam here for two hours. Then, after a break, she will receive a behavioral psychology evaluation. Greg, Emily, and I sit in the office, juggling Emily back and forth. She would prefer to be on the floor, but we keep her up in our arms, jiggling and singing. Finally, a resident comes into the room. He will administer the developmental test and then confer with the main doctor here on staff for the results.

The resident, Christian, who is younger than us, pulls a series of blocks and balls from a box on the floor. He places these items on the desk in front of him and begins the test. For every item, there are numerous things he asks Emily to do. She is to stack the blocks two high and then three high. Instead, she picks them up, mouths them, and then bangs them together. I gulp. Already this is not going well.

Christian erects a plastic transparent panel on the desk and places a ball behind the panel. His goal is to see how Emily solves the problem of how to get the ball. Predictably, Emily knocks on the plastic and then whines in frustration. She wants the ball, but doesn't know to reach over or around the panel. She starts to melt down, an event I knew would happen eventually, but I had hoped not quite so soon.

I shift Emily to Greg's lap, hoping a change might distract her. She regroups long enough to show that she can wave, clap, and touch her head. Toy after toy is introduced, and we watch Emily inspect each one vaguely and then discard it. Her attention span and focus are nil, and she is tiring of this. Christian pauses and suggests moving to the physical exam part of the test to give Emily a break. He is intrigued by her rare syndrome and complicated medical history. The rundown of surgeries in one year of life is pretty impressive, and he furrows his brow and nods, yes, yes, as if to sympathize with what we have endured.

He checks Emily out from head to toe, noting her high (tight) muscle tone, poor head rotation, and stiff legs. He notes her "frontal bossing," the way her forehead overhangs her face. He spends a great deal of time with her ears, which are oddly wrinkled. The geneticist did the same thing, and I suspect this oddity is one of those markers for chromosomal syndromes. Christian won't say directly that Emily has cerebral palsy, but he says she does have certain aspects of it. We have heard this before.

That's Emily, impossible to pin down—she has a little bit of many conditions. When we're in a joking mood, we say that Emily just has a little something "extra," a reference to the additional genetic material on her 13th chromosome.

Emily is so stressed by this appointment that she falls into an exhausted sleep in Greg's arms. The resident leaves to find the lead doctor. Greg and I sit for an interminable time, growing distressed by what has happened. We know Emily can't do a lot, but at home she has shown glimmers that she is smart. I feel the test here hasn't adequately demonstrated what Emily can do, and I am anxious to correct any misperceptions.

Finally, the doctors come in, an elderly gentleman following Christian. This leading developmental specialist greets us warmly and shakes our hands. We repeat what we know about Emily's condition and her life thus far. The doctor says that, given the test just administered, he would place Emily at the developmental age of a four-to-six-month-old with a probable IQ in the moderately mentally retarded range.

We are stunned, really just too shocked to speak. I guess we knew she was behind, but her condition has never been spelled out for us in black and white like this. The doctor can't say for sure what Emily's prognosis is, medical or academic, but it is clear she is very low functioning on the charts. Faced with this information, I am sorry we even came. My spirit is dampened, and the sadness we feel must be palpable. The doctor excuses himself after I sniff a few times. We are shown back into the waiting area for the behavioral/psychological component of the testing, to take place in an hour.

Suddenly, Greg and I look at each other, then at our beautiful sleeping child, whose blonde hair has fallen across her face, and we stand in tandem to leave. With a hurried excuse, we make a beeline for the parking lot and load everything into the car. We hold hands all the way home, united in this escape. We may not be able to elude Emily's diagnosis and her long-term impairments, but we can leave this place, where children are plotted on a chart.

# CHAPTER 13

To be Emily's mom, to get through the day doing the best I can for this little girl, I am cultivating a hard exterior that at first seems impervious to pain. Everyone around me says how well I am faring, how great Emily is doing because of me. But there are chips in my facade that I do my best to hide. My heart contracts in pain every single day. I am guilty of wishing for an easier life, guilty of wanting a perfect child, and guilty of being a little bit angry at the child I do have. To assuage this guilt, I go to the mat, fighting for Emily, pushing her, and researching her condition until her disability encompasses me. Knowledge is indeed power, and if I become an expert on Partial Trisomy 13, I will at least feel I am doing something.

The cooing adorations that strangers used to bestow on our daughter have segued into looks of bafflement by now. Anyone who knows anything about children can tell that this child is way too big to be a baby, yet she acts, sounds, and moves like an infant. By two years old, she is not crawling. We hoist her around in our arms and in a vast array of backpacks, wagons, and strollers. I transport her everywhere I go, but, left to her own devices, she still rolls like a log or sits with her legs splayed like a marionette. People don't wonder IF something is wrong, they wonder WHAT is wrong.

Of course, all our friends are sensitive and compassionate, but none of them has a child with disabilities, so they can't possibly know. I try not to dwell on Emily in their presence, as the awkwardness is unbearable. One day I am at the gym with my friend, Heather, and she asks how the evaluation at Kennedy Krieger went. Unbidden, I choke on tears as I tell her the moderately mentally retarded diagnosis. She absorbs this information with aplomb and I realize maybe I need to stop selling people short. They can handle it—it is actually me who needs to get a grip.

Emily sits well, but her balance is off, so we requisition a feeding chair from the Early Intervention Team. The high chair is industrial style with a high back, padding, and numerous straps to support Emily as she eats. It is ugly, even frightening, reminiscent of a pint-sized electrocution chair. Our neighbors from across the street come over for a cookout with their two children, one of whom is nine months old and already walking. They gape at the feeding chair before they can help it and then scramble to hide their expressions. Such tiny adaptive equipment is difficult to see, and I feel both embarrassed for our friends and then shamed that we have such an obvious symbol of Emily's disability on display.

I can't decide whether to accept my role as Emily's mom, really embrace it, or fight against it, using denial as my weapon. Most days, I am in a sort of limbo, an outward show of resolve and calm, and an inward pleading with God to make all this not be true. I am fighting, constantly battling within myself, and it is taking a toll.

My family's biennial reunion rolls around, the first we attend since having Emily. My dad and stepmom choose Stowe, Vermont, as the destination. Greg can tell how overwhelmed I am feeling, how strung out I have become from nonstop caregiving. He invites his parents to come out to Maryland to watch Emily while we head north for a week without our child. Getting this break is like a life ring thrown out into turbulent waters.

Stowe is all pine trees and mountains. Our family's cabin is at the Trapp Family Lodge, up a winding drive, wedged into the side of a mountain. Greg and I sleep late, lunch in town at touristy restaurants, and generally find ourselves again. I'm thrilled to discover a little health center on the Lodge property, complete with a treadmill. The mountaintop gym is sauna hot and unventilated, but that doesn't deter me. I take walks gazing out a picture window, facing the mountains, mentally climbing to the peak.

There are trails galore here, and Greg and I explore them all. On one hike, we find a nearly perfectly circular pond situated on a plateau of land, a necklace of pine trees surrounding it and Adirondack chairs by the edge. Sitting with Greg, listening to our exhalations after the rigors of our ascent, I am at peace. Any guilt I have felt about leaving Emily is assuaged.

Grandma is with us on the trip, picked up by Dad on the way up. She's not a frequent traveler, so her company is a treat. She can be counted on for hearty German cooking, funny family anecdotes, and words of wisdom.

Grandma has some words for me this time, things she couldn't say when I last visited her on her mountain. She sits on a reclining chair on the deck overlooking the valley, relaxing with a glass of wine. When she is sure we are alone, she broaches the subject of Emily.

"Jude," she says, "I know Emily has lots of problems. Please promise me, though, that you won't let her complications stop you from having more children."

I'm pretty shocked by this statement, although Grandma never holds back, so her frankness isn't unusual. What is unusual is that no one else ever mentions this, that Emily is an only child, that we avoid speaking of adding to our family. It is the taboo topic, brought out into the open now. I guess Grandma fears we will let Emily govern our entire world.

But I can't make this promise to her. I am way too shell-shocked by Emily's effect on our world. Even contemplating another baby upsets the apple cart in my mind. I think about Grandma's words later in the day and wonder. She had seven children, had none with problems. How can she know my fear?

By the time fall rolls around, Emily's diapers begin to smell strange and she develops a high fever. The pediatrician inserts a catheter into Emily's urethra to get a urine sample. It comes back positive for a urinary tract infection, despite the powerful antibiotics she is taking. We are referred to a urologist at the University of Maryland, the same place where Emily was diagnosed over two years ago.

The pediatric urologist is Dr. Voigt from New Zealand; he has a charming accent and an excellent manner with children, most of whom are sick and in pain. He performs a renal sonogram and a kidney test and declares that it is time to do the surgery. We put it off because it never seemed urgent, but Emily is growing and the tube from her kidney to her bladder is not growing with her. She will get more infections and risk kidney damage if we don't get moving on this now.

Emily is admitted to the hospital for a pyeloplasty the week before Christmas. Compared to the heart surgery, renal surgery is a breeze. She sails through and is released two days later. She comes home with yet another scar on her little body, this time on her side. Her entire chest area is a sad patchwork of scars.

Running out of her kidney incision is a tube attached to a drain whose purpose is to pull bloody liquid away from the surgery site, much like the chest tube after the heart surgery. This time, however, we are in charge of keeping track of how many cc's of liquid are present each day. We also must empty the drain, sterilize it, and reinsert it every four hours. At the rate we have been going the last few years, we will soon have the expertise to be nurses or doctors without having to attend medical school.

There are some tense moments when the amount of liquid in the drain increases over time and turns a darker pink. We think surely something has gone wrong—isn't the fluid supposed to taper off and become clearer? After calling the doctor in a panic, he assures me this is all normal, and I feel silly for worrying. But I am acutely aware of our responsibility for Emily and our inadequate preparation for most of our experiences with her.

The kidney surgery marks a huge turning point. Barring any unforeseen events, it is the last corrective surgery Emily will need. That is not to say she is home free because we have been warned that children with chromosomal syndromes can develop a myriad of problems. But for now, the faulty plumbing she was born with has been fixed as much as possible. The main focus presently will be developmental and behavioral.

I bid farewell to the hospital compound with mixed feelings. I feel enormously grateful to all the staff who have helped Emily, yet I can't hurry fast enough away from the brick walls, the sea of blue scrubs, and the medicinal smell. I am hopeful that the crisis is over—that of Emily's life and of my own—but somehow I know that it is just beginning.

# CHAPTER 14

During the spring when Emily is two-and-a-half years old, I suddenly explode with a burst of adrenaline. One day while I am on a walk, I wonder if I could possibly run to the end of the block. I make it, but I'm winded. I am in pitiful shape for a thirty-two-year-old woman. All of my life, I have been active, even athletic. I have been a power walker, an aerobics instructor, an exercise biker. But these physical pursuits have fallen by the wayside somewhat after Emily's birth, and the subsequent malaise I feel is uncomfortable. I am cooped up inside myself and literally need to run off all the emotions I have been pushing down.

The next nice day, I run around the block two times, and I'm still winded, but I'm on a mission. I begin tentatively jogging on the treadmills at the gym, enticed by the exact measure of distance covered and speed. It appeals to my nature to have such a precise accounting for one's efforts. I am victorious when I reach the three-mile mark, so I up it to five miles, which becomes my new daily goal. I buy actual running bras and shorts and research the best shoes for my feet. Greg gets me a running log so I can keep track of my mileage, and he does the morning routine with Emily so I can get outside on weekend mornings.

I call Heather and shyly announce that I have started running. She is thrilled and immediately invites me to run with her. We hit the local trails or pick side-by-side treadmills at the gym and pound away the miles. We talk about our lives, our husbands, our kids, and I can feel the shell that has encased me for years beginning to fall away. The physical exertion is liberating me from my self-imposed exile. I am happier to see Emily and to work with her when I have had my workout, and I begin to incorporate exercise into my life in a way that is unapologetically selfish.

I quit teaching aerobics when I got pregnant with Emily, and now I am ready to begin again. I am hired right away at the local gym and begin teaching three times a week, high and low impact. The people are friendly and inspirational, praising me for my snappy music and well-choreographed routines. I am comfortable in front of a group, despite my reticent nature, and I thrive on the energy. Emily is in the gym nursery while I shout into a microphone, dance, clap, and stretch. I teach my own classes and sub for other instructors when needed, so I am constantly, almost frenetically, in motion.

On days when I am not at the gym teaching, I run outside, logging the miles, the weather, and my perceived exertion in my little black book. I feel lighter and look fitter than I have in years. I feel liberated to have something for myself, and I pursue my new fitness lifestyle with abandon.

It is a slippery slope, though. For most of my life, beginning in adolescence, I have struggled with eating and exercise issues. I was hospitalized at sixteen with anorexia and did manage to recover, but the residual effects are there, at the fringes. When life gets stressful, I cope by not eating or by exercising too much. The endorphins from working out must be my sedative from pain. I know all of this. I have talked about it in therapy, yet it still has a hold over me, is still the tool I reach for when things get rough. I rationalize that at least I am not addicted to drugs, or a smoker, those harmful crutches. A little compulsiveness about food and exercise doesn't seem too bad.

But my obsessions are like a barnacle, firmly attached to my sense of self, almost impossible to remove. I fall back into my old patterns with ease. It is something I know, a predictable routine. If these last couple years have taught me anything, it is that we cannot control much, and that idea is poison to me. I crave control, and I'll get it any way I can, even if it means depriving myself of food or running myself into the ground.

I'm not unaware of the irony. Emily struggles to move at all, and I spend countless hours jogging, running, sprinting. My pent-up anxieties and the sadness I feel for Emily's disabilities are left on the pavement. The ease of movement confounds Emily, yet it sets me free. I return to Emily fresher and somehow cleansed. Maybe I'm fooling myself and all the running is just running away instead of really coping, but at this point I don't care.

Emily's physical exertions are just as arduous. She is over two years old now and still no closer to crawling. The physical therapist decides she may never crawl, so we focus on "pulling to stand," a move that has Emily pivoting from a sitting position up to one knee, then pulling herself up by holding onto the coffee table or the couch. This movement is a series of four separate steps that her body must perform. Alas, her "motor planning" deficits make this extremely difficult. It takes her one month to get to one knee, with my help. We ply her with toys and food again, dangling things just out of her reach so she will rise up and take the bait.

Once in a standing position, Emily grabs onto the surface in front of her for dear life. Her balance is wobbly at best, and she has no clue how to reverse the sequence and get back down. Once she is up, her choices are to remain standing until her legs give out or fall clumsily to the floor. I can't move more than a foot away from her for fear she will hurt herself. I set out an array of musical pop-up toys along the couch in hopes she will be enticed by them and scoot along. She is content in one place, however, scared to upset her tenuous grasp on the upright position.

One morning, though, I go in to wake Emily and find her standing in her crib. I gasp with surprise and disbelief. I know how long it takes her to get to that position and with how much effort. I am touched by the thought of her, working quietly on her own in the dark room. She looks at me with a calm, focused gaze, and it is then that I realize how much she will be able to do.

For several weeks after that, Greg and I are wakened in the night by Emily's cries. She practices her new skill in her crib, but needs our help to get back down. It doesn't occur to us to be upset at the night wakings—we are just happy she is progressing. The physical therapist notes in her paperwork, "goal completed." It is a small thing, really, to come to stand by oneself, but to our little girl, it is Herculean.

Upright, Emily is another ball of wax, and it takes some adjusting. Rolling around on the floor, literally being on a different plane than the rest of us, kept her out of touch with the world, but now she is up and is a force to be reckoned with. Suddenly she is more smiley, more engaged, and more fierce as well. She has a mind of her own. At an age where most of her age-group peers are talking in complete sentences, Emily doesn't say a word. That doesn't mean she's quiet, though. She squeals, giggles, and makes long utterances consisting of a series of vowels strung together. Now that she's standing in place by herself for a period of time, she seems to feel more comfortable joining us with her own form of conversation.

So now she's Standing, Talking Emily, and she seems so big. But there's quite a lot of fussing on a daily basis, still, and I am resigned to it. I figure she is tired all the time from the effort it takes her to do the littlest thing. Plus, she is frustrated by her inability to move well and communicate. I think this will become part of Emily's temperament, the pseudo howl, the squeals of indignation at the hardship that is her life.

# CHAPTER 15

An entire subculture exists for stay-at-home moms. It consists mainly of toddler and preschool classes, anything from music, to gymnastics, to art and dance. It includes places that little children go to learn and occupy themselves before they begin preschool. A chasm of time exists between when children can walk and when they can separate from their mommy, at around two or three years old. Hence, toddler classes.

These classes are a lifesaver, actually, for both the child and parent. A break in the endless routine of feedings, errands, playtime, and naps is a saving grace. It gives young families an excuse to get out of the house and mingle with others. It is also a venue for the parents, usually moms, to meet and have some social life. I jokingly mention to Greg that I never noticed the "stroller brigade" at the mall until I became a mom. Little kids and their moms are everywhere, playing, talking, and partaking in this envelope of time before the onset of teachers, buses, and school.

But we are not part of it, Emily and me. I put on my hard shell when I go anywhere with her, impervious to the stares, or so I would like to think. We are not the typical mommy-child unit, that is glaringly obvious, and there is no place for us. At the park, I push her in the swing for hours, but she can't do much else. Even standing next to a play structure is precarious, so I hold her all the time. There are slides, a fort, and dozens of kids running around, but we just watch. I overhear a child asking his mom, "Why isn't that little girl walking?" and I turn away before I can hear the answer, my face flaming and eyes burning. It seems I am either ashamed of Emily or myself, and that is the biggest hurt of all.

We try the library story hour, which seems like a safe bet. Story time is held in a carpeted ante room with a cheery librarian, pastel artwork on the walls, and scores of kids. Emily sits obediently throughout the story, but she is not really looking at the book or her surroundings. She starts to flap her hands rhythmically, usually a sign of over-stimulation, and I am unnerved by all the women who notice. I wonder what she looks like to them—a cute little girl who is jittery with excitement or a weird little girl who might have something wrong with her?

Despite my best efforts not to compare, I do, and I am shocked. Children Emily's age are fully and gracefully mobile, of course, able to traverse any surface, scale any structure, swing, dangle, bounce, climb, and twirl. Emily is stiff and awkward, her gross motor skills on par with a ten-month-old, at best. But the language, the words! These other children are talking with their moms, really talking, and pointing, and giggling, and having a relationship. There is no relationship with Emily and me yet, just caregiving, struggle, and work. I am trying to get her to a place where we can relate to each other, but all I know how to do now is push and push. It is folly to think she will ever catch up—I am not deluded—but I want her to be the best she can be.

Envy of the other moms with their perfectly developing children just swamps me, along with an anger that I am not able to do more, to make Emily do more. We soldier on through story hours, playgrounds, and the pool and I hope she is getting something from all these excursions. What I am getting is more alienated and afraid.

One Tuesday night, I am teaching low-impact aerobics at the gym. One of the clients, Teri, is a regular. She is there every week, in the same outfit, the same spot in the room. She is friendly and caring and so I let down my guard. I tell her I have a two-and-a-half-year-old-daughter with special needs and she is interested. There is no pity, just curiosity, and the vise around my heart loosens a bit.

The next week, Teri introduces me to her friend, Jeanne, also a participant in the class. It turns out that Jeanne has an autistic daughter a bit older than Emily. Jeanne seems to have a grip. She has accepted her child's disability and integrated it into her life. She is almost matter-of-fact, reeling off names of organizations, resources, and websites. I am dizzied by all that I don't know or have refused to investigate. It occurs to me that being Emily's advocate might involve more than working with Emily every day. Help is out there if I would just ask.

Jeanne says there's a local mom's group just for mothers with disabled children. It is simply a dinner, once a month, no obligation. This is not like me. I'm not a joiner and definitely not good at meeting strangers, but I need to try it out. Emily stays home with Greg for the evening when I go to my first dinner at a local Mexican restaurant. The women at the long oak table are talking, laughing, and trading information. Some of them know each other, and some are first-timers. There is no shyness here. The question "What's your child's diagnosis?" is flung about casually, as if it is the most ordinary thing in the world to have a child with problems.

Up and down the table there are stories of cerebral palsy, spina bifida, autism, pervasive developmental delay. I am blown away that these women have children—some more than one!—with serious issues, yet they manage to laugh and enjoy themselves. I have been punishing myself without knowing it, and their laughter is releasing me from my self-imposed jail.

I sit next to a petite, blue-eyed woman with a kind smile and a penetrating gaze. She turns to me and, over the appetizers, we begin to share stories. To my surprise, her daughter also has a chromosomal syndrome. Her condition is different from Emily's, on an entirely separate chromosome, but there are striking similarities. We are the only two at the dinner, and in the group as a whole I am told, whose children fall into this category. Sue's daughter is sixteen months old. She was diagnosed at three months old, just like Emily, and by the same geneticist.

The clamor of the restaurant and the chatter of the women fall away as we share that moment when we found out. I want to cry in utter relief that I'm not alone. That someone else can say their world was destroyed in that moment and not feel like a horrible person for saying it. We love our little girls, we would do anything for them, but we are shattered. We live day to day with the truth of our situation while simultaneously wishing it away. We feel guilt, blame, and sorrow, and now there is a friend who can understand.

I return to Greg that night weeping. He thinks something is wrong, that I am upset, but when I can finally talk, I tell him. I am not alone, I say, there are other people doing this exact same thing and they can help us. Greg's hurt that I have felt alone because he has been at my side this whole way, and I try to explain. I need to talk about Emily, about our life with her, and I need to talk about it a lot. He doesn't always want to hear, and he definitely doesn't want to see me cry. But I have found a place where that is okay, and for this I am overjoyed.

# CHAPTER 16

I am galvanized by the mom's group, just energized. I have not done enough for Emily or myself, it is clear. I sign up for newsletters from three foundations that support children with disabilities. They arrive all glossy and promising, but it is a mixed bag. Profiles of children are displayed, along with photos, and it is scary. All these problems, all the things that can go wrong.

One of the publications is from the UK, with contributors hailing from around the world. Despite the cultural and language barriers, the children and their families are all the same—wounded and in pain. But I plow through, trying to turn this into a good thing. Before long, I can read the profiles as more than just sad stories— there is hope and advice. Pages and pages of information about adaptive equipment, doctor recommendations, and cutting-edge therapies. I realize we are all looking for answers, no matter where we live or what language we speak. It is sobering to realize how many damaged children there are—and this is just the tip of the iceberg. A community exists out there, a club made up of people with special needs children, and we are part of it whether we like it or not.

One of the women in the mom's group asks me if I use the ARC Respite House. I am clueless about this, and she explains that the Association for Retarded Citizens (ARC) is an organization serving the entire network of disabled people and their families. They provide equipment, services, and occasionally even funding for the expenses that accompany having a special needs child. One of the things they do is provide respite care for disabled children from eighteen months old to adults. The respite program employs adult babysitters with medical training, it is reasonably priced, and it is local; I jump at this gift.

So far, we have never had anyone watch Emily for us except family members, and not often at that. The opportunity to have a bit of child-free time sounds like heaven. I call for an application, fill it out, and supply the necessary medical history and personal information on Emily. Our application is approved within a week, and we are set to meet the caregivers at the ARC House. It turns out that the facility is actually a single-family home purchased by the ARC and maintained by the employees. The home is comfortable with high ceilings and toys galore. Best of all, it is located right down the street from our house. I take a short walk through the woods, pulling Emily in the wagon. We arrive to a staff of four and a total of four children. This is what they call a 1:1 ratio, and it is exactly what Emily needs. She will have an adult with her every minute, keeping her safe and entertained.

I spend some time filling the staff in on what I call Emily's "quirks"—her unsteadiness in a standing position, her funny noises, and her flapping hands. I also show them a few signs they will likely see Emily use, like "drink" and "eat." I park Emily in the midst of a sea of toys and slowly back out of the room, double-checking the paperwork I needed to sign, making sure I have written down my phone number correctly. Everyone looks happy and capable, definitely up to this task, so I leave them to it.

The ARC House becomes my savior. Emily and I are together all the time, and I need a break. Now I know what my friends are talking about when they discuss babysitters. It is a concept I have all but dismissed, given Emily's condition. How could I leave a teenager with a child I can barely manage? But it is clear that the ARC understands the needs of families with disabled children.

I schedule Emily once a week at the ARC House, just four hours of respite at a time, but it feels like a lifetime. At first, I stay at home during the hours, convinced that something will happen and they will need me to come pick her up. I clean the house until it is spic and span, turning on music I haven't listened to since college. Sometimes I read a book in the quiet house. I feel edgy, though, and slightly guilty to be enjoying this time, in angst that I am not getting something big accomplished. Occasionally I run errands, amazed at how simple it is without the car seat and the constant singing I do to calm Emily. I can buzz in and out of four stores in an hour.

After several months of dropping Emily at the Respite House, I begin to feel more comfortable. I am wound pretty tight these days, and I can feel myself unwinding during this time every week. I come to look forward to the babysitting days as time that I absolutely need to stay grounded. I find it hard to ask for help, even when I am in desperate need. This realization that I need to care for myself, too, is a new one. Caring for Emily has become a job for me, an undertaking that's called on all my efforts and energy. But it is wearing me down, even I can recognize this, and a short break now and then is heaven.

In fair weather, I wear my running clothes to the ARC House, drop Emily off with a kiss, and literally dash out the door. I plan running routes of various lengths depending on my time or energy on a given day. I set my watch, establish a comfortable pace, and head down the road. I traverse suburban streets and walking trails, and I distract myself from the exertion by looking at people's houses and gardens, admiring or critiquing their style. I file away things to tell Greg, a stone walkway that's attractive, cottage-style red shutters, an interesting screen porch. I greet other exercisers with a wave, but no words. I am silent except for the slapping of my feet on the pavement. I am sweating profusely by the end, and panting, but it hardly matters. It occurs to me that I am not so much leaving Emily on these precious days as trying to find myself.

# CHAPTER 17

Emily is ready to graduate from the Early Intervention Team to a preschool in the fall when she is almost three. It is a complex turnover, involving lots of paperwork and many meetings. We are asked to develop an Individual Family Service Plan (IFSP), which is basically a list of goals and objectives we want Emily to accomplish. This plan is a way to document her achievements as she enters the school system. She will never follow a regular curriculum. Rather, she will have an adaptive curriculum fashioned for her every year based on what she can do. I remember from my education classes in college that that is the law. People with disabilities are due the same chance at an education, and accommodations must be made.

In the time since I was in school, people with disabilities have come out of hiding and have been included in mainstream education. Greg and I wonder to ourselves if we remember any disabled children in our classes, and we are hard pressed to come up with one. But it's different now, or so the team tells us. Children with disabilities, if they can, are included with typically developing children all the way through their education. Our job is to properly assess Emily's skills and weaknesses every year so that her progress can be documented. She will fall through the cracks if we are not diligent, and we can't have that.

At almost three years old, Emily can "cruise." She sits, turns onto one knee, grabs the couch, and pulls herself up to stand at the couch. From there she side-steps down one side of the couch to a toy, plays for a minute, and then side-steps the other way. When she wants to get down, she releases her grip on the couch and plops on her diapered bottom. This movement is not pretty, in fact, it is laborious to watch, but it's amazing to us. How many physical therapy sessions to get here, how many hours of massaging her muscles and loosening her joints? We are thrilled to watch her, but never satisfied. Getting Emily to walk, unassisted, will be the primary goal for the next year.

The IFSP is discussed and drafted. There is a section for everything: Gross Motor Development, Fine Motor, Expressive Language, Receptive Language, Self-Control, and Academics. Greg and I want to laugh when we see the "Academic" section—we are giddy just thinking of Emily learning her numbers and letters, but it is sobering as well. Emily cannot utter one word. We are scared to expect too much, but we follow the lead of the intervention team, which reels off goal after goal, placing hurdles in front of Emily that we can only hope she will surmount.

Life is a whole new ball game now that Emily is a preschooler. Instead of home visits and once-a-week therapy sessions, she will be in school all day, every day except Wednesdays. She will attend a local elementary school and her teachers, aides, and therapists will be onsite. The school has a classroom, hallways, a cafeteria, a real school. On the orientation day, Emily and I arrive to check it out. It's an affluent school, a new one in the county, served by a proactive parent—teacher group. We are lucky to be placed here. Not every school in the county has special needs preschools—it's sort of luck-of-the-draw. Every summer, the eligible children are shuffled around from school to school until everyone is situated.

Emily's program is called Multiple Intense Needs Class (MINC). The program serves kids with more than a little bit wrong. The mom's group routinely debates whether these classes are any good, but Greg and I know it is where Emily needs to be. We observe a

MINC class before making our decision and know without a doubt
that Emily would be lost in a less rigid program. We know her
limitations and don't much care that she is in the "retarded" preschool. She is where she needs to be, and that is just a fact.

The MINC classroom is brightly lit and colorful. Mobiles dangle
from the ceiling, and vibrant rugs cover the floor. Alphabet puzzles and Disney character bulletin boards abound. Tiny potties are
stationed against the wall, and the chairs and tables are miniscule.
It smells like school in here, all waxy crayons and rubber erasers.
You would never know this was a classroom for disabled children
except for the pint-sized wheelchairs and walkers stationed at the
outside door. I wheel Emily into the room in her stroller and offer
her some Cheerios to munch on while the orientation proceeds.
The adults are invited to sit while the teacher does her introduction. I am anxious to see who will be Emily's first teacher.

Rachel Morey is beautiful, no question about it. She has thick
red hair cascading down her back, a la Nicole Kidman, held in the
center with an ornate clip. Her bangs just skim her green eyes, and
freckles decorate her ivory skin. Her fingers are long and thin, she
has a soft voice, and she exudes confidence plus. I am immediately
intrigued and hopeful that she has what it takes. I am entrusting
Emily to her care every day of the week, and I need to believe in
this person. She hands us a packet of classroom information and
then asks us to introduce ourselves and our child. There is a rundown of classroom procedures, a basic supply list, and then a tour
of the various centers in the room.

I am impressed with the organization of the room and the school
day. An activity takes place every fifteen minutes. Each child is
assigned a color (Emily is yellow), and that color is used to transition the students from activity to activity. A tiny chair, complete
with safety straps, is all ready for her, with a yellow sailboat taped
to the back. Emily's seat at the group table is also marked with a
yellow sailboat, as is her own private potty against the wall. I am
taken aback by the obvious attempt at toileting—Emily can't even
walk yet. But Rachel explains that the entire goal of education,

especially special education, is to get the kids to be as independent as possible, including toileting, self-dressing, and self-feeding.
I have been underestimating what Emily should be trying to do,
that is clear, and the lump in my throat won't go away. There is so
much she cannot do.

Rachel shows us the "bus bay" where all the buses pull in every
morning. The preschool kids are dropped off by their parents, so
there's a special area for us. Rachel has requisitioned a large, plastic wagon for Emily so she can be transported from the parking
lot to the classroom in safety. This teacher has done her home-
work and it shows. She shakes our hands as the orientation session draws to a close and schedules a home visit prior to the start
of school. At home that night, I tell Greg I have a good feeling
about Rachel—that if anyone can help Emily achieve her goals,
this woman can.

A week before the school year begins, we are close to ready. We
have a Blues Clues mini-backpack for all of Emily's papers, a princess lunchbox, and five quart-sized Ziploc bags. Each bag contains
a complete change of clothes—shorts, shirt, diapers, and socks—
in case of a mess or potty accident. Each item of clothing has been
labeled with indelible marker and affixed with a yellow sticker to
claim it as Emily's.

The backpack also contains a composition notebook, which is
the main venue for communication between Rachel and me. At
the close of every day, she will describe the day, noting Emily's
behavior, mood, accomplishments, and setbacks. The notebook is
also a place for me to note whether we had a rough weekend or a
bumpy night so Rachel can be prepared. I think this idea is ingenious because Emily certainly can't tell me anything about her
day, and I can't expect the teacher to call every day.

The Saturday before school begins, I am shaky. It seems ridiculous to send a nonwalking, nonverbal child to school. I pace the
length of the house, waiting for Rachel to arrive for our home visit
so I can quell some of the fears. I am excited for Greg to meet her,
to see whether he shares my opinion of her.

At 10:00 a.m., she arrives at our house, laden with folders and a large box. She greets Emily first, squatting down where Emily sits and beaming into her face. Instead of taking one of the chairs we offer, she sits cross-legged on the floor. She places a bulging folder on the coffee table and a moment passes before I realize that it contains notes on Emily, lots of notes. It appears to be her complete (very large) medical file; all the therapy notes from more than two years of physical, speech, and occupational therapy; and her recently completed IFSP. I get it now—our little girl is supported by a vast network of people whose sole job it is to help her grow and advance. They pass her along with an array of notes to help the next person. A chain of service providers helps little Emily.

Rachel plays with Emily like she is a regular kid. She is not surprised that Emily plays like a baby, gumming everything and squealing. She takes it in stride, following Emily's lead. The big box comes out, filled with toys, most of them way too advanced. Rachel just wants to see what Emily will do. She puts Emily through the paces, helping her operate little levers and push buttons. She calls it "hand over hand" and encourages us to help Emily in this way for everything. Emily will feel the object she touches and be successful at operating the toy because we help her. Her frustration threshold will not be reached, and she will be more likely to stick with the activity longer.

Rachel says this will work for self-feeding, too. Instead of feeding her myself, which I admit to doing, I am told to make Emily hold the spoon, using my hand over hers to guide the spoon to her mouth. Over time, I will reduce the pressure of my hand in increments until Emily can do it all herself. To help her cruise more smoothly, we are to put toys just out of her reach, encouraging her to step farther than she is used to going. Greg and I stare at each other. It sounds like we are going to have to harden our hearts. We are used to pushing Emily, but we balk when she starts to fuss, and we tend to do too much for her.

I envy the ease Rachel has with Emily. She has an innate sense of calm and knows instinctively when Emily's had enough or when to continue. We take a break when the whining gets too much. Emily lies on her back with her teeny while we chat with Rachel. She tells us the team this first year will consist of her, a physical therapist named Diane, a speech therapist named Maureen, an occupational therapist named Megan, and two classroom assistants. I take it as a good omen that two of the women working with Emily this year have the names of my dear sisters, Rachel and Maureen.

We take a look at the class schedule and then Rachel pulls out a mysterious looking machine, approximately the size of a shoe box. Rachel explains that this is a Cheap Talk, an adaptive communication device she hopes Emily will learn to use. The device has three panels in the top for an assortment of interchangeable cards. The cards have pictures on them and are used to form sentences. Before she gets to that, however, Emily must get familiar with the cards.

This is our introduction to the Picture Exchange Communication System (PECS), a widely used tool for communication for the disabled. PECS has been monumentally successful at helping the nonverbal to "speak." By simply pointing to a picture, a person can identify a want or express an emotion. In the beginning phases, a child like Emily can simply point to a picture of "milk" to indicate what she would like to drink. In the more advanced phases, words can be combined into phrases to answer questions or carry on a conversation. The machine Rachel shows us can be programmed to "talk" every time a card is pushed.

What we are looking at is Emily's voice, right here in our family room. This will be the way—finally—that this little girl can be heard. She does use sign language, but sparingly and not gracefully given her lack of fine motor control. We know she can understand most of what we say, but that is not enough. Giving her a voice of her own will open up a whole new world.

# CHAPTER 18

Emily is in school every day, and suddenly I am all alone. I take Emily to school first thing in the morning and watch as she and a classmate are wheeled into the building in the green plastic wagon. Emily's class looks downright pitiful next to the hordes of elementary kids at this upscale school. They are tiny, for starters, but that is a given because it is a preschool. But these kids are different and it shows. They screech instead of talking; their gait, if they walk at all, is uneven; and many have repetitive behaviors such as clapping or twirling their hair. I take a deep breath every day as I unstrap Emily from her car seat. It takes all the strength I can muster to face the masses of perfect children.

Once Emily is at school, I am on my own for four hours until she needs to be picked up. I am at loss at first and walk around the house like a zombie. So much of my energy has been directed toward Emily's daily care, and now I am aimless. But then the lists come out, all the projects I have ignored for years, all the cleaning I've meant to get complete. I become a dervish, spinning in frenetic energy until every surface is dusted, every tub scoured, and linens folded just so.

I up the ante on my physical exertions. Not enough to merely teach my own classes at the gym, I substitute for anyone who asks. Some weeks I am teaching five days a week. On nonteaching days, I run outside or on the treadmill at the gym. The miles blur by as I hit my stride, and the rhythmical pounding of my feet soothes me. Still I add more, usually lifting weights or riding an exercise bike before teaching a class, or alternatively running three miles after a complete aerobics session. Most weeks I run forty miles total. I know it is crazy, no one needs to exercise two hours a day, but I keep on.

The food I take in to offset these strenuous feats is minimal. Fat-free pretzels are the lunch fare, and sometimes grapes, if I'm really hungry. I make popcorn every night and eat huge bowls full, trying to assuage the hunger pangs with pure bulk. I am headachy a lot, and tired, but I push on. My hands shake when I skip too many meals, but I ignore this. In fact, the buzzing in my head is addictive, the constant motion strangely calming. I shut myself down at night with sleeping pills and awaken dulled.

Emily takes to school right away and has no trouble adjusting. She loves Ms. Rachel, and the feeling seems to be mutual. Notes come home every day in the communication notebook documenting what toys Emily played with, what therapies she had, and any difficult moments. Rachel is working on getting Emily to focus on tasks for longer periods of time, and she gives me tips to try at home. Rachel convinces Emily to sit on the potty, even without any success, as part of a consistent schedule. She encourages us to do the same at home. Emily seems to like stacking rings on a ring toss toy, so we get one for home that is the same as school. The idea is to provide a learning environment wherever Emily happens to be.

By late fall, Emily is the last of her classmates still not walking. She side-steps, or "cruises" down tables and couches very timidly, tumbling often. On a home visit, Rachel encourages us to push for more. She surveys our family room, then moves the coffee table closer to the couch and buts the end table against a far wall, creating an unbroken train of surfaces for Emily to cruise along.

It works—we line up toys, snacks, and books along the furniture, and Emily takes the bait. She transfers from couch to coffee table, to love seat, to end table, and then cautiously turns and goes down the other side. The span is a total distance of twenty-five feet, but it is easily the farthest she has traveled. She gets more confident with each go-round and then poops out. We are elated, and Rachel is just glowing. It is clear Emily can walk, we just need her to leave the comfort of the furniture.

After a month of this, Rachel says to separate the furniture so there is a gap between each structure. Emily will have to transfer from one piece to another because there will not be a continuous line. This is scary for her. Her little fingers grasp the edge of the couch until her nail beds are white. She stretches out the other hand as far as it will go and grunts audibly. Her feet move ever so slightly, and she inches toward the coffee table and finally with a lunge, she's got it. Soon she is cruising comfortably, doing an ugly lunge fall from one piece of furniture to the next, applauding herself at the end. I buy two packs of corner guards, big wedges of rubber that I attach to all the sharp edges because now Emily is a hazard.

Greg's mom gets Emily a Little Tykes plastic grocery cart for her third birthday, and one day Emily transfers to it from the couch and toddles along with it. The look on Emily's face is priceless, pride mixed with fear. She begins staggering around with the cart, first in the family room, then into the uncharted territory of the kitchen, and then the foyer. She bashes into walls and can't manage to turn corners at all, but in a straight line, she's on fire. We weight down the cart with toys and bean bags so it is slow and less dangerous. I bring it with us to school every day so Emily can practice there. The cart offers a new-found freedom of sorts, and our daughter is starting to look like a big girl.

In case we forget that Emily is disabled, there appears to be a whole line of accessible equipment for the toddler set, and we are ready for it now. Rachel orders a walker for Emily to use—a metal contraption with plastic grips for handholds and a sturdy, four-legged base. Emily looks like a miniature geriatric patient with hers, and we would laugh if it were not so sad. She ambulates down the hallways of the elementary school, drawing glances of adoration and pity. People seem to feel sorry for this little blonde girl who is trying so hard. The physical therapist works hard to convince Emily to step away from the walker, but she is not ready yet. Still, to see our daughter upright and moving about is such a leap from a year ago that it seems like a miracle. We wonder if she will walk by herself or if this will be her mode of transportation.

On a lark, I decide to enter a local running race. It is a 10K, which is a tick over six miles, and the course runs right by my house. I would be out running on race day anyway, so I might as well try running with a crowd of others. To my immense surprise, a competitive beast lurks within me. At the start line, I am all nerves and a jumpy stomach. I go out too fast, a big mistake, because the last few miles are fiercely painful. But despite the warm weather and arduous hills, I finish in the top quarter of women runners. My mom takes a picture at the finish line and I look victorious. I immediately head out to buy a training manual for racing—I figure if I am going to push myself like this, I better know what I am doing.

My running takes on a new purpose—not just putting in the miles or the time, but actually having a plan. I run hills one day, do speedwork the next, and run a set pace the next. I buy a running watch, top-of-the-line shoes, and a subscription to *Runner's World*. Greg is proud of my little hobby, but he knows my penchant for going to the extreme. He is worried I will get hurt and urges me to scale back.

In December, my town hosts a Dazzle Dash, a short race run through a five-acre park filled with elaborately decorated Christmas displays. The path winds through nutcrackers, gingerbread men, Santas, and reindeer, all illuminated and twinkling brightly. Heather and I dress in tights, heavy windbreakers, and mittens. At full dark, the race begins, and we dart to and fro, leaping around slower runners, trying to avoid pits in the trail. The air is crisp, and Christmas carols are piped in over a loudspeaker. We finish, panting white puffs of air, and high-five each other. Sipping hot cider and milling around, we run into a friend of Heather's, a woman named Wendy. She is taller, with copper-colored hair and freckles. She finished way before us and uses the jargon of a seasoned runner. I ask if anyone is interested in running from the park to my house, a distance of perhaps two miles. Wendy agrees and we leave the holiday landscape.

As we traipse the roads to my home, we talk the talk of people who don't know each other. We share stories of how we met our husbands, how many kids we have, the basics. I feel a connection immediately and am surprised. I am the kind of woman who does not have many woman friends. I am picky and kind of an introvert, so it is hard. But Wendy has spunk and energy, and I am drawn to her. Without knowing how I know it, this woman will become my friend, a person who will never judge me or Emily and who will help me through the struggles of life.

# CHAPTER 19

The new century opens. Greg and I have been married ten years, and we have a three-and-a-half-year-old daughter who is more like a one-year-old in most ways. I know it is a blessing she has come this far, but it never gets any easier or less painful. We have settled into a routine of Greg's work, Emily's school, and managing the house. The external structures of a middle-class life are all there, but the details are in the fine print.

Emily is on a roll with the walker. She transfers from the walker to other surfaces and cruises down tables with ease. Without something to hold on to, though, she topples like a felled tree. She lacks protective reflexes or the ability to throw out her arms to block a fall. She can get seriously hurt from even the smallest stumble, so we have to watch her all the time.

The physical therapist says it is time to wean her from the walker, but that will be a hard sell. We are supposed to try a strap she says works for some kids. It is basically a knotted piece of multi-colored rope that Emily holds as the therapist tugs on the other end. It reminds me of playing a tugging game with a dog and a chew toy. The strap is not for balance, but for security. The idea is that the therapist will gradually loosen her grip on one end of the strap, eventually enticing Emily to walk holding the strap all alone. But Emily is having none of it—she whines and looks fearful, so we scale back.

The speech therapist sees Emily twice a week and writes to us regularly in the notebook. She is getting more vocalizations from Emily, but they are not real words and still unintelligible. The therapist is not saying it directly, but we know anyway. Emily may never talk in a standard fashion, may never be understood by most. That is why they are pushing the technology. Emily's "talker," as we call it, will be her mode of communication. She has adapted to using the device at school and regularly requests things and answers questions with it. It is still the most basic machine that the school system offers, but I see a day when Emily will move on. Greg does some research and finds that disabled people use all forms of computer-generated voice output devices for everyday life. Another dream is dying—the dream of having an actual conversation with my child, of hearing her say, "Mommy," of hearing her little voice.

Wendy and I sign up to run the Cherry Blossom Race, a ten-miler down in Washington, DC. We train all winter for the April race, slogging through the snow and slush, inventing new routes to get the miles in. We are able to talk while running and it is as I predicted, Wendy does not judge Emily or show pity. She has four kids of her own and has seen the gamut. It is a relief, a gargantuan validation just to have a listener. Sometimes I just vent, other times I complain, and Wendy's always spot-on. She reminds me that even though Emily is a kid with disabilities, she's got a lot right with her, too. I vow to take a page from Wendy's book and not be so mired down in the disability part of it. My optimistic streak has been flagging, and I need a primer now and then to get me back on track.

The day of the race dawns brittle cold and windy. Some of the runners wear trash bags as makeshift windbreakers, to discard later on the course. The race is out-and-back, meaning that we will see the front runners heading to the finish line as we are in the early miles. And see them we do. The race features an international field of runners, with fleet Kenyans and Ethiopians barely touching the ground. I am mistaken to think I am a runner after seeing them—I am merely jogging and will be happy to finish.

In the time it takes us to run four miles, the winner has crossed the finish line. He is probably on a bus to his hotel by the time we finish with the rest of the midpack, but it is a victory anyway. This race begins a tradition—as I cross the finish line, I whisper, "Emily," dedicating the race to her. Emily is running her own race every day, huffing and puffing and giving it her all. If my own child can be an inspiration, she is.

On Greg's 34th birthday, Emily gives us a surprise. I am playing with her, but distractedly. We have the milk and cookies toy out—a plastic milk bottle with a slit in the top. Multicolored plastic "cookies" get inserted in the slot and the bottle goes "MOOOO!" Emily could play with this toy forever, compelled to fill the bottle, hear the sound as she dumps it over and begins again. I have the bottle by the coffee table with a few of the cookies, but the remaining cookies are on the couch, six feet away.

Emily starts her task, filling the bottle halfway. She turns, eyes the other cookies, pauses just a minute, and then launches herself away from the coffee table. She is walking—actually walking—with no grocery cart or walker. The edge of the couch breaks her momentum, Emily grabs the cookies, turns, and comes back. There are cheers all around and clapping. Emily's on a mission the rest of the afternoon, carting toys back and forth from one surface to another. It seems holding a toy makes her feel secure, gives her that anchor she needs.

And so it goes. Rachel calls it "target walking"—as long as Emily can see an endpoint, she will walk toward it, stop, and turn around. Given an empty swath of space, however, and it is a no-go. We shoot endless video of Emily going back and forth, toting items and completing tasks. I joke that she sure is productive, multitasking. Our kid doesn't just walk, I say, she has a job to do. At school, Rachel literally measures the number of feet between the table and desk. Once Emily feels secure going from one to the other, Rachel separates them by a fraction. More than a few inches and Emily's too nervous, so it's is slow going. But she is going, and that is what counts.

When the distance gets pretty far, Emily holds her toy in one hand and pulls on her shirt with the other. Alternatively, she chews on the collar of her shirt or pulls the shirttail up to her mouth and stuffs it in. It is clear she is worried, but she will not stop. This little girl with bobbed blond hair, a lumpy diaper bottom, and sturdy legs is something to see. Both hands are tied up with holding or twisting her shirt as she lurches along. Her way of walking is not graceful, and definitely not the way it is supposed to be done, but we are beyond caring about that.

There is a month left until school wraps up for the year. The goals we outlined at the start of the year have been hit or miss. Some have been achieved, like mastering the voice output device, and others, like independent walking, will have to be recycled for next year's teacher. I have to get used to seeing "Incomplete" on Emily's reports because that is the norm for kids with special needs.

But she has got something up her sleeve, this girl of many surprises. On a sunny May day, Emily is walking to and fro, couch to couch to table, wearing an invisible path in the carpet. Greg has the video camera, and I am luring Emily from one surface to another, prattling on about what a big girl she is.

All of a sudden, Emily veers off course and trundles into the kitchen, a room that is off her usual course. She bypasses the table and refrigerator, likely surfaces for holding, and continues into the dining room. She proceeds around the table and into the foyer. I scurry to keep up with her, actually picking up speed to catch up to my daughter. I gasp and say, "Where are you going, Emily?", and I whisper hushed commands to Greg to get this all on tape. "Oh my God, Greg," I keep whispering. I watch a miracle and I can't quite believe it.

Now we go out to the playground and the mulch is no problem, the pavement does not deter Emily, there is no stopping her now. We call the whole family, crowing, exultant. Most kids walk on their own at a year or thereabouts and here is Emily staring four years old in the face. But that is neither here nor there. I think about the geneticist who said Emily wouldn't walk or talk, and I want him to see her now.

The next day we are off to school and I am jittery. I unload Emily from the car and instead of carrying her to the wagon at the school entrance, I put her down on the asphalt and let go of her hand. She spots Ms. Rachel in the distance and totters toward her, pulling on her shirt, squealing. Rachel squats down, crying, arms out to receive Emily.

"Well, look at you, Emily," she says, "Look who's a big walking girl!!"

I don't know who is happier, Rachel, Emily, or me.

# CHAPTER 20

That summer, my sister Rachel gets married in Maine. The trip would be too much for Emily, so Greg's parents agree to watch her in our home while we attend the wedding. We will be gone for a week, the longest we have ever been without Emily, if you don't count the brief trip to Stowe and all the hospital stays. Emily's in a good place right now and, by proxy, so are we. Reaching that developmental milestone of independent walking is huge. We smile every time we see her toddling around and keep repeating the mantra, "The sky's the limit." After all, she is already doing more than any expert, or we, had predicted.

But despite her recent strides, Emily is never completely healthy. She keeps getting urinary tract infections, even after the kidney surgery, so she takes antibiotics all the time. The kidney surgeon assures us that Emily's ureter will grow as she does and her infections will cease. We take him on faith and ride out one infection after the other. The antibiotics give her secondary yeast infections, compounded by diaper rashes and chafing. So, the poor little girl is never totally comfortable or medicine-free, but she is a trooper anyway. Despite these lingering issues, Emily is more pleasant than she has ever been and actually fun to be around.

Notwithstanding, we need to get away, and the wedding is a perfect excuse. Greg and I operate in two different orbs, his world of work and my dealings with Emily, her school, the therapists, and the doctors. I cannot remember the last conversation that didn't have Emily at its center. We fly up to Manchester, New Hampshire, and rent a car for the drive to Camden. The pine trees and rocky shores are a balm, and we drive along in companionable fashion.

The wedding is on the grounds of the Norumbega, an old Inn on Route 1. Upon our arrival, my sister throws herself into my arms, and it is a mass of curly hair and old memories. I do not see Rachel much, and it has been too long. She is in wedding frenzy mode, dashing here and there attending to details. But she and her fiance, Pat, have time for lunch with us prior to the rehearsal dinner. Over corned beef sandwiches and draft beer, we talk about love and the future. Greg proudly shows them the beautiful ring he had reset for me from a family diamond for our 10th anniversary, just passed. I begin to think about our own wedding, so long ago, and all that has transpired since then. I can't even remember that young woman or what was important to her. In effect, I have buried myself in Emily and her needs, and all that remains is a living corpse.

It is a sobering frame of mind, and it colors the whole week. Amid the gorgeous ceremony and reception, I sense a longing, either for times passed or for a future not filled with so much angst and worry. I am distant from myself, and certainly from Greg, and neither of us can articulate what is happening. The time alone illuminates my inability to relate to my husband the way I once did. He wants to relax, make love, putter around the town, but I am too distracted. I go for runs out on the country roads, five miles out, then five miles back. If asked, I would have just said I'm grumpy, but no one asks, so I put on a happy face and go on. Whatever is happening with me feels objectionable and contrary to my nature, so I push it down.

Emily goes to a different school this fall, another elementary school, this time one closer to our house. It is not as new or upscale as the previous one, but its reputation for special education is stellar. Emily is not good with change in routine, so the first week of

August, we go to meet the teacher and the aides. Ms. Rachel has turned Emily, along with her voluminous paperwork, over to a young woman named Mindy.

We meet Mindy as she rifles through boxes in a room topsy-turvy with kid-friendly decor. Mindy is young, very young, and in fact this may be her first job out of college. I am afraid to ask. She is a soft muffin of a girl with a round face and straw-colored hair. She is shorter than me and is sweating in a grey t-shirt. She sticks her hand out confidently, welcomes me to the classroom, and immediately kneels down to talk with Emily. I give her points right away for knowing she needs to be literally on a child's level. She talks animatedly, with large gestures and big eyes. Emily crows with her sound, which means she is won over.

As Emily plays around the room, I meet the two instructional aides, Rebecca and Barbara, as well as the occupational therapist, Dee, and the speech therapist, Karolyn. It is a bonus to meet this many of the staff so early in the year. I chalk their early presence up to professionalism and preparedness, and I feel relieved. Despite being young, Mindy has got it together. She has read Emily's file and has already come up with a protocol to manage her day. I am impressed with her efficiency and knowledge of Emily's many needs. She is serious about her job and it shows.

Mindy explains that this preschool program, unlike last year's, enrolls typically developing children as well as those with special needs. These "peers," as they are called, serve as role models to the others when it comes to toileting, attention to tasks, and behavior. The Peer Program in the county has been well established and has gotten great reviews. Many of the mothers in my moms' group have their (non-disabled) children enrolled as peers, and they feel strongly that the system works. I feel fortunate that Emily is in such a preschool.

But I am nervous as well—it means more students and more chaos, which is troublesome for Emily, who melts down when things are noisy and overwhelming. Mindy reassures me that Emily's service plan dictates a one-on-one teacher/student ratio.

She will never be unattended. After another half hour of chatting and roaming the classroom, I scoop Emily up to leave. There will never be another teacher like Rachel, but Mindy is good, too, and I have high hopes for this school year.

Two weeks later, I am back to school for the Orientation Night. Parents and their children enter the classroom and it is a model of order now. There are "stations" everywhere, sections of the classroom for each activity. An art corner is filled with tables, easels, tubs of crayons, paint, chalk, and Playdoh. The gross motor area is positioned over soft gym mats, and houses a plastic jungle gym, slant boards, and all manner of balls. This indoor playground helps the kids let off steam and work on their motor goals. A multi-colored rug is in another corner for circle time, surrounded by shelves stocked with books. Up front is a chalkboard with all the children's names on it, plus an elaborate schedule. I notice the school day is broken down into fifteen-minute segments. That must be the longest anyone can stay on task, at least at first.

Next to each activity is a set of initials for which adult will be leading that activity. Each child seems to be assigned to one adult during the separate activities. It looks like the staff rotates responsibility for each child on a daily basis. The schedule is complex, and I can see immediately the genius of it. The children are kept busy and so are the adults. There will never be a dull moment nor will any adult be "stuck" with the same child day after day. These folks know how important a fresh face is.

Mindy has got her work cut out for her. There are four disabled children in the class matched with the four typically developing peers. Seated next to us is a boy named Brandon. He is clearly autistic, with the textbook flapping hands and averted gaze. But his receptive language is great—when his dad tells him repeatedly to sit down, he does--repeatedly. Chiara sits one row up, a sweet-faced black girl who is as quiet as can be, but prone to awful tantrums. I soon learn she is also autistic and nonverbal. She has some serious impulse-control issues, making her the wild card of the bunch. Little Kelvin is in back, an Asian boy who looks so much

younger than the rest, only he isn't. I don't know what is wrong
with him, but it is something pretty major. He has trouble even sitting up on his own, and the bright lights in the room bother him.
He clings to his mother, a wisp-thin woman with the softest voice.
Kelvin needs to crumple paper in his hands to calm himself, so
his mom has brought an arsenal of brightly colored construction
paper, enough to last the whole session.

I hate myself for gaping at these children, and I try not to be
too obvious. I can't seem to stop the age-old comparison game.
How does Emily stack up against these children? Is she better off
or worse? In truth, it is impossible to tell. They are all so different
from one another; the proverbial apples and oranges. I do not even
know if Emily is capable of making friends, if these children will
become her friends.

At one point, I shift my gaze from the children to their parents. A new fascination of mine is to study other parents of kids
with disabilities to see how they are faring. I practice this game at
the moms' dinners every month and also on visits with my friend,
Sue. Sitting here, welcoming in the new preschool year, I get to
do it again. I am rewarded with tired eyes masquerading behind
brave smiles, a courageous resolve alongside the devastation. I
squirm and am uncomfortable in this environment, and I can't figure out why until I glance over at Greg. He has the same eyes, the
same steely facade as all the other parents. That must mean I have
it, too, and I swallow hard to realize that I am not the onlooker I
pretend to be.

# CHAPTER 21

The despair I felt at the wedding last summer persists, but I quash it every day with activity. I find that being busy is an antidote for pain, so I embrace a self-imposed schedule of relentless motion. Despite the fact that I see Emily less, given her full days at school, I do more on her behalf. I lobby for private speech therapy for over a year, and finally my efforts have paid off. A program nearby uses graduate students in speech therapy to take on special needs clients as part of their practicum prior to graduation. Emily has been moving up the wait list and now she is finally in. Every Wednesday, we drive to the Loyola campus for an hour of therapy. The cost is exorbitant, but after some arguing, I get the insurance company to pay for half.

Our therapist is a fresh-faced student named Angela who is overjoyed to work with an actual person. She takes Emily to the motor room first, swinging her on a tire swing to calm her in preparation for the real work. If Emily wants to swing more, or to quit, she has to vocalize a particular sound. Angela models the sound, tapping on her own cheek to draw attention to her mouth. Emily tries to echo the sound, usually making a guttural effort instead. But it is something, and the therapist responds with claps and smiles.

They use the PECS system here, and Emily is familiar with that. The twist is that she can't just point to or grab a picture. She has to say, or try to say, the word. If Emily wants to move on to the slide, crawl through the tunnel, or even stop for a break, she has to articulate the sound that accompanies the picture. Emily does a lot of screaming in frustration and a fair bit of writhing to get away, but Angela is tough. Emily learns quickly: make a sound, get something in return. The simplicity of cause and effect works for her, and she flourishes.

They use a two-way mirror during the speech sessions, and I get to watch my child without her seeing me. I sit in a small, warm room with a chair and video equipment. If Emily or Angela moves to a section of the room that is out of my range, I have been taught how to train the video camera on that area so as not to miss anything. I take notes throughout the session, observing the sounds Emily does well and those that need work.

After the motor room, we progress down the hall to another therapy room, a sort of miniclassroom. I am again escorted behind the two-way mirror as Emily and Angela go next door. This portion of the session is harder for Emily. Angela pulls out all manner of horns, straws, bubbles, and toothbrushes. The idea is to make Emily more aware of the muscles in her mouth by performing various exercises with her mouth. I had never thought about the complexities of speech in this much detail before, and it is shocking. Even as an untrained person, I can tell that to form certain sounds the lips need to come together and the tongue needs to pull back. Emily struggles with this, and that is where all these instruments come in.

Angela holds a bubble wand up to Emily's mouth and urges her to blow. Emily tries, but she can't. Her lips just won't meet up that way. Angela tries a small horn, a kazoo, really, and Emily inhales instead of exhaling. She is confused and frustrated. Angela decides not to push it, but not to give up either.

In subsequent visits, Emily gets her teeth and gums massaged with a Nuk brush, a knobby, brushless apparatus that stimulates the gums. Angela explains that Emily has poor sensation in her mouth. She can't necessarily feel where her own tongue is, and that is why proper placement is so hard for her. It also explains why

Emily stuffs her mouth with food. She can't really sense how full her mouth is. This Nuk brush is designed to heighten awareness of sensation. Emily hates the brush, hates being interfered with. Angela uses a count of thirty to give Emily an endpoint, and that seems to work. No one claps harder than Emily when Nuk-time is over.

Angela asks me to bring a snack and a drink to the sessions with us, and she uses these as reinforcers to entice Emily to cooperate. One vocal utterance equals one graham cracker. It is the tried-and-true Pavlovian conditioning, and it works. Emily uses a sippy cup for drinking, one of those closed bottles with a long straw attached. Angela asks if it is okay if she modifies the cup, and I nod yes. Before I know it, she takes a pair of scissors and lops the straw down to a nub. Now when Emily wants to drink, she has to work her tongue back and purse her lips closed tightly to get a purchase on the straw. This handy little trick trains her mouth to close every time she sips. Soon all the cups we own have whittled down straws, and Emily, for the first time in her life, can regularly get her lips close enough together to kiss. It is one of those little things that is a landmark to us.

Angela uses puppets and flashcards as well, and gives me a take-home set. I am intimidated, so I watch Angela like a hawk as she prompts Emily. She opens up the puppet crocodile's mouth as wide as it can go and then presents Emily a flashcard to "feed" the crocodile. Each flashcard has a sound affiliated with it, and the game is that the crocodile only eats if the sound is uttered. Angela prompts Emily with the sounds—first vowels because they are easier and take less physical skill to form.

Angela makes an exaggerated face as she makes the sound "EEEEEEE" and brandishes the flashcard. The crocodile gobbles it up with gulping, chewing noises. Emily thinks that this is the funniest thing she has ever seen and is anxious to do it herself. She tries five times before she can say "EEEEEE" to Angela's satisfaction, and then Emily gets to feed the crocodile herself. The puppet grabs the card with a flourish and chomps away, glub glub glub.

And so it goes—make the right sound, get a snack or a drink or praise or an exciting puppet snatching away your flashcard. Emily is in heaven with all these rewards for her efforts. Angela is smart, this whole program is ingenious, and my child is responding. Moving along to the harder things, like consonants, is a real challenge, but the early success and payoff are motivating for Emily. When I announce every Wednesday that it is time for speech with Ms. Angela, Emily flaps her hands with excitement and squeals with glee.

The graduate students at the center, as well as their supervisors, are bowled over by Emily's cooperation and enthusiasm. By the end of the school year, they ask whether they can make a videotape of Emily's sessions to show as a model to future students. Usually loathe to publicize Emily this way, this time I say yes with certainty.

At home, my copy of the flashcards lies in a stack in the family room. Three days a week, we get out our own puppets and do the drill. Say the sound, puppet chomps the card, Mommy and Emily clap and get a snack. It is repetitive, but Emily loves it, and I dig deep to summon up a portion of the energy that Angela has for this task. Emily is nowhere near talking, she can't even say one word, but if anything will help her to learn, these drills are the ticket. She is already more organized and specific in her sounds. Instead of random, unintelligible noises, we can actually pick out clear vocalizations. Our daughter emits the type of babbling an eight-month-old might make, which is depressing to be sure, but so much more than she could ever do before.

# CHAPTER 22

Work is everywhere, it seems. Mindy says she is developing a behavior modification plan for Emily. The behavior goal is to reduce or eliminate "stimming," which is a special needs term for "self-stimulation," something almost every special needs kid does. Despite its masturbatory sound, that is not what it is. A child "stims" to regulate the world, to produce motion, and to organize his or her senses. Indeed, most stimming is a sensory experience, eliciting a calming feeling.

Most children with autism have recognizable stims, with the tell-tale flapping hands the most prevalent. Emily flaps as well, but has branched out from there to include shirt chewing, hand biting (her own), and tag rubbing. The sensory input she derives from these actions makes her content, but they detract from her ability to learn and are inappropriate as well. We decide to add this component to Emily's class routine, addressing her "stimming" behaviors. Suddenly, her education seems so complex.

Although Emily walks independently now, her gross motor skills are still lagging terribly. She has no upper body strength to swing from playground bars, nor can she walk up or down steps. When going from a standing to a sitting position, she plops down in an ungainly fashion, instead of folding her body piece by piece. With any change in surface, such as from blacktop to mulch, Emily stops and feels with her toe to make sure there is no drop-off. She requires hand-holding up and down the halls in school to negotiate comfortably amid the moving sea of students. She is unsure of where her body is in space, and she looks both stiff and tentative in almost every position.

Her struggles are due, in part, to our old friend, "motor planning," the complex set of steps that must be sequenced to complete a task. A lot of thinking is required for Emily to maneuver basic physical feats. But there is also the component of her heart surgery. Performed almost three years ago, Emily's scar from the surgery is faded to a white-pink, but the muscle hasn't healed as fast as the skin. Emily's shoulders, arms, back, and chest are weak and must be built up if she is to regain flexibility.

To this end, the physical therapist recommends two things: a routine of upper body exercises that we are to perform with Emily at home, and swimming sessions. A special school is nearby, outfitted with a therapy pool that is perfectly suited to our needs.

The Cedar Lane School is a facility for special needs children with "profound involvement," the euphemism for kids who are badly off. Going into Cedar Lane is grueling. During the school day, the students, most of whom are non-mobile, are wheeled through the corridors in their wheelchairs. Some are even in beds, and it looks like they are restrained to keep them from hurting others or themselves. The children here sway and crane their necks, howling and banging. But the staff is cheery and seemingly immune to the chaos and sadness around them.

I sign up for swimming lessons in the therapy pool and am relieved to discover that the sessions will be at night. The less I have to see of these severely involved children, the better. I find that it is a peculiar relief that, although I often think of Emily as terribly affected, in truth she could be a lot worse.

Therapy pools are great for kids with high tone. The pool is heated, and the lights are low. Every Tuesday night at 7:30, Emily and I don bathing suits and get into the pool with six other parents and their children. The goal here is not to learn to swim, but to

operate the muscles of the body within the weightless environment of the pool.

The warm water and dim lights are relaxing from the get-go.
Emily allows me to hold her in a variety of positions that are normally pretty uncomfortable for her. Stretched out, face down in
my arms, Emily's mouth and nose skim the water. She needs to
hold her head up to breathe, so she cranes her neck and tilts her
forehead up. This position is non-preferred and always has been;
it is the reason that Emily never crawled. Holding her head at this
angle is just too difficult. But here in the water, she is less rigid and
can sustain the movement a bit longer.

Holding Emily's slippery body is a joy, and I am happy for the
opportunity. As an infant, Emily was not a snuggler, just a crier.
She never molded herself to my body or clasped her arms around
my neck. If I hold her on my hip, her shape does not conform to
my body. Instead, she holds herself at a rigid reserve, backing off
and pulling away. She likes to be patted and hugged briefly, but not
held, and there is a big difference. Here in the water, she has no
choice but to cling, and I lap it up.

I wrap Emily's bony legs around my waist and fasten her arms
around my shoulders. We skim along in the water, bobbing down
and up, just getting comfortable. I hum quietly in her ear, slick-
ing her hair back and squeezing droplets from the ends. I flip her
from front to back, practice kicking and paddling. Emily would
rather slap the water and tries to splash wildly, but I guide her
arms around in a circular fashion.

The instructor doesn't give a lesson, per se, just shows us some
moves and gives us safety tips. Some of the kids at the session are
swimmers already and work on their strokes, whereas some hover
near the edge of the pool, reluctant to get in at all. We are here to
get some pliability into Emily's limbs, to introduce ways for her to
move that dry land makes too difficult.

It must be called a therapy pool for that reason—it is magic the
way Emily relaxes and becomes like jelly in my arms. Her limbs,
although still tight, are more adaptable in the warmth, and she

feels comparatively droopy. I help her flex her legs and then bend her knees to kick. We practice neck rotation, blowing bubbles, and treading water. The water is as warm as a bath, and it is almost sensual to be touching Emily's little hands, legs, body. The half-hour session goes by too quickly, and suddenly we are out of the water and into the bright cold of the locker room.

I towel Emily off with brisk strokes and bundle her chlorinated self into a diaper, t-shirt, and zip-up sleeper. She is asleep by the time I strap her in the car seat, and she transfers easily into her bed at home. I question whether we are learning anything at swimming—certainly not how to swim. I can't even tell whether it pays off with enhanced motor ability in her daily life. But I am loath to part with this slice of the night when I can hold my daughter and feel warm and safe with her.

# CHAPTER 23

As fall turns into winter and Emily settles into the preschool routine with Ms. Mindy at the new school, I up the ante on my running. Partly it is to fill the time—the endless day when Emily is away at school. But partly I am addicted to the endorphin rush of the physical exercise. I begin to plan a race schedule for myself and map out training mileage and running routes. Wendy and I decide to run a local Metric Marathon— a distance of sixteen miles over locally hilly terrain. This is farther than I have ever run at one stretch before, and I feel intimidated. But the challenge suits me and mollifies the angst that is my daily companion.

Wendy has been a runner since high school, and next to her I am a novice at this long-distance thing. She knows all about hydration, energy drinks, and shoes. I pick her brain for training ideas and am motivated by her speed and energy. As the training runs are long and arduous, it is smart to train together for a race of this length. Company helps to pass the time. Our routine is to begin a long run of two hours or more by at least six in the morning. That way, we are done before the day has really started and have time to spend with our families.

Greg is on board with the whole running thing, in as much as it makes me happy, but I sense his growing dislike for this athletic side of me. He does morning duty while I am out on these training runs—waking Emily, changing her, and feeding her—and all this he does happily and well. He is never resentful, but there is an undercurrent of dissatisfaction. I urge Greg to find a hobby of his own so his life is not just work and Emily, but he is reluctant. He feels guilty about leaving me in the lurch with more child-care duties. I try to explain how it helps everyone if parents attend to their own lives, but again Greg desists. What he really wants is more time with me, he misses me. I am selfish, he says, to over-look him in favor of running. A bone of subdued contention rises between us. I feel certain it should be clear to anyone that I need, absolutely crave, this time for myself.

I have to renege on these hard feelings, though, when I cross the finish line of the Metric Marathon, worn out but jubilant, to see the cheering faces of Greg and Emily. He has bundled Emily up in an enormous snowsuit, loaded her into the stroller, and located me at the end of the race—no small feat. I chastise myself for thinking Greg unsupportive, and I resolve to do better by him.

It doesn't happen all at once, but rather sneaks up on me. The eat-ing disorder I conquered in high school is back with a vengeance. The rigid diet and excessive exercise have a relentless hold over me and I can't get out. I feel for my hip bones in all my clothes, and I get panicky if they don't feel sharp enough. Feeling full scares me, so I am empty most of the time. Running and teaching aerobics on little food is an act of will. Sometimes I think I will topple over from fatigue and stabbing hunger pangs. The buzzing headaches are still there, but I have learned to ignore them. I drink no-calo-rie Crystal Light, Gatorade, and lots of water. Social events are torture because I want to eat but can't bring myself to. I push food around my plate in an effort to disguise the fact that I am not eat-ing. I wonder if it's normal for a 34-year-old mother of one child to need a nap every day. I am tired, bone tired, all the time, but compulsively driven to ignore my body's warning signs.

Why this old demon has taken hold of me now is not a mystery. My life has been out of control these last few years. I have turned myself over to the caring of a disabled child, and I wing it every day. I am tormented by guilt and inadequacy, and I feel nervous all the time. I fool myself into thinking that if I can control one element of life—my eating and exercise—the other, more chaotic parts will fall in line as well. None of it is rational, none of it makes sense, I am aware of all that. But it's not like a leaky faucet that can be turned off at will. This coping mechanism has a tight grip on me.

On a dare, Wendy and I decide to get our belly buttons pierced. For two moms in their 30s to sport belly rings is ludicrous, really—downright trashy. But we are proud of the slim bodies we have achieved from all the running, and we want to have something to show for it. Greg is adamantly against the idea and is horrified that I would even think about it. But we will not be deterred.

On a Monday afternoon, we meet at a tattoo and piercing parlor in the historic district of town. The tattoo and piercing artist is a scary looking young man with holes all over his body and colorful art everywhere the eye can see. You could easily push a tube of Lifesavers through the enormous holes in his ears. But he is nice enough, and the upstairs anteroom where the procedure takes place is clean and sterile. He asks what type of ring I want—simple, silver, not too showy—and I lie back on the drape-covered table. He rubs betadine on my belly, pulls a wedge of skin taut, tells me to anticipate a small pinch, and it is over. I have now got jewelry in my belly button. The tiny hole throbs and the waistband of my pants rubs a bit, but it is done. I sit up slowly, check to make sure I feel okay, and then hop off the table and let Wendy see before her turn.

When Greg gets home from work that night, I am stirring chili on the stove, and Emily is watching "Baby Songs" on the TV. I must have a strange look on my face because he asks, "Did you do it?", to which I answer by pulling up my shirt. Greg squats to look at the ring and says, "I can't believe it." He is part joking, part serious, but I know. He has lost a little respect for me. This person to whom he is married is changing before his eyes, and there is nothing he can do. I used to be predictable, always happy, even-keeled. But now there is an edge he can sense, all this crazy running and

now the belly ring. He knows better than to tell me to stop, and I
know I am scaring him.

This spring, I have two races back to back, first the ten-mile
Cherry Blossom Race that I have run before, and then a 10K the
next weekend. This schedule is intense, but I feel certain I can pull
it off. The ten-miler goes well, and I add another race T-shirt to
my growing pile. Mom got me a scrapbook for my last birthday,
and I use it to document these races, my times, and the weather. I
am greedy for more pages and more races. The week in between
the two events goes as usual. I do not think of scaling back on the
aerobics or finding a substitute.

By Friday, I am wiped. The daily household tasks seem daunting, and I catch myself nodding off while folding laundry. The Friday before the 10K, I get my usual hunger headache, but I think
nothing of it. In the shower the next morning, I am washing my
hair and all of a sudden I need to grip the wall. I fall before I can
call out, and Greg hears the thud from downstairs. He pulls me
out of the shower and places me on a towel in the vestibule. I come
to with him holding my face and calling my name. He pulls me
into bed and piles blankets on. I shiver there while we decide what
to do. Greg's sister, who is a nurse, is visiting for this weekend. She
takes one look at my face and we are off to the hospital.

In the Emergency Room, I am triaged into a small area. My
urine sample is dark brown, and I know before they tell me that
I am severely dehydrated. Two IV bags of saline later and I am
restored. Greg tells me my cheeks aren't sunken anymore, and I
can see that my rings aren't rotating around my fingers. I am all
plumped up with liquid. The doctor on call gives me a stern talking to about overdoing it. There will be no race for me this weekend. I cry on the way home, partly from the shock of fainting, but
also from the shame of letting things get this bad. I thought I was
in control when I don't have any control at all.

# CHAPTER 24

Ms. Mindy gives me a project in the spring. Emily will be five in the fall and needs to get potty trained. Now that she can walk, we have got to get going on this. The brunt of the chore falls to me because I am with Emily the most. Mindy tells me to find a method I like, set the protocol, and the school will follow my model. Learning to use the toilet is a huge milestone for most kids, usually mastered at age two or three. As with everything else, Emily is delayed. She learns everything differently than a typically developing child, so it stands to reason that she will accomplish this in her own way as well.

I visit the library, scouring shelves for literature on potty training. Most books I find are for "normal" kids and will not work for us. Emily can get herself to the bathroom; that is not an issue. Rather, the challenge is all the little things, like pulling down her pants, seating herself on the toilet, wiping, and pulling the pants back up. With her fine motor impairments, these steps are challenging at best. The Internet yields a more fruitful supply of books, and I order several. I feel pressured to get this right because the school is counting on me to say how I want this toileting program to run. Surely they know I am no expert, that I am in fact just guessing at this motherhood thing from day to day.

There is an Early Childhood Support facility in town. They serve the community of children and parents by providing resources for a myriad of needs, from names of doctors to food allergy-friendly grocery stores. One day a flier arrives in the mail from this agency. A list of parenting seminars is offered and, voila, one of them is Toilet Learning for the Disabled Child. The class is timely and inexpensive, so I phone right away to sign up.

For four Tuesday nights in a row, I head out after dinner to hear speakers discourse on potty training. I bring home folders, pamphlets, and reams of notes. The other parents at the workshop are a mish-mash. Some have children with behavior problems and will be a challenge with anything. Others have children in wheelchairs, for whom independent toileting may be an ambitious goal. Many, like me, have a child who can't be pigeon-holed neatly into the "special needs" category. We all have our own separate issues, and we are all hoping the answers are here.

We learn that a child has to be physiologically ready, first of all. They need to know when they have to go. Then, they have to be able to negotiate the steps that it takes to get to the bathroom and manage the entire toileting routine. This involves a long sequence of awareness and events, and all the parents look on, baffled, as the speakers discourse about rewards charts, keeping a potty log, and various brands of training diapers.

If anything, the course has made the whole process more complicated, not less. I get frustrated, so I pull back a bit and spend some time thinking about how Emily learns best. She thrives on praise, she depends on a daily schedule, she loves to eat, and she loves music. There must be a way I can come up with something that uses all these characteristics. Greg and I sit down and map out Emily's day. We earmark several times a day, roughly after waking, mid-morning, before lunch, before nap, before dinner, and before bedtime. These will be designated "potty times," when we will bring Emily to the bathroom and sit her on the potty. It is too much to expect her to manage the pants-down portion, so we will do that for her. We will make her meals contingent on going to the bathroom, we will praise her ebulliently when she goes, and we will incorporate some music in there, somehow.

It works like a charm. The regimentation of our schedule appeals to Emily, as does our enthusiasm and "big girl" chants. When she has success on the potty, she gets our praise, a hug, and then a snack or, if it is mealtime, her full meal. Greg even makes up a potty song to the tune of the "ABC" song. He launches into a spirited rendition whenever Emily is on the toilet, and sure enough, she goes. I throw out her diapers, except the heavy-duty ones we use for nighttime, and now Emily wears little girl underpants. This process is way easier than we anticipated, but not without snafus. Because we take her to the bathroom on a schedule, her body is conditioned to the clock. If we are late, she is wet. If there is any variation to her fluid intake, she often overflows instead of holding it. We need to devise a way for Emily to tell us when she needs to go.

Greg suggests using sign language, and I wonder why no one has ever tried that before. There is no sign in the sign language manual that is simple enough for Emily to use, so we make one up. A flat-handed pat to the upper thigh with her right hand means Emily has to go. We show her over and over as we take her to the potty, and by the third day we drop the sign to see what she will do. Sure enough, she pats her right thigh as she walks to the bathroom, crowing to herself. She knows she has done something major here.

Now we have to get the school on board. I write up our entire plan, complete with the toileting schedule, the words to the potty song, and the sign Emily uses. I also pack three fresh outfits in Emily's backpack because it will be a rough start and I know to anticipate accidents at school. Mindy is pleased with our progress at home and supports our regimen whole heartedly. The notes home in Emily's notebook reflect mostly successful ventures at school. She is the first of all the disabled kids to use the potty, so she has an audience every time and seems to enjoy being a model.

I am not fooled into thinking she has this mastered, but it is a good start. She may never be trained all the way and certainly not at night for a long while, but still the whole experience is a feather in our caps as parents. Emily has been in capable, trained hands since her diagnosis, whether it be doctors, therapists, or teachers. This is the first time we have been called on to take charge of a portion of Emily's development. This lesson is a testament to parents' intuition and an enormous boost to our parenting egos. I still wing it every day, but at least there is this, little as it is, that I can point to and say, "I tried something out on Emily, all by myself, and it worked."

# CHAPTER 25

School is out for the year, and for the first time in Emily's life, we are going on a beach vacation. Greg's folks have rented a house in Duck on the Outer Banks of North Carolina. The house is right on the ocean, with water views and sand galore. Our whole summer leads up to this vacation as we consult the calendar and make plans. I am a little concerned about how Emily will take to the change in routine and location, so I decide to keep the early part of the summer as stress-free as I can.

Emily attends summer school three days a week, basically a truncated version of the regular school day. We find ourselves with a bit more time together, so I plan pool outings and trips to local playgrounds. It feels liberating to be more flexible, out from under the tight regime of school and therapies. Having a vacation to plan for makes me feel like we are almost a normal family.

However, we are anything but normal, a fact that is hammered home on an almost daily basis. I go to the gym every day, and now I bring Emily along to play in the nursery as I teach a class or work out. It has been a while since I have observed Emily in the company of this many regular kids, and I am taken aback. In the privacy of our home, I look at Emily and forget she is disabled. I see her as a plump-cheeked, white-blonde little girl who plays vigorously and is moving around nonstop. But in comparison to the other kids racing around the nursery, she sticks out like a sore thumb. Her face is not maturing at the rate of a typical almost five-year-old. The plump cheeks I adore make her look babyish. The motoring around that I take such joy in—after all, she is pretty new to walking—looks staggery and uncoordinated next to the fluidity of the other children.

Emily's play with toys is also odd. It takes me a while to determine what it is that sets her apart, and then I realize. To Emily, a toy is always what it is. She lacks the capacity to imagine that a toy car might morph into an airplane or that a series of blocks might be formed into a boat. To her, a block is a block. She bangs toys together, manipulates the parts, but doesn't pretend. She doesn't have any interest in dolls or play figurines because they don't do anything. She simply can't imagine a plot or enact a scenario. Her play is functional, basic, and very telling.

The kinds of toys Emily does enjoy are those that require the least effort, simple cause-and-effect toys. We have an entire toy box filled with battery-operated push-and-hear toys. Push a button and hear a letter of the alphabet, the MOO of a cow, or a color. There is instant gratification to these toys, sure, but no real complexity. Emily also likes to hold pretend phones up to her ear, listening to the warbling ringing tone over and over and over. It keeps her occupied, but it is not creative play.

One of the early books I read on mental retardation talks about this concept, and I get the book out again now. I seem to remember a passage about what the lack of abstract thought means. I tremble as the passage reveals itself to me. Complex, higher order thinking involves the ability to imagine. Pretend play is the cornerstone of cognitive development. If a child cannot form imaginative characters or assign abstractions to their play, they do not possess higher order cognitive skills. I am floored and then immediately chagrined at myself. What did I think—that despite a major chromosomal syndrome, she would nonetheless be normal? The evidence that she does not have higher order thinking has been there all along, but somehow I fooled myself into thinking it was not so.

I pause to take inventory of all that Emily can do, and the list is long. She can walk, eat by herself, follow simple directions, go to the potty regularly, and make word approximations. But the truth is there right in front of me, in black and white. She is limited, severely so, and there is nothing I can do about it.

I guess on some level I have been living under the false assumption that she would catch up. But the chasm between Emily and all the other kids, whether at school, the gym nursery, at the pool, or the playground, is startling. I know this disparity will only become more pronounced as Emily grows from a preschooler to an elementary student and beyond. I must accept this truth, but feel I just can't. In fact, I have never felt less prepared for anything in my entire life.

Emily is figuratively crippled by her abnormal chromosomes. I try to be strong for my daughter, but it seems I am crippled, too. The dreams I had for her, and for myself as a mom, are dying more and more every day, and I can't seem to find a way through this pain.

# CHAPTER 26

July opens as a swampy morass of humidity. The Washington, DC, area is known for its torpid summers, and we are not getting off easy this year. Emily and I swelter through the days, staying in the air conditioning or visiting the pool. Even with SPF 50 sunblock on, our pale bodies are getting tan. Greg fights the commuter traffic every day and comes home with sweat rings under his arms. We count the days until we can head to the beach.

Our Ford Explorer is packed to the gills with everything we need. We even have a travel TV so Emily can watch her favorite videos as we drive. I stuff an entire bag full of snacks, and a basket of books sits right next to Emily's car seat. We agree to split up the driving, and I take the first shift. To our surprise, Emily travels well, mesmerized by the "Little Bear" and "Blues Clues" tape that Greg has made for her. We stop occasionally for gas and bathroom breaks, parsing out the snacks one after the other. We have brought along a travel potty so that Emily won't have to brave a Shell station bathroom, and it is a success. I am sure I look ridiculous toting around a vintage wooden mini-toilet with a lamb applique on the back, but people can think whatever they want. My daughter pees at rest stops and I am proud.

The trip is six hours, the last hour stop and start up the only access road to the colony. Our development in Duck is three miles up this road, and we chomp at the bit to arrive there. Our rental home, called Farmer, is set back from the beach by only one house, so it is virtually oceanfront. The house is all weathered wood siding, scrubby landscaping, and crushed shells on the sidewalk. I can smell the salt air and hear the seagulls, and I can't wait to show Emily the ocean.

Greg's folks meet us at the house, having traveled from Indiana. Emily and I skim into our swimsuits while Greg's mom sets up the kitchen. The walk is a short jaunt along a scalding boardwalk to the sea. Over a small dune, and there it is. Emily's footing is unsure over the sand and she is fussy with the heat, so I lift her up to my hip and cart her down the dune. A tangled mess of seaweed winds around my ankles before the soft surface of yellow sand, so it is a good thing Emily is in my arms. Once the sand turns wet and hard nearer the water, I put Emily down and watch for her reaction. Emily has no sense of danger and doesn't know that the surf and undertow could be scary. I hold her hand as she advances. The water laps over her toes and she wiggles with the cold shock of it. She squeals and walks farther in. Here we stop and let the waves come over our feet, up to our legs. Emily is entranced, all flapping hands and eyes darting around. The delight on her face is a gift.

I am coming unwound this week, though, and instead of enjoying this vacation, I feel miserable. Whatever has been wrong with me is escalating. I am out every day at 5:30 a.m., struggling into a sports bra, running shorts and shoes. I creep out of the house and down to the running trail, a great paved sidewalk that runs parallel to the access road, so there is no chance of getting lost. The trail is marked every mile with sign posts, so I can keep track of how far I go. The route is flat, which should mean easy going, but the heat is just brutal. There are no trees for shade, and the sun glinting off the water, even this early in the morning, is torture. I sweat little chunks of salt on my face after only fifteen minutes.

Every day is the same, out the door at the crack of dawn, down the trail for 3.5 miles, turn around at the t-shirt novelty shop, then back. It takes an hour most days and wipes me out for the rest of the day. I am relentless with myself. I won't shorten the route, or take a day off, no matter how tired I am.

One day I run alongside a man who is wearing a marathon shirt. We hit our stride together, and I ask about marathons. Wendy and I are thinking of training for one in the fall, and I am intrigued by the idea. This man is a veteran of marathons and reels off the ones he has run, citing the hills, his finishing times, his favorites. He has specific ideas about training programs, nutrition, and hydration. I latch on to his enthusiasm.

I decide at that moment to get more serious about running and can't wait to run a marathon of my own. Never mind that I am fatigued after only an hour—the appeal of long-distance running is intoxicating, and this racer-man is just the impetus I need. He sprints ahead of me as I peel off for home, leaving me with a final bit of information. The mile markers here on the Outer Banks, he says, are off by 1/4 of a mile. During all these days I thought I was running seven miles in an hour, I have only run a bit over six. I am devastated.

The days revolve around meals, trips to the beach and the pool, and naptime for Emily. I am a whirling dervish all day, pushing through fatigue. If I sit down, I might fall asleep. At the beach, we line up the beach chairs, cover them with towels, grease Emily up with sunscreen, and get out the sand toys. I bask in the sun while Emily bangs shovels and buckets together. Typical Emily, she does not build sandcastles or fill buckets with sand. She just bangs, taps, and drums on the buckets.

I am uncomfortable on the beach, not at home in my body and as self-conscious as ever, despite the years of fitness. I am thinner now than I have ever been, but I still feel bulky. Greg's folks look askance at the belly ring, and I feel weird about that, too. Greg can relax on his chair with a Pepsi or a beer, but I am wound too tight, always fretting and worried.

Our 11th anniversary has just passed, and Greg's folks offer to watch Emily while we go into town for a meal. The restaurant is family-style and noisy, but our booth is tucked in the back and not too bad. We order scallops and steak and talk about the vacation so far. We are proud of Emily for dealing well with a different routine and a new environment. But it is not Emily that Greg wants to talk about—it is us. He is tired of the way I am acting and wonders what is wrong. Why am I so rigid, so controlling, why can't I relax? He reads me the riot act about the morning runs. Instead of getting up to run every day, he says, why can't I stay in bed and make love with him? He thinks I am obsessed and selfish. He has lost sight of me and misses the person I used to be.

I understand everything he says, I do, but I react badly. I am being criticized and it hurts, so I lash back defensively. I accuse him of being unsupportive and demanding more of me than I can give. It is a poor talk, and we are both wounded by the time the meal is over. We stop for ice cream at a shop overlooking the sound, and I gaze out at the water. What Greg doesn't know is that I have become as foreign to myself as I have to him. I do not recognize myself anymore, but I will not admit that to anyone. The hard covering I have been wearing ever since Emily's birth has tightened and crystallized until now I am petrified in a shell of my own making.

We form a truce, putting on a happy face for Greg's parents, but a palpable rift lurks, seething. It was a big fight for us, and it has left its mark. On the way home the next day, I study Greg's profile, as familiar as my own. Marriages shatter easily under the rigors of having a disabled child, I know the statistics. I thought we would be the exception, but now I am not so sure.

# CHAPTER 27

In the fall of 2001, Emily is in her second year of MINC preschool, again with Ms. Mindy. With an October birthday, Emily has just missed the cutoff for kindergarten. She is nowhere near ready for kindergarten anyway, even a special education class, so we are just as glad to wait. With the same school, teacher, aides, and therapists, Emily is in her comfort zone. She greets everyone at the school doors with a confident flap of her hands and a yelp of happiness. Even the teachers who don't have Emily in class, the 1st- through 5th-grade teachers, seem to know her and give her a smile. Being in Emily's wake is like walking with a mini-celebrity.

But it is not as happy a comeback for me. I have been hit with a ton of bricks and can't get out from under them. My husband is perpetually annoyed with me, I am always exhausted from non-stop running, and the reality of Emily's condition is just now hitting me. It is a delayed realization, to be sure, but maybe it has just taken this long to finally sink in. I have read about post-traumatic stress syndrome, and I wonder if I qualify. I was able to hold it together through Emily's early years, the hardest times, but now I am floundering when life is comparatively easy-going.

My heart aches, actually contracts in pain, as I watch the hordes of children entering the elementary school this year. They chat amiably with each other, hoisting backpacks over their shoulders, running to greet teachers with summer tales. As if someone is speaking directly in my ear, the thought occurs: Having Emily is not enough. I absolutely need the experience of a "normal" child to mend my wounds. Almost as soon as I think this, I feel like a traitor, as if I have betrayed Emily. I love her, I do, but it weighs heavy, a guilty love, one borne out of worry and pain.

At home that night, I broach the subject to Greg. Emily is almost five. I will be thirty-five on my next birthday. Why don't we try for another child? Greg won't entertain the thought for an instant. He is dead set against it, thinks I am being sentimental instead of practical. Emily demands so much of our time, so much of our emotional energy. We would have nothing left for another child, he says. It just wouldn't be fair. Plus, we don't even know if we can have a healthy child. He is right about all this, so I reluctantly shelve the idea. But buried inside is the idea that I have not met all my children yet.

September 11, 2001, dawns a crisp, cloudless blue. It is one of those fall mornings that feel like a true respite from the summer's torpid heat. Emily and I have breakfast and then play in the family room before we get ready to leave for school. Emily is a haphazard player, careening from one toy to another, lurching as she walks. On one of these ricochets around the room, she stumbles and I see what is going to happen before it actually occurs. Before I can get to her, Emily has fallen hard against the coffee table. We have long since removed the corner guards, and she falls right on the point.

Her head slams hard and there is a horrible silence before she screams. A huge gash opens right at her hairline, and it sends arcs of blood across the room. I know head and facial wounds bleed a lot, but I am not prepared for this amount. Quick as I can, I scoop her up and take her into the bathtub upstairs, wet a towel, and attempt to stanch the blood. It soaks the towel right away, so I lay another on top. Emily cries long wails of pain and fear. I try to remain calm, but am scared, too.

Somehow I get to the phone and call my mom to come over. She is by my side in a flash, helping me remove Emily's blood-soaked clothes and tamp down another set of towels on her head. I am covered as well, so when Emily seems relatively calm, I change to a fresh t-shirt, bundle Emily in a blanket, and set off for the emergency room. On the way, I call Greg to let him know what is happening, and then I call Mindy to give her a heads-up.

Just before 9 a.m., we are admitted to the pediatric wing of the ER. Once they clean up the wound, it is really only an inch long, and not too deep. But it needs four stitches. I explain Emily's history in brief while we wait for the doctor on call. Emily has been in hospitals a lot, I say, and doesn't like to be messed with. She won't be easy. But they have just the trick, a blanket that wraps around Emily like a burrito and fastens with industrial Velcro strips. In effect, they have her in a straight jacket. Two nurses hold her head while the doctor sutures her hairline. Emily's screams are piercing, but short-lived. They work fast and soon Emily is freed from the blanket. We are told to wait a bit for the paperwork and then we can leave.

Something is wrong, though. A hush falls over the emergency department, a surreal cessation of all noise. Not a soul is talking. Mom and I walk the halls with Emily, looking at the fish tanks and checking out the playroom. For the life of us, we can't figure out where everyone has gone. As we round the corner to the waiting area, we see a group of people clustered around the wall-mounted TV. They are all open-mouthed, chins up, watching something in utter horror. I have most of my attention on Emily, but I do see footage of an airplane and some smoke. The most I think is that there has been an accident with an aerial stunt plane. Whatever it is doesn't even look real.

By the time we get home with Emily, we know what has happened. I am frantic to reach Greg. He works down in DC, right across from the FBI building, so maybe he is in trouble, too. I don't know what to think when I can't reach him. All lines are down, and his cell phone is silent. Emily is oblivious to my mounting panic, thank goodness, as I pace the length of the family room, up and down. Her school has been dismissed, so we are at home for the day. I try to have the reading time that she loves, cuddling her on the couch for all the Dr. Seuss she can take. But I am distracted by the news footage and do not give Emily my full attention anymore.

Wendy calls from her cell phone, which somehow transmits. Her dad works in New York and she is beyond worried. We compare notes on what we know, which newscasts we are watching. She wants me to call back when I hear anything at all from Greg. I hang up and run around the house locking all the doors. I have never felt so unsafe.

At 2:00 in the afternoon, I hear a rattle at the side door. After a tussle with the lock, Greg bursts in, looking greasy and disheveled, but here. I throw myself into his arms sobbing. He is stunned by the events of the day and of the panic down in the city. He is one of the lucky ones who caught a ride home with a coworker because all the public transportation was shut down. I am so relieved as to be speechless.

We sit on the couch watching the news for the rest of the day, breaking periodically for dinner and the bedtime routine. The carnage is all real, but not real at the same time. The disbelief that this has happened to our country, in our country, is an assault on the senses. I am on adrenaline overload and know I will struggle to sleep tonight.

But sleep I do, the restless, fitful sleep of a soul in trouble. My dreams are like a montage of images, first a plane striking a building, then blood squirting from my daughter's head. The two events comingle until they seem one and the same; the strike against our country and all the assaults against Emily. By morning, something within me has unraveled, and I know I will never be the same.

# CHAPTER 28

The day after 9/11, I drive Emily to school, which in itself seems unbelievable. For normal life to resume, and so quickly, is staggering. But I understand it is part of our message to the terrorists: We shall carry on. As I turn the car onto Cedar Lane, I notice a vehicle one lane over. The small pickup wears an enormous American flag draped just so over its entire length. The owner has obviously taken considerable care to secure the flag in meticulous fashion. The flag is pulled tight and shown off in its full glory. The sight is so majestic and so humbling that I am near tears. A simple thing of beauty in this horrendous aftermath is a sight I will remember my entire life.

Wendy meets me at Emily's elementary school and we run until lunchtime, almost two-and-a-half hours. We are training for the Montgomery County Marathon in the Parks. We have signed up, so it is official. But this run today is not about training or miles or minutes. We run to make sense of what has happened. My dreams of Emily's bloody head and the airplanes' impact are still fresh in my mind. Usually these runs are rife with banter and light gossip, but today we are sniffling and interrupting each other as we wind through neighborhoods and across busy thoroughfares. I try to tell her how bad I am feeling lately, how unwound, but my personal struggles seem trite compared to what is going on in the world.

So, like the nation, I fly my flag at half staff for a while and then carry on as normal. A fault line runs underneath my life, yet the surface looks fine. I still yearn for things to be less difficult with Emily, and I still crave another baby. But the way things are with Greg and me right now, I don't dare bring up dissatisfaction or unhappiness or babies. I hunker down and play the Mom Who Can Handle It All. But underneath the brave façade I show to the world lies a disaster, dormant.

The month after 9/11 blurs by, and the bottom falls out. I will do anything to erase the pain, or just to escape it for a little while. I avoid mirrors, not daring to glimpse the countenance I can no longer recognize.

On the weekend just after Halloween, Greg and I are out at the tot lot behind our house. Greg has Emily hoisted on his shoulders and he is loping down the path. The sunlight glints off Emily's hair, illuminating the golden strands. Greg turns to catch my eye, grinning from ear to ear. I can't even swallow for the egg-sized lump of shame in my throat. What I am doing will kill this man, this family. I run into the bathroom and crouch on the floor, digging the heels of my hands into my eye sockets. I can't bear what I have become.

# CHAPTER 29

The marathon I have been training for is finally here. Held on a Sunday in mid-November, Wendy and I arrive at 6:30 a.m., well before the start time. Most of the runners appear to have run this distance before and are participating in their little pre-race rituals. Some have trash bags over their running clothes, as a makeshift windbreaker that they will shuck by mile three. Some of the men are taping their nipples to prevent chafing, and everyone is tying and retying their shoes for that perfect feel. Running twenty-six miles is nothing to sneeze at, and the people we see here seem to respect the distance. Men and women alike are pacing nervously and lining up at the bright blue Porta-Pottys.

Wendy and I have trained smart, maybe even over-trained. We have run over three hours at a time and have the gel to water ratio down pat. Still, we are nervous, bouncing up and down on the balls of our feet as we wait for the starting announcements. A veteran runner tells us about the course, how hilly the first ten miles are, and how it flattens out by mile fourteen, for sure. We listen raptly, filing away this information like fuel we will need. Just before the start, Wendy extracts a promise from me that, if her energy flags, I should go ahead, and I tell her the same.

As the starting horn blows, we can hardly see our feet. The chilly fog has clustered at ankle level and won't budge. We mince along, trying to find our pace as the crowd chugs and puffs along with us. When the fog lifts, we are already at mile five and comfortable. We talk during the race, dissecting the fall, how our kids are doing in school, our husbands at work.

By mile ten, we forget what our expert course guide said about the hills, and we are spent. It will take a lot of mental strength to finish this. At mile fifteen, we can see runners behind us at a bend in the road. One of the men is wearing red, white, and blue shorts and is, incredibly, carrying a regulation size American flag, complete with flagpole. He bears it in front of him, and the flag ripples in the wind. His effort is a beacon, a statement, all right, enough to leave us choked up for the next portion of the race.

By mile twenty, we hit the proverbial wall. My legs feel heavy, my knees swollen to resemble cantaloupes. Wendy is getting tired and urges me ahead. Only when she shoves me down the leaf-strewn path do I surge ahead, maintaining a quarter mile distance in front of her. But I feel too loyal to keep on, so I run back to her, impart a few encouraging words, and then go on ahead. After several laps like this, Wendy says she will see me at the end and if I hold myself back she will be mad.

So I push myself, mind over matter, through a highway tunnel that marks the last mile. There are balloons at the end, and a big crowd, and my sister Maureen clapping to see me finish. I am only two minutes in front of Wendy so I wait for her, draped in a silver warming blanket. We clasp finisher's medals around our necks and rehash the course together. I am triumphant to have accomplished this goal. We walk through a neighborhood to find the Metro, legs tightening up as we stride, but mindful that we need to keep moving. We have both heard horror stories about people whose thigh muscles locked up after a marathon, and we don't want any of that.

With coffee in hand on the ride home, Wendy and I congratulate each other. I can't believe I have gone from a non-runner to a marathon runner in the space of a few years. I never thought I could do it. But ricocheting against my own pride and amazement is the knowledge that I'm doing other things I never thought I'd do either. And of these things, I am not proud at all.

# CHAPTER 30

When I get home from the marathon, Greg has pulled out all the stops. On the kitchen table, there are a dozen roses, a huge card, balloons, and a pound of the peanut M & M's I love so much. I am touched and a little scared. His excess tells me he knows all is not right.

I am jittery all the time, strung out on coffee and nerves. Whenever I take Emily to school or pick her up, I check out the other moms. We have daily banter about our children, and I am known as the Mom of Emily, garnering praise and admiration for all the challenges we face. How would they think of me, I wonder, if they knew what I have been doing in my spare time?

Emily's fifth Christmas is bearing down on me, and I am in a frenzy of toy buying, wrapping, and decorating. Christmas is my favorite holiday, filled with tradition and joy. But this year, I am a real mess. Greg wonders why I cry all the time, what on earth is wrong. I don't know how to get out of this, and there is no one I can confide in. I have felt out of control since Emily was born, but now it is worse than ever.

On December 8th, as we circle the twinkling white lights around our Christmas tree, I tell Greg I think we should take a break from each other. He is floored. I tell him that separating for a time might help me to figure things out. I just say I am unhappy, I have been unhappy for a long time, and I need us to be apart. Greg pleads with me to wait until after the holidays, and I agree.

This separation idea came out of thin air and doesn't feel right. But it is the only way I can think of to work this out. Greg is propelled into action. He decorates my car with cards and flowers, so when I come out after teaching a class at the gym, I am greeted with a profession of love. Greg bends over backward to be supportive, wordlessly taking Emily when I want to head out. He buys me a treadmill so I can continue running despite the shorter days and colder weather. I chug along on the treadmill in the basement, watching grainy TV and collapsing inside.

Greg's folks come to visit over the holidays, and they can sense the tension in the air, but we don't say anything. We focus on Emily, talk about her school, and busy ourselves with meal preparation and cleanup. We play happy, but the fault lines are riven, almost palpaple.

When Christmas ends, the days together before the new year are squandered with silence and odd looks. Greg is sad but determined, and I am hollowed out, a husk of myself. One grey morning, it is all I can do to fold the laundry while the clinking sounds of breakfast curl up the stairs.

Suddenly, I snap to attention, literally pull myself up, smooth my sweatpants, and descend the stairs two at a time. My gallop is met with questioning eyes as Greg and Emily greet me with Cheerios and waffles littering the kitchen table. I plop down, face this husband of mine and let the tears flow. I tell him I don't even know who I am anymore, that I am barely holding it together. But the words aren't working right, so I give up and repeat, "I am so sorry, so sorry, so sorry," until my voice runs out.

# CHAPTER 31

And I am truly sorry that I have visited more hurt on a family already in pain. With Emily's birth and subsequent diagnosis, we had the wind knocked out of our sails, but I have never really recovered, only soldiered on. Greg's integrity remains intact while I mourn the loss of myself.

After a few weeks of recriminations and tears, it is obvious we need outside help to mend our wounds. I call my friend Heather and she suggests a therapist. We drop Emily off at my mom's one evening and walk up the street to a counselor who works out of her house. Our session is close to Emily's bedtime, so she is in her sleeper, drowsy and aching for her crib. But it is the only time we can both be available for therapy.

Lee is a slender woman in her mid-60s. She greets us with a smile and leads us down the stairs of her townhome to her office. Her home is modern, with geometric artwork and bright colors. The couch where we sit is red with chrome footings and armrests, evoking a retro look. Lee wears a tailored sweater and wool pants, looking more like a librarian than a therapist.

But she is good, this woman. She listens intently and jots notes as we talk. When I have the floor, Lee queries: "Tell me about yourself, Judith," and I am not sure where to start. So I begin with the obvious, my resume of sorts. I am a former high school teacher, I say, now I am a mom. Oh and, by the way, our five-year-old daughter has severe disabilities. This stops Lee in her tracks and she makes me explain Emily's condition. She is suddenly nodding, really bobbing her head. Our case, our story, is not a tough nut to crack, she says. She knows exactly what is going on.

When a couple has a child, any child, they turn themselves over for a time to that child. The care, feeding, and development of that child eclipse the couple's relationship in the early months. But as things get easier and the child becomes more independent, the couple can usually reclaim their lives, at least somewhat. This time period is primarily when couples entertain the thought of having another child. The introduction of a child into a marriage puts the marriage on hold, if only temporarily.

With a disabled child, it is a different ballgame. Even at five, our child is hardly independent. She needs an aide with her at all times and relies on others for everything. She is vulnerable and needy. We are too busy taking care of her needs and have forgotten our own. The energy we used to spend on fostering our relationship has been poured into Emily, and there is nothing left at the end of the day.

This all makes a sort of academic sense to me. It is a nice package. But there are a lot of parents out there who have sublimated themselves to their children, and not everyone is messing up like me. I personally know several moms who are all about their kids and fine with that. I wonder why I went the way I did, what is wrong with me.

Lee schedules a session for us every week as a couple, and I go by myself once a week as well, during the day. Greg is uncomfortable with this plan, sure I will tell secrets and leave him out when I talk alone. He is paranoid and fearful, wanting to rehash everything we say in the sessions. But I look forward to my sessions alone. Time with Lee is my safe space, where I can finally unfold and be myself.

I take care not to wear mascara for these sessions, not to schedule them right before I need to pick Emily up. I need time to clean up. My talks with Lee are exhausting, cathartic, and just what I need. We work on the Emily Connection, as I have come to call it. I am loath to blame Emily for anything I have done, but I know there is a link. Despite that I seem to have dealt with Emily's diagnosis in a stalwart, courageous way, the opposite is true. I collapsed under the weight of it, folded in two. Instead of rising to the occasion, I chose unacceptable coping mechanisms.

I tell Lee one day that I had a single perfect day with Emily, the day she was born, before any problems surfaced. Then it was as if that perfect child evaporated and an imposter took her place. I still grieve for the child who went away, and I can't seem to give my whole heart to the girl who is with me every day. Lee looks at me levelly, pauses, and leaves me to consider who the real imposter is.

# CHAPTER 32

No one can be in pain forever. Somehow we stumble on, like an amputee still feeling the phantom limb. Our relationship maintains the outward trappings of a marriage, but it is just window dressing. Every day we repeat the same dance—anger, apologies, recriminations, fear, and doubt. Greg and I decide not to split up, so there is that to cling to, but it is a Herculean task every day.

I talk to Lee every week, and I talk to my mom a bit, too. I depend on their input to offset the vitriolic dialogue that often occurs at home. By the time the worst of the pain has subsided, when the majority of the smoke has cleared, I look up and find myself a hermit. I have hardly left the house in weeks, only to transport Emily to school and to teach a class or two. But I haven't seen a friend in forever. I need to see whether I have any friends left.

I talk to Heather about how it is going, and she takes my hands in hers. Her eyes are the kind eyes of a friend who has seen me through thick and thin. Heather is spiritual, wise beyond her years, and can be counted on to be thoughtful. She tells me she was shocked by my behavior. I think about this, and I agree. It wasn't about hate for Greg or really about anybody but myself. I was medicating myself from the pain of life with the balm of running away. Heather says Greg is courageous to stay with me, and

for a minute I am insulted. But she is right. This man I married is a
better person than I will ever be, and better than I deserve.

Wendy and I are training for our second marathon this spring.
I am so exhausted I don't know how I will make it through the
training runs, but somehow I muster the strength. Armed with
gel and water bottles, we meet every Saturday at my house and
head out for increasingly longer runs. One brutally cold morning,
we struggle around the town center, circling the mall. We need a
distraction to get us through the next hour, so I take a leap of faith.
I have held back with this friend of mine, and it is time to come
clean. I tell her that Greg and I are having a really hard time. One
good thing about running is that I can't see Wendy's face directly,
just her profile.

She is not appalled, just surprised. She wondered all fall if something was the matter, but just figured I didn't want to be close
friends with her, that I was content to be just running buddies.
So here is another person I have hurt with my actions, although
inadvertently. I blather now, trying to explain why I didn't say anything, when she stops me cold. She is in the throes of marital dis-
cord herself, and I didn't know anything, so we are even.

From that moment on, Wendy is another safe place, a friend
who doesn't cut me any slack, but who doesn't judge me either. In
a time of terrible pain, having these friends, as well as my mom
and sister, Rachel, keeps me afloat on days when it seems easier to
drown in the misery.

# CHAPTER 33

We pass into spring trying to be tender with one another. Our conversations, once taut and mechanical, are morphing into actual give and take. I am careful with my little family. I mince through the days as if on ice and am grateful for the winter thaw.

Lee has a suggestion, a psychology trick, that works like magic. I envision Greg wearing a t shirt emblazoned with the word FEAR in all capital letters right across his heart. I tell myself that Greg is so angry because he is scared of losing me, and that helps me stay patient, focused.

My second marathon is the Baltimore and Annapolis Trail Marathon, so named because it is run entirely on a paved trail rather than city streets. The race is organized as a half-marathon as well, leaving runners with the chance to bail out at the halfway mark or continue on to complete the whole distance. I have been one of the bailers before, so I eagerly anticipate going the full distance. At the start it is 40 degrees, so Wendy and I wear shorts and long sleeves. We will be cold at first, but it only takes a few miles to get acclimated.

This race is a much smaller field than the marathon in the fall, so we find our stride immediately. We made some strategic errors in the first race, and we look to correct them this time around. We start out slowly and stay there, one foot in front of the other, mile after mile. The course is relatively flat, and after we pass the halfway point, the number of runners thins considerably. It is lonely out this far, and I am grateful for Wendy's company. Her husband has recently moved out of the house, and my own marriage is tenuous at best. This marathon is not just about running; it is a metaphor for the tumult in our lives. If it hadn't been for the constancy of the training program or the loyalty of Wendy's friendship, I might have truly unraveled this spring.

As it is, I run strong despite the trauma that has taken place. My legs never really tire, and my breathing is rhythmic and steady. At the twenty-mile mark, where we fell apart last time, we sing old songs from the 80s and joke around. A woman passes us on her bike, a pacer helping to buoy the spirits of a runner friend. She asks us how old we are, and we are stumped. Wendy can't even give the correct age, and we giggle hysterically. We must be hallucinating from dehydration, but luckily the finish line is not far off.

Mile twenty-six is at a local high school. I round the curve and sprint as best as I can to the finish. Greg is right there, with Emily in the jogger stroller. My heart is heavy with exertion, but it takes flight when I see Greg's sweet face. He is helping Emily to clap her hands and he is yelling, "Go, Mommy!!!" He embraces me and says he is so proud. I limp into the gymnasium, kneading my thighs and circling my neck around. It seems like everything hurts. At the makeshift tables in the gym, I pick up a finisher's medal and hobble towards the buffet of carbohydrates. I load up on bagels and bananas, wrapping them in napkins and rolling them in a spare shirt.

I can barely squat to get down to Emily's eye level in the stroller. I hunch over, offering her a bite of bagel, when it occurs to me that I forgot to say my traditional "Emily" at the finish of this race. My celebratory accolade to Emily is so programmed into my racing repertoire that I can't believe I forgot. Just another scathing reminder of how I have lost track of my priorities this year.

The sky opens up as we drive home, a relentless downpour. I know there are still runners out there on the course, and I am thankful to be in the warmth of the car. I look over at Greg and wonder if he will hold my hand. I snake my hand closer to his and slowly entwine my fingers, weaving them with his. Greg's hands are strong, square, and capable. He can fix anything. A few seconds pass before I feel a little squeeze and then he rubs my thumb with his. For the first time in more than three months, I feel close to my husband, feel like maybe, just maybe, we can work our way back to each other and be a family again.

# CHAPTER 34

Emily's second year of preschool is drawing to a close, and it is time to prepare her for kindergarten—or, more precisely, prepare her paperwork. She has a mountain of documents already, and they need to be passed along to the next teacher, aides, and therapists. Having Ms. Mindy for two years in a row was a true bonus. The continuity and routine is just what Emily needs. But it also means that her transition to a new teacher will be that much harder.

Luckily, we know the new teacher, at least by sight. Her name is Ms. Renee, and her classroom is right next to Ms. Mindy's. In fact, you have to walk through one to get to the other. The nearest bathroom for the special needs preschool and kindergarten is located in Ms. Mindy's "pod," so kids are constantly walking back and forth. The suite of classrooms provides a collegial environment, reminiscent of dorm living, where students are one on top of the other. So Ms. Renee is no stranger to Emily or to us.

Renee is young, just like Mindy. She is a Phoebe Cates look-alike with olive skin, a slender body, and tiny features. I stifle the urge to question her capability because of her youth. I know better by now. These young teachers have energy to spare and are up on the latest theories and methods of teaching.

Renee has me stay late one day when I pick Emily up. She wants to say how much she is looking forward to having Emily in class, how she has watched her for the past two years and loves her spirit.

She hands me the voluminous stack that is Emily's Individualized Education Plan (IEP) and asks me to go over it. I am to look at all the services the school deems crucial to develop Emily's skills and see whether I agree with the school's assessment. I rifle through page after page, skill after skill that Emily needs to master. I have got my work cut out for me.

The purpose of the IEP is to design a plan for students with special needs that addresses their areas of weakness or skills they need to accomplish. In some cases, the IEP follows the school's curriculum fairly closely. A typical kindergarten skill is learning to read, involving letter recognition and sounding out vowel—consonant blends. With a child like Emily, who can't vocalize, that skill has to be adapted drastically. Because Emily cannot speak in the traditional sense, it is hard to determine whether she recognizes letters. So the IEP is designed to address that quandary. An IEP is broken down into goals and objectives, and then it lists steps the teacher will take to help the student reach the goals.

I am impressed as I leaf through Emily's draft of the IEP, but saddened as well. If the thickness of a folder is a marker of all the assistance a child needs, then Emily has got a doozy. This stack of papers rivals her medical file in thickness and sheer verbosity. Page after page spells out Emily's shortcomings, areas with which she struggles, and then the corresponding goal. Many of the goals are academic, such as "Emily will learn to identify and organize the letters of her name (first and last). She will identify the days of the week and colors and match letters with letter sounds." Reading this makes me smile, envisioning Emily actually knowing her name in written form, tackling early literacy.

But other goals are wrenching, things Emily needs to work on that most two-year-olds can do: "Emily will independently eat a variety of foods with minimal spillage. She will also wipe her mouth after eating with minimal prompts. She will don her coat and shoes independently and use the potty independently on 4/5 occasions." These goals are called Self-Care Goals, the title of which reminds me of a level in a nursing home hierarchy. Most of

Emily's education, truth be told, is not intended to be academic. Her teachers' role, and ours as parents, is to help her be as independent as possible. The degree to which she can care for herself will largely determine what her life will be like after formal education has run its course.

Greg works with a woman who is a "differently- abled" employee. She is maybe forty, with noticeably altered speech patterns and social awkwardness. She brays when she laughs and stands too close. But she does her work adequately, copying and filing, and is proud of her job. Greg says she has her own apartment in a complex with other disabled people. She is checked on regularly by staff at the complex or by her parents, but she lives alone. She can write her own checks, does her own marketing, and commutes to and from work on her own, using public transportation. This woman's independence is a stunning achievement for a person with special needs, and what all parents with disabled children hope for.

Flipping through Emily's IEP, rife with "self-care" goals, my mind strays to when Emily will be grown. I wonder, will she have mastered the self-help areas or will she need round-the-clock assistance to function? Will she live with us always or with others? Recognizing that all futures are uncertain to a degree, I know that Emily's future is more uncertain. She is uncharted territory. No doctor or teacher has yet ventured to guess what her young womanhood will hold. I can only plow forward, trying to help Emily as best as I can.

A kindergarten bonus that Emily receives this year is a school loaner of Intellikeys, an adaptive keyboard for typing. It is a plastic sheet positioned over the regular keyboard, providing letters that are bigger, much bigger, than standard. The hope is that Emily will learn to type as one method of communication. After a few false starts with the new keyboard, Renee's educational savvy shines through; Emily takes to it like a pro. She is mesmerized by typing, loves looking for and pressing the keys, and enjoys looking at the letters and words she has written. Greg takes a special interest in this device, buys a home version, and works with Emily every night.

When I am at the conference room table at the elementary school for the late spring IEP finale meeting, all the big guns are there: principal, assistant principal, Ms. Mindy and Ms. Renee (representing the last two years as well as this coming year), the "regular" kindergarten teacher, and a cavalry of therapists and aides. Extra chairs have to be siphoned off from the media center and crunched around the table. The excitement is palpable, and I am struck with what a big deal this is for them, too. Emily is going to kindergarten in a regular school. With support, true, with this army of helpers, but still. It is more than we hoped for, an event we never anticipated all those years ago in the geneticist's office.

The big file makes its way around the table, with each staff member saying his or her piece. We make revisions here, tweak the language there, and, after two hours, emerge with a document that pleases everyone. It is a roadmap of Emily's upcoming year, outlining practically every day. As the minutes are read back, I glance around in what I hope is a surreptitious manner. The teachers are packing up, shifting in their chairs, considerably wearier than when we all came in. The entire meeting has the air of a military maneuver, maybe a flight plan or a war strategy.

As I pick up my things to go, I right the papers in front of me so they line up precisely and I gather my pen, spring jacket, and purse, I notice something in the middle of the table. A rectangle of glossy paper, smaller than an index card, is strewn amidst the larger sheafs. It reminds me of a wallet-sized photograph, flipped over. And that is in fact what it is. I scoop the picture to the edge of the table and use my fingernail to flip it over.

My Emily stares out at me from the picture, her pageboy bob of white-blond hair ringing her head. Her red shirt has an elephant on it, I can tell without even looking. I am the one who picked out her outfit for school picture day, so I should know. The look on Emily's face is of a child startled by the bright flashbulb popping unexpectedly. She is a deer in the headlights, bug-eyed and open-mouthed.

Mindy blushes and explains. She has had Emily in class for two years now and loves her. There is no telling whether their paths will cross again. She keeps this picture in her paperwork as a memento of my child. Mindy seems shy, embarrassed, as she admits this. I hand the picture back to her and thank her for all her hard work with Emily. I turn away, in essence leaving Emily's preschool years in stacks on the table. She is launched now, a schoolgirl for real.

# CHAPTER 35

Two things happen as spring turns to summer that year. When I am getting ready to take Emily to the pool for Opening Day, Memorial Day, Greg accosts me in the vestibule next to our master bathroom. He kneels to the floor and lifts my cover-up, exposing my bikini top and stomach. He looks at my belly, then up at my eyes. Can we take this belly ring out, he asks, but it is not really a question. I know he wants me to do this for him, to prove I have stopped being crazy.

I bend my head down so I am almost double, my head touching Greg's from his kneeling position. We examine the clasp on the belly ring, circling it around to find a gap. The ring is similar to an earring without a back, only with a thicker post. Greg wrenches the ring apart slightly, and I pull back on the skin of my belly. The ring pinches free, leaving a hole surrounded by an angry pink. I douse a Q-tip with rubbing alcohol and pat the hole with the cotton tip. It stings and burns. I am all clean now.

Greg is happy about this. He sees the belly ring as a reminder of the ugly past and a harbinger of bad behavior. They are trashy and entirely too sexy, and he doesn't want me to be either one. I am glad to do anything to soothe him.

Life at home with Greg hovers near normal, whatever that is. We still occasionally spin around each other like boxers in a ring, throwing jabs and hooks, and then backing off. We need a project or hobby together, any distraction to keep our minds off the pain that nearly destroyed us.

That distraction comes in a furry, white package. Greg has wanted a dog for years, and now I can't see why not. A pet will be fun for us and fun for Emily. We start researching breeds, talking about supplies, and tossing around names.

We settle on the West Highland Terrier breed and comb the paper for local breeders. I am on this task like a hawk, eager to prove my enthusiasm for this new addition, this new direction to our relationship. I find a Westie breeder who lives in our neck of the woods. One Saturday in early summer finds us at her town-house, looking into a wire pen in her one-car garage.

Five puppies cavort in the pen, all running around on newspaper, yelping, and trying to scale the wire gates. We pick the two smallest, easily the cutest, and the breeder sets them out on the lawn. They hop on top of one another, rolling pell mell down an incline. The breeder tells us they are brother and sister, and for one hysterical moment I think I may have to take both.

But I come to my senses. Taking care of Emily is hard enough, and one new puppy will be pushing it, never mind two. So we set Emily down and teach her to pat gently. She is hesitant at first, but warms to it quickly. It seems that the female pup is especially affectionate, not nipping Emily once, instead just curling into her lap and licking her hand.

We settle on this one and write a check. We have a crate and leash in the car, so we are serious. All the way home, we vacillate between "What have we done?" and "We got a puppy!" Emily is whirling around in her car seat, craning her neck to catch a glimpse of the puppy, who is clearly terrorized to be in a crate in a moving vehicle.

Once home, Greg sets out for the store to get dog food while we take the puppy for her first walk. Walking a puppy is harder than it looks, and I am a bumbling novice. The puppy won't walk in a straight line, the leash gets wrapped around my legs and then Emily's, and we plop down on the sidewalk, defeated already. One of our neighbor ladies is out walking her Springer Spaniel and she gives me some tips. We get underway again, this time keeping the leash tight and pulling the puppy along. We are in the front yard when Greg gets back, letting the puppy sniff everything. Greg is actually smiling, something I haven't seen for a long time.

Maybe this will be it, I think. Dogs are supposed to be therapeutic; it has been proven medically. This puppy might be the way we mend ourselves, our family. This responsibility is a big load to heap on a dog, but it just might be the ticket. We decide to name the puppy Gretchen, calling her with echoing voices as the twilight engulfs the yard.

# CHAPTER 36

In the spirit of mending fences, I tell Greg I want to move, to start fresh. Another project, like the acquisition of Gretchen, is always a good distraction and this one is perfect. He gives me the go-ahead to contact a realtor who lives on our block, and we are on our way. We put together a list of priorities we have for a new house, and I am off.

Emily is in summer school this summer, what they call an Extended School Year. The days are shorter than the regular school year, but it still gives me plenty of time during the day to house hunt. I feed Gretchen, take her for a walk, and then put her in a crate in the basement. Our realtor, Karen, slips information about houses she thinks we would like into our door every morning. I grab a map, chart a course to see these houses, and hop in the car. I call Greg after every sighting, giving him the particulars and my thumbs-up or thumbs-down rating. Greg seems as excited as I am about this new project, and it is heartening to hear the lilt in his voice.

Greg's parents come out for a visit and watch Emily for us while we go on a long weekend to St. Michael's, a small tourist village on the Eastern Shore of Maryland. We have rented a set of rooms, a rehabbed barn, really, at the Inn at Christmas Farm. Our abode features a downstairs sitting room and bathroom, then a loft for the bedroom upstairs. The eyelet curtains ruffle with the breeze, and the quiet is a luxury. Peacocks roam the property, as well as goats and donkeys. The man-made pond is surrounded by Adirondack chairs and umbrellas. For the first time in a long time, we can sit in silence and be comfortable.

We tour the town, feasting on steak and then ice cream for dessert. We stop at a souvenir shop to get a t-shirt for Emily. We hold hands, swinging them even, as we walk through the village. One of our favorite things to do is to watch people, so we sit on a bench ogling the passers-by. We think about buying an antique lamp from a charming store, but decide it is just one more breakable doo-dad we don't need.

When we make love that night, it is as close to forgiving as we can get. Greg's hands on me feel familiar, strong, and right, and when he says he loves me, I know he means it. An ache pulses between us, the pain we bear from things both our fault and things for which we are blameless. But this ache has a sweetness to it as well. Greg and I have been through the mill together, we are bruised and battered, but we made it through to the other side. We fall asleep wrapped up in each other, breathing in tandem.

We sleep until 8:30 the next morning, positively sinful by parenting standards. The Inn has a full breakfast of Belgian Waffles and fruit. The coffee is syrup-thick with real cream. I eat every last scrap and look around for more. I practically moan at how good everything tastes and how relaxed I feel. Before we leave, we tour the entire Inn, followed by the resident dog and the Innkeeper. The getaway has been glorious and healing.

All the way home, we sing our favorite 80s songs at the top of our lungs, laughing as I bungle the words. We eat sandwiches in the car and nosh on Twizzlers until we finish a one-pound bag. My face actually hurts from smiling, a sensation I haven't felt since I rushed a sorority in college.

Later that week, I go in to see my obstetrician to have my IUD removed. If she wonders why we have waited almost six years to try for another baby, she doesn't let on. The device releases from my cervix with a pinch, and when the doctor pulls it out I am amazed at how little it is. She says we can start trying right away. She also says that if we conceive, we need to get genetic testing right away, given Emily's condition. The testing is an obvious step, especially because I am over thirty-five, but one I have overlooked in my enthusiasm. I decide to cross that bridge when (and if) I get to it.

The house hunt continues, escalating as the days tick by. I spend my days either cleaning our house in preparation to sell it or driving around, scoping out prospective new homes. The market is hot now, so I feel rushed, but energized. If any houses seem likely, Greg hurries home from work, jumps in the car with me and Emily, and accompanies us to the house. We play the pro and con game, tallying up what we absolutely must have in a house and what we can do without.

Our house sells in three days, for $5,000 over the asking price, cash. The new owners are in a hurry to get in, so we have to scramble. If we don't find something right away, we will be homeless in one month. I accelerate my efforts, whizzing past house after house, dismissing some without even slowing down or calling our realtor for a closer look if one seems intriguing.

One day, I zoom past a neighborhood adjacent to a lake where Wendy and I trained for our marathons. The lake is beautiful, and it is a desirable location to live. Just by chance, one of the cul-de-sacs near this lake has a house new to the market. I call Karen and ask her if we can see it. The first showing is on a Saturday, and we are the second couple to see it. We take digital pictures so we can remember details when we get home, but we know as soon as we set foot in the door. This is our home. The floor plan is traditional, and the rooms feature bold paint colors. The yard backs to dense woods. The basement is Greg's dream, with a sports type bar and a spot for a pool table.

We make an offer right away and are accepted the following day. For the next two weeks, life is a barrage of phone calls, paperwork, and moving plans. I drive to the loading dock of a liquor store and make off with dozens of sturdy boxes. I spend days packing, sorting, and labeling. I feel bittersweet to leave this house. Our little starter place was our first home together, and we redid every room, painted, wallpapered, repaired. Emily was conceived here and has never known anywhere else. Her fingerprints are on the sliding glass door, and her footprints are embedded in the dirt by the back deck. This house is where she learned how to sit up, walk, and then run.

But at the same time, it is good to leave. The ache of disappointment pervades this house and it will be good to take the lessons learned to a new abode. As I pack all the detritus of our lives, deciding what to keep and what to throw away, I throw away more than just material possessions and junk. I toss away a segment of our history that is better off left behind.

By closing day, we are all cleared out and squared away with the moving guys, who will meet us at the new place, only ten minutes from the old place. We just have to sign a few more things and we are good to go. My stomach is doing little flips, and whenever I swallow I feel nauseous. Come to think of it, I have not felt well for a few days now.

# CHAPTER 37

On July 27, 2002, my period is a full week late. I have not been feeling myself, and Greg is convinced I am pregnant. I want fish one day for dinner, and I never eat fish. At first I attribute my tiredness and stomach trouble to the impending move and all its stresses, but I know better. I am used to going full-out all day, and this lingering fatigue just won't let up. I examine my breasts in the shower, looking for the tell-tale fullness. Every time I go to the bathroom, I wipe vigorously, inspecting the toilet paper for traces of blood. Finally, I take a pregnancy test. They come in packs of two, so I take both with me into the bathroom first thing in the morning.

Peeing on a stick is a delicate act, and messy. I decide to pee into a cup and dip the sticks, which is infinitely easier. Greg is on the other side of the door, waiting. I try not to glance at the sticks before the allotted three minutes is up, but the two blue lines are there as soon as I pull the sticks out of my urine. Two seconds is all it takes to confirm what I already know. I am pregnant.

I am ecstatic and reeling at the same time. This is fast, almost too fast, but a blessing nonetheless. Less than a month has passed since we started trying to conceive. I open the bathroom door and hold the pee sticks aloft for Greg to see. He picks me up and twirls me around the room, yelling, "I love you, I love you!!" We tumble back onto the bed and hug each other. A lot is happening right now, and we cannot even absorb it.

We tell Emily right away, over Cheerios and yogurt. She cannot comprehend what a big sister is, looks at us blankly, in fact, but it makes it seem more real to tell her. At a decent hour, we put in calls to our families, who cover their shock with congratulatory words. I can tell that my mom thinks we are moving too quickly, selling our home, buying another, and now a baby. But she covers her trepidation well.

My OB will not see me until I am six weeks along, so I have a little while for this to sink in. I am far too busy, anyway. Summer school is over, leaving the entire month of August free. August is always the hardest month of the year. I try my best to give Emily fun things to do, venturing out to new playgrounds and going on errands. But I cannot compete with the perpetual stimulation provided at school. This summer will be the hardest of all. The house is in a shambles, and the bone-crushing fatigue of early pregnancy is settling in.

My energy flags in the late day, so I schedule all our activity for the early hours. To get some last-minute packing done, I park Emily in front of a "Baby Songs" video with a snack. She has loved these videos for years, clapping at the same dance sequences, squealing with glee. I am a dervish of energy while she is occupied, folding, stacking, and throwing away. This move seems like a gigantic purge, not just of all our stuff, but also the emotional baggage that has plagued us for the last several months.

My relentless activity comes to a screeching halt when the churning nausea sets in, like clockwork, right at six weeks. I cannot even lift my head from the pillow some days, curling up in a ball until the queasiness passes. Night is actually worse than morning, which is a godsend, because Greg is home to help with Emily while I retreat to our bed. The only upside to nausea is that it means the pregnancy is, hopefully, taking hold. I feel terrified of a miscarriage, so I take every sign, even the vomiting, as a positive omen.

My miscarriage before Emily, Emily's birth, and the subsequent diagnosis of her syndrome have given me a lesson in the fragility of life. Not every pregnancy lasts, and not every child is born normal. This I know. I have not had good luck in the past, and there is no reason to imagine that things will go smoothly this time. Yet I have hope, a tentative fiber that I test every day. I allow myself to think of a tiny little girl or boy, a sister or brother for Emily, to add to our family. I take the prenatal vitamins, eat lots of cheese and chicken for protein, and scale back on the exercise. I will do what I can to give this baby a chance.

The day before Emily goes into kindergarten, I have my first ultrasound. The sonographer weighs me, asks me to disrobe from the waist down, and then has me take a seat on the exam table. She asks why I am here this early in the pregnancy, and I explain our history, Emily's condition, and our need for genetic testing. The exact age of the fetus is a must for genetic tests of any kind, and the early scans are the most accurate. The sonographer hands me the vaginal sonography wand, and I insert it awkwardly. Then she takes over, circling the wand about, tilting it up, then down, to locate the sac.

Then it pops up—the sac of blackness on the screen that is my uterus and, within, a raisin-sized nugget with a glittering middle. The center flickers like a lightening bug, the heartbeat of this tiny babe, alive and strong. I feel so overjoyed I begin to cry, and I want to hug the technician right there on the table. It looks like we are having another child for sure.

# CHAPTER 38

Going off to kindergarten is a landmark milestone for most kids and their parents. It marks the first time the child leaves the parents all day, every day, and joins the academic world. Enough of all the playing at preschool, kindergarten is serious stuff. Kindergarten is backpacks and homerooms, the cafeteria, and recess. But for our Emily, kindergarten will seem like old hat. After all, she has been going to all-day preschool for two years already, so she knows what it is like to conform to that schedule. She is familiar with the school building, her classroom, and her teacher. Her backpack and lunchbox are the same this year, on purpose. When she strides into the building this fall and treks down the hall to Ms. Renee's room, she should feel right at home.

Emily at five years old (almost six) is something to see. From a brief glance, she is a petite blonde girl with a blunt-cut hairstyle, whose short layers fall onto her full-cheeked face. Anything more than a brief look, however, and you know something is wrong with this little girl. You just wouldn't know what.

Although Emily is categorized as "nonverbal," she is not quiet. In fact, she vocalizes all the time. She has a repertoire of hoots, howls, and word approximations, most coming from the back of her throat. These guttural noises, the majority of them vowels,

sound like excitement, pain, or somewhere in between. Most people are startled at first and then quickly get used to the constant
barrage of noise. We hardly notice anymore.

When Emily walks, she can cover some ground. For a child so
late to the gross motor milestones, she has made huge progress.
But her gait is unusual, a lurching, careening, stomping walk that
is awkward and strangely quick. She weaves her head back and
forth as she walks, and I wonder that she doesn't get dizzy. Each
physical therapist who has worked with Emily explains that she is
very vestibular, or motion-seeking. In other words, she creates her
own whirling, calming motion if not provided for her. That is why
she likes to swing so much.

The walking, although strange to watch, is considered a goal
accomplished. It represents a section we can effectively check off
on the IEP. But Emily still struggles to walk up stairs; in fact; she
crawls up, leading with her head down on the floor, if we let her. In
addition, simple navigation on a jungle gym is excruciatingly difficult for her. She cannot squat with ease, dangle from monkey bars,
or keep her balance on an uneven surface. As far as riding a bike,
even a tricycle, it looks like it will be a while on that, too. Greg
likes to say that Emily does her best work on the straightaway. She
has come so far, but has such a long way to go.

Returning to the same school for the third year in a row definitely has its perks. Everyone already knows Emily, except for the
incoming kindergarten students. She is an old favorite with all the
teachers and other students. I guess she is quite a presence in the
hallways with all her hooting and clapping for herself when she
successfully completes a task. We have no first-day jitters as we go
down the hall to find Ms. Renee.

Ms. Renee's aides this year are Olga and Bertha, the occupational therapist is a plump woman named Dina, and we have Ms.
Karolyn back for speech therapy. I ask everyone if I can snap their
picture with my Polaroid camera. Our tradition is to post pictures of Emily's teachers on the refrigerator, mounted on a piece
of construction paper. Emily points to these pictures every day.

Her teachers and therapists are flattered by the attention, so I pose them against a bulletin board and snap away.

Renee shows me the schedule for the day, similar to Mindy's schedule, with slightly longer blocks of time because the kids are older. The staff has a rotating schedule, too, so that Emily can take turns with each adult. This year, there will be Alphabet People in the room, inflatable, life-sized dolls formed in the letters of the alphabet. Each doll gets a week in the room and a weekend home with the students. Plus, each letter has a special song assigned to it, which helps the students identify and remember that letter's sound. It seems like a fetching way to teach a concept, especially for these special needs kids. Anything with bells and whistles is a winner.

Renee also tells me that Emily is the only one in the class who will be "pulled out" of her classroom and mainstreamed into the regular kindergarten for periods of time during the day. They think she is ready to sit with the "regular" kids, or at least ready to try. They will start small, at first maybe only ten minutes a day. Renee's vision is to have Emily attend class in kindergarten for at least forty minutes in the morning and the same in the afternoon. The idea sounds daunting, but I am thrilled with the prospect. As much as I like the self-contained, special program Emily is in, inclusion with the typical class is always preferred.

Before I say my goodbyes to Emily, Renee shows me the updated technology she hopes will be successful for Emily's communication device this year. It is a larger model of the "talker" Emily used all through preschool. This version is like a computer, only with a touch screen. Each screen has panels with a word or picture on each panel. The computer can be programmed to speak the words as they are pressed. The hope is that one day Emily can generate her own sentences using a device like this.

As I bend to kiss Emily's soft cheek, I reel. What I thought would be the same-old is turning out to be more than I expected. Ms. Renee has upped the ante for Emily, stretching the boundaries of what she might be able to achieve. It looks like there might not be as many limits to what she can do after all.

I turn to leave, hoisting a hand up in the air, momentarily exposing a bit of my tummy flesh. Greg and I have decided not to tell anyone about the baby until after the genetic testing, so I guard my little secret safely behind a pair of loose-fitting running shorts. I look like any regular mommy who might be going to work out after dropping her child off at school. But this day holds momentous significance for me. Kindergarten is the launching pad for the rest of academic life, the starter. I have been waiting for this moment, a moment I never thought would get here. I figured Emily would be in a special school, at the very least. And yet here she is, special, to be sure, but in a regular elementary school, where she passes other kids in the hall, waving like a princess on a parade float. I careen about, just like Emily, as I retreat down the hall, the school's industrial carpet turning to a soupy mass as my eyes blur with tears.

# CHAPTER 39

The pregnancy lasts, and I count down every day, then every week, until the magical Week Twelve, when I can get the genetic testing. I start to show, a little pot-belly poofing out my shorts, and my breasts are definitely fuller. When I lie down, a mushy pear-shaped object rises up between my hip-bones. I cradle the pear with one hand, begging the baby to be okay. At my last appointment, the doctor used a Doppler device to locate the baby's heartbeat. Hearing the rhythmical whooshing of the heart is gratifying, of course, but a huge hurdle remains.

I have a chorionic villus sampling (CVS) scheduled for late September. This test is akin to an early amniocentesis, which is generally performed at eighteen weeks. The sampling of fetal tissue is merely a less well-known method of early genetic screening. The CVS is known to be somewhat risky, but the benefit is that results are back early, allowing us to make a decision in these young weeks of the pregnancy if need be.

We do not talk about it, but Greg and I know the unusual circumstances of our case and how much this test matters. Emily's condition is one of two things: a random fluke or the result of a chromosomal problem with one of us. If it is the former, another baby is highly unlikely to suffer from the extremely rare syndrome. If it is the latter, our chances of having a "normal" baby are pretty slim. I bank on Lady Luck to smile down on us. We have experienced a lot of pain and disappointment, and we are due a break. Greg is landlocked with fear, espousing his familiar credo, "Hope for the best, prepare for the worst."

While we dance around the subject of the genetic test looming, we skirt the "what if" question as well. What if this baby has disabilities, what would we do? The question hovers in the air above us like a swarm of bees, dangerous. We are afraid to go there, yet acknowledge that, by agreeing to the testing, we are entertaining all the options available.

The CVS will be performed at the same hospital where Emily's heart condition was diagnosed and where her geneticist resides. There is a certain symmetry to this. This hospital is where our journey with Emily began, so why not revisit the site, this time not filled with pain, but instead with hope.

The Center for Advanced Fetal Care is on the third floor, an office filled with standard issue grey chairs and a huge reception desk. I announce myself and then sit down with Greg to wait. The clientele here are a mix, some upscale suburbanites like us and others from inner-city Baltimore, the neighborhood where the hospital is located. By the looks of the others in the waiting room, high-risk pregnancies are everywhere and early fetal screening is done for a myriad of reasons.

There are the Young Girls, skinny black child-women who giggle with their moms and swig Diet Dr. Pepper. They bust out of their street clothes, proudly sporting swollen bellies. I guess being thirteen and pregnant is a risk factor in itself. Then there are the Older Mothers, women who are well into their 40s, maybe IVF recipients, here for yet another medical procedure to safely ensure delivery of a healthy child. We are somewhere in the middle, not old or young, kind of normal-looking, but really anything but.

The office is busy and we have a long wait. One expectant mother is loud on her cell phone, haranguing her caller, reading him the riot act about something. It comes out during the call, which is impossible to ignore, that the caller is the father of her baby, and he is in prison. I give Greg the raised eyebrow look that means, "And we think we have problems." It does put things in perspective to be here, one of many, to realize that our lot is not as bad as it could be.

We are called to Step One of the procedure, a meeting with a genetic counselor. Her name is Amanda, and she is Ally McBeal thin, wearing a pencil skirt and clacking heels. She is definitely younger than us, but chic, polished, and professional. Once again, as with Emily's teachers, I feel baffled by how all these experts can be so young. Amanda leads us down the hall to a windowless cubicle of a room with a round table in the middle. She needs to get our history, our medical information, before we can start the procedure.

I begin by pulling out Emily's karyotype from my purse. A karyotype is a map of Emily's chromosomes, wiggling like so many worms across the paper. Amanda is intrigued by Emily's syndrome, peering at chromosome thirteen as she tilts the paper back and forth in the bleak fluorescent light. She has never seen a duplication and inversion of this sort before, she says. We know the syndrome is rare, all Emily's doctors are fascinated by the clinical aspects of her genetic makeup, but to us she is just our little girl.

Amanda explains that we are wise to get this genetic testing. With a syndrome this rare and debilitating in our family history, we need to take every precaution. She is a believer in information. She says if we are armed with as much information as possible, we can make the right choice. I sit there knowing what choice she is referring to, and I quiver at the thought. She then explains the CVS procedure and tells us that it will be about ten to fourteen days until we get definitive results. By then I will be almost fourteen weeks pregnant, into the second trimester.

Amanda takes us back down the hall to a dimly lit room where I have an ultrasound. The sonographer checks to make sure I am water-loaded, and I assure her my bladder is quite full. I put on the speckled hospital gown and lie back for the scan. The ultrasound wand smears warm goo across my belly, and I hold my breath. The baby is readily visible—there is no searching around. The fetus is about the size of a shrimp, the head much bigger than the limbs. This tiny person is wiggling, kicking, and whirling so much so that the sonographer says, "Whoa!", as she attempts to get measurements. She tries to check the age of the fetus, as well as pinpoint the placenta's location.

I love this baby already, no question about it. I told myself that, because of all the complications with Emily, I would not bond with this baby until we were sure it was okay. But that idea is a joke, I see that now. This little shadowy self, all web-footed and squirmy, has my heart already. I place my hand on my side, just slightly distended with the pregnancy. Some of the ultrasound goo trails down my waist and I wipe it away with a finger and then trace little circles, up and down. "Hi baby," I say.

Once the measurements are taken, I hop off the table, gather the hospital gown together in the back, and go next door into the procedure room. The doctor has me lie in the stirrups, and he swabs betadine on my inner thighs and on the catheter he is holding. The catheter will be inserted into my vagina, through my cervix, and into the uterus. A tiny pinch of genetic material will be taken from the placenta and then the catheter is removed. The genetic material goes to a lab out in California to be analyzed under special lights. The chromosomes will be highlighted, counted, and checked for any rearrangements, duplications, or deletions.

I can see from the doctor's face and from the ultrasound, which is tracking the entire procedure, that he is struggling with the catheter. The catheter looks like a tiny white worm snaking through my insides. The doctor is not getting where he needs to be, and I start to feel lightheaded. Greg tells me to relax as he rubs my thumb, our code for "I love you."

The problem is that the placenta is too close to the baby, and going in this way, transvaginally, poses a risk to the baby. So the doctor decides to approach the procedure through my belly, or transabdominally. He puts a pump device in the center of my stomach, through which the catheter winds. Changing the angle allows him to get to the top of the placenta without getting near the baby.

The pump reminds me of a bicycle pump and feels like that, too. I try to relax, but the hissing of the pump, combined with my anxiety, makes me tense. My jaw is locked, and I can't stop staring at the ultrasound screen, willing this whole ordeal to be over.

And soon it is. With a few decisive pushes, the doctor extracts as much material as he needs, removes the catheter and pump, and wipes the betadine off my legs and belly. He advises me to lie on the table for a while before getting up. He repairs to his lab to put the placental tissue in a test tube, and I finally allow myself to breathe.

When the doctor comes back in, I'm sitting up and back in my clothes. He motions us over to the counter where there is a microscope. He wants us to check the information printed on the test tube—our names and social security numbers—to prevent any mixup. Then he tells us to take a peek through the microscope. I haven't used one of these since high school, but find they haven't changed much.

With one eye closed and the other squinting, I can see little red fibers in a pinkish, viscous solution. That is the placental tissue, the doctor points, and that is your blood. The red fibers are bands of chromosomal information that will be dissected and examined. This information will tell us whether this baby is normal. Suddenly my knees give out and I'm squatting on the tile floor, lowering my head between my knees. So much is at stake in those little tubes.

# CHAPTER 40

In the months after 9/11 and my subsequent escape from the reality of life, we are primed for something good. We continue to go to therapy together and separately, I deliver Emily to kindergarten every day, and I wait for the results of the genetic testing. This period of days is like suspended animation. I know the time passes, yet it seems not to move at all.

A week after the CVS, my abdomen is definitely poking out. It takes a concerted effort and some costume work with my elastic waist clothes to disguise this baby. I am ready to burst from my clothes and with the news of this new child. Call it superstition, but I am still waiting to tell most everybody until we know for sure.

I'm folding laundry one day when I swear I hear a voice. The voice is that of a little child, a girl's high whisper. "I'm okay," the voice says. Nothing more. I look around, spooked. When I call Greg, he thinks I am crazy, blames the pregnancy hormones. But from that moment on, I am convinced I am having a girl and that she is as healthy as can be. Now if only the test results would come in to confirm that.

Lucky for us, we just moved. I have tons of work to do in the new house, and that keeps me almost too busy to think. I haul boxes from room to room, trying valiantly to keep Greg's admonishments about not straining myself in mind. I unpack, dust things off, and put them in their rightful places. This house is bigger than the old one and organized differently, so it is trial and error with the furniture. I like the silence of the house as I work, and the feeling of starting fresh.

The house is located at the end of a cul-de-sac, backing to woods and a lake. I feel safe here, comfortable even, and that is something I haven't felt in a while. I entertain myself by taping paint swatches to the walls in several rooms, envisioning vibrant, cheerful colors. We decide on an airy, light pink for Emily's room, and a perfect place for a nursery is right across the hall. But superstition won't let me linger in there or make any plans.

Emily turns six at the beginning of October. Her birthday coincides with day ten of waiting for the genetic test results, and I am on pins and needles. We decide to have a big party, which is a good thing since I am distracted by shopping and decorating. Emily cannot tolerate huge hordes of people; it is just too stimulating, so we are limited to family members, but it is still a lot. My dad and stepmom fly in from Indiana, and Greg's folks are there as well. My mom and stepdad make the quick trip up the road, and Aunt Maureen is there, too. The party is simple, just a cookout followed by cake and ice cream, and it is exactly right. Emily gobbles the food, rips open her presents with panache, and then falls asleep in a heap on the couch.

I am tired from all the party prep, the pregnancy, and all the nervous anticipation of the test results, so I sit on the couch next to sleeping Emily and stroke her cornsilk hair. I watch all my family and Greg's as they talk and mingle. At one point, my mom sits at the table with my Dad and stepmom and they talk like old friends. I can't believe after all the strain, the bitter divorce, and then the stilted civility of the past few years that they are finally, miraculously, in a comfortable spot. The tableau at the table, my parents whom I love more than anything, moves me to tears.

I am still stroking Emily's hair as I look across the room at Greg, who is seated in the green Lazy Boy, talking with his father. I am filled with the hope—no, the absolute certainty—that things will continue to improve for Greg and me. If my parents, despite their pain, can forge a new bond of sorts, then we can, too.

Four days later, I am still waiting for test results and chomping at the bit. The weekend looms, and I just can't wait another day. I decide to call the Center for Advanced Fetal Care to see whether I can hurry things along. Julie, the tech with whom I speak, isn't sure what is causing the holdup. Usually results are back by now. She puts me on hold while I tear a cuticle off my pointer finger, unlacing a ribbon of red. When Julie returns to the phone, she apologizes for the delay. With the lab in California, she says, sometimes things get delayed. They will definitely have the results by Monday.

Although not assertive by nature, something in me snaps. I tell Julie I am not waiting one more day, that I have a severely disabled six-year-old with a rare chromosomal syndrome and a pregnancy that is advancing by the minute. I need to know—NOW—what the future holds. Julie is all efficiency, takes total responsibility for this situation, and says she will call the lab in California, herself, right away.

Two agonizing hours later, I get the call. I have stepped out to get the mail when Julie initially calls back, so all I get at first is the cryptic message that "everything looks wonderful." I am on the horn immediately and can hardly believe it when Julie says this baby has normal chromosomes—no trisomy, no duplications, and no deletions; everything is perfect. She can tell me the gender, if I wish, and I definitely wish. The sweet little voice I heard was right. It looks like Emily will have a baby sister.

# CHAPTER 41

Almost immediately, I sport a full-blown pregnant belly, as if the good news from the genetic testing finally makes the pregnancy real. We tell all our friends, and even our new neighbors take note and extend their congratulations. We can paint the nursery now and get the crib out of the basement. The time is right for new beginnings, a time to feather our nest and revel in the lucky hand we have been dealt.

I show Greg my ever-expanding belly and have him touch it. He marvels at the baby growing inside, but is scared as well. I don't think he will relax until he sees that this baby is fine. Almost on cue, one week after we get our genetic test results, our little girl gives me a swift kick. From then on, I always have a hand on my belly, waiting for the next one. The kick is my barometer that everything is fine. Greg doesn't have such a barometer, so he vacillates between loving and believing in me and suffering from intense suspicion and fear. This harsh combination puts added tension into the relationship again.

This pregnancy is easy, made more so by the absolute knowledge that the baby is okay. I revel in my bizarre food cravings, joking to Greg that we will have to name the baby Olive Provolone if I can't stay away from the cheese and salty condiments. When the baby kicks and rolls over in my belly, I marvel at the wonder of it all. Thinking back to my pregnancy with Emily so long ago, I now know I should have been more aware of the fetal movements (or lack thereof). Emily's high tone prevents her from ease of movement even now after years of physical therapy; in the womb, she was virtually motionless. Denial is a powerful thing.

Every other year Emily visits her cardiologist at Johns Hopkins for a checkup, and it's time to go again this fall. Mom accompanies me because Emily is getting bigger and harder to control during any procedure. This appointment is more than one pregnant lady can handle. Emily's cardiologist is thrilled to see her, and he is amazed at how she has grown and how much she can do. When I tell him that Emily is mainstreamed into "regular" kindergarten for periods of time every day, his mouth gapes open. He tells me frankly that a child with her diagnosis is usually greeted in the medical world with a poor-poor prognosis. He explains that this means poor life expectancy and poor prediction for cognitive development. Emily is defying this definition across the board.

The cardiologist needs to see an extensive picture of Emily's heart, and this is done with ultrasound. Mom and I struggle to get a hospital gown on Emily. I anticipate another huge fight to get Emily to lie down on the examination table, but to my surprise, she cooperates, collapsing back in a heap. She begins to suck her fingers, so I know a nap is on the way. This visit is going better than I ever thought, so I call the technician in right away, telling him time is of the essence. Given Emily's relaxed state, he is able to get comprehensive pictures of Emily's valves and arteries using a gelled transducer, similar to the one used on me at my OB visits. The room is warm and dark, and I find myself getting drowsy as well. I know for sure that Mom is drifting off.

Emily looks like an angel, lying flat out on the bed, golden hair splayed and white skin fairly glowing. I finally cover her up with a blanket once the tech is done. He goes next door to consult with the doctor, who has been watching the exam on a monitor in his own office. I tell Mom the plan—Emily is out like a light, so now is the time for a haircut. She doesn't blink, simply accepts that this is the unusual way things are done with this unusual child. I remove the hair scissors, wrapped in tissue, from my purse. The sleeping haircut is my modus operandi for Emily, so I always travel prepared. Mom props up Emily's sleeping form, and I snip away, clearing a straight-enough path across her forehead and clipping an inch off around the back.

The tech and the doctor return with an all-clear heart report, catching us red-handed in the midst of our impromptu haircut event. They chuckle and say they thought they had seen it all, but this takes the cake. Giving a child a haircut while she is limply asleep is parenting at its best, I retort. The doctor gestures toward my pregnant belly and says that Emily sure has been good practice for this next child. Emily broke the mold, he says; you'll be ready for anything

I ponder his words on the drive home. I don't feel ready for a second child at all. I wing it every day with Emily, wondering when someone will figure out what an imposter I am. I am hardly an expert on child-raising. In fact, I feel I have failed in so many respects. But one thing I know I have done is to love Emily the best that I can.

I ask Mom, what if I can't love this new little girl the way I love Emily? What if I only have a finite amount of love and I have used it all up on Emily, who needs so much? Mom is quietly wise as she says, with the certainty that can only come from having four children of her own, "You won't have to divide the love you have for Emily and give some to the new baby—your heart will grow and fill to create new love that you never knew you had."

I hope she is right. I remember when Emily was born. A new compartment simply opened up in my heart, a place reserved just for her. I struggled to love her, to give her wholly that place in my heart. But I did, and I hope I can do the same for this next little one.

# CHAPTER 42

Right before Christmas, we lose our little dog, Gretchen. Overnight, the first snow of the season falls, and the flakes are soft and fluffy. Emily and I go down to the basement where Gretchen is crated at night. I leash her and take her to the sliding glass door, which leads to the backyard. I have boots on with my maternity sweats, and I have put a snowsuit on Emily, so we are ready for the winter wonderland.

The dog freaks out. She has never seen snow before and is crazed and disoriented. She pulls on the leash, wanting to dash around in the snow. I stay on the patio, holding Emily's hand as she stands tentatively beside me, and Gretchen barks and pulls. She refuses to pee or poop out in the snow, no matter how long we stay out there. I decide to take the dog back in, let Emily warm up a bit, and then try again later.

When we return to the basement, I unleash the dog. She dashes around, shaking her fur vigorously, snow flying off in tufts onto the carpet. I turn back around to latch the slider and put the security bar on the floor when Gretchen dashes past me, squeezes through a gap in the door, and runs outside before I can stop her. She is out in the snow, unleashed, barely visible as a white-on-white whirling ball of energy.

I yell for her, jingling the leash, saying, "Here girl!" Emily is giggling like something funny is happening. I try to keep the panic

out of my voice as I tell Emily we are going out again. This time
I put on one of Greg's coats, the only thing that will close around
my body anymore, and we go out the front door. The snow is knee
deep and falling fast, so I have to hoist Emily on my hip. She's no
good at walking in this uncertain terrain.

We circle the cul-de-sac, looking and yelling. Then we walk up
and down the cross streets, back and forth. We must make quite
a picture, a rotund pregnant woman with a large child precari-
ously balanced on her hip, traipsing through the snow, hollering.
Despite our efforts, there is no sign of Gretchen. I wonder about
going out in the car to search, but decide to call Greg first.

Greg is level-headed in a crisis, always has been. He has had lots
of experience as a child with runaway dogs, so he has a plan. He
tells me to stay put, don't attempt to drive anywhere, for heaven's
sake, and keep casing the neighborhood whenever we feel up to it.
He will help out when he gets home.

By nightfall, there are two feet of snow and no sign of Gretchen.
We have been out four times and just can't do it anymore. Greg
arrives home at 6:30 and heads out right away, but it is as dark
as pitch, so it is a fruitless attempt. We remind each other that
Gretchen ran away before briefly and found her way back. Maybe
we will be lucky this time. I make up "Lost" flyers on our computer and copy a stack to disseminate the next day.

Despite our efforts, we never see Gretchen again. Our flyers turn
yellow with age on the light poles and fence rails. Once in a while,
I take a walk around the block, getting some air, working the knots
out of my muscles. I spot a woman a few blocks over with a West
Highland Terrier, walking along jauntily. I can't help but stare. I
want to ask her, is this your dog? Where did you get your dog? Is this
our dog that you stole one snowy night? But of course I don't ask.
That Gretchen could possibly be living so close is unbelievable.

Gretchen's disappearance leaves a hole in the family for a while,
a loss that hurts. Greg especially misses patting Gretchen at night
while we watch TV. Gretchen was a dog, a pet, but also part of
what healed us during a very rough patch.

Instead of patting the dog at night, Greg's hand rests on my belly now. Once in a while, his fingers jump with the gymnastics of the baby and he starts in surprise. A knowledge creeps in that, even without our beloved puppy, the closeness we have come to savor is here to stay.

# CHAPTER 43

My friend Heather convinced me to take up running all those years ago, and now she tries to sell me on swimming as the next great exercise. Before I can argue, we meet at the gym and I don a maternity swimsuit. Heather has done this before, so she gets me set up with goggles and shows me the lanes for lap swimming. I am 7-and-a-half months pregnant, it is mid-January, and I am about to get in a pool.

I was a swimmer way back when in high school, and the sharp chlorine assaults my nostrils with memory. I haven't been back to an indoor pool since. Walking is getting more uncomfortable for me every day, with the weight of the baby pressing on my spine and bladder. But I still need my exercise, so this will have to do. Heather assures me I will feel weightless in the water and that swimming will be easier than walking. I will judge for myself.

Swimming seems to be all about adjustment—making sure the suit bottom is pulled down modestly over my hind end, pressing the goggles tightly into my eye sockets so water can't get in and render my contact lenses useless, and tightening the swimsuit straps over my shoulders so my breasts hoist up. My dear friend Heather says I am beautiful when I am all exposed this way, self-conscious, and I decide to believe her.

There are two lanes open, side by side, so we scoot in and make a plan. We will swim one lap and then check with each other. If all is well, we will try segments of ten laps before the next break. My body is heavy with the lethargy of late pregnancy, but strangely itchy for the adrenaline rush of movement. I put my feet flat against the wall, give the goggles one last grind into my face, and I am off with a solid push.

The water is strangely quiet. All sensation is cut off, and it is just me and the engulfing wetness. Heather is right, I can't even feel the extra thirty pounds packed on my frame, and I slide through the water gently. It takes an entire length to remember how to time my breathing with the strokes, but it does come back, and soon I am in a groove. Four strokes, flutter kick, turn my head for a quick breath, repeat. There is a real calmness to the repetition.

Heather and I are well matched, just like with running. She is way smaller, of course, but I am pretty strong. We touch the wall after our first lap at exactly the same time and emerge to shake droplets from our hair. We compare notes on what stroke we are using—I do freestyle and she does breaststroke—then we turn and push off for a longer segment. The sameness of swimming is lulling, even more so than running. With running, there are always obstacles to watch for, potholes, chunks of dirt, slippery terrain, but with swimming I can just zone out. I even imagine the baby likes the feel of it, as she curls in a ball and seems to sleep.

We swim an entire mile that first day, seventy-two lengths of the pool. This exertion is tons harder than running a mile, that's for sure, and it takes almost an hour. It becomes a routine, twice a week, to do our swimming workout. I look forward to it every time, not only for the exercise and bone-deep fatigue that compels me to nap for hours right afterward, but also for the time spent with my friend. I have a heightened sense that everything is ending, that the new phase just about to start will change everything in my life.

We leave the pool, patting ourselves dry and rubbing out the deep indentations left around our eyes by the goggles. Heather tells me when she looked over into my lane, all she could see of me was the big baby belly plowing through the water, such a part of me, but so separate as well.

We go swimming one day in late February, a day when Emily is off from school. I reserve a spot for her in the nursery and get her all set up with the attendants before I suit up. This time, when I am in the water, it is not just me and the baby cutting through the lane, back and forth. I can feel Emily. I can absolutely sense her physical being, right there with me. It occurs to me that I only have a few weeks left for just Emily and me—that this long phase of us as a twosome is coming to an end. I am already nostalgic for it. I wonder whether I have done a good enough job, if I have done enough for Emily.

For the past six years, my life has been all about Emily—and about how I have adjusted (or not adjusted) to having a disabled child. I wonder if I am up to the task of nurturing two children. Truth be told, Emily is not the only disabled one around here. I have been crippled as well, and I am just now beginning to heal.

# CHAPTER 44

On St. Patrick's Day, I venture down to Greg's office in DC where they are having a surprise baby shower in his honor. He doesn't know I am coming, and I take great pains not to spill the beans. He is superstitious about pregnant women traveling, even on the Metro, so I have been staying close to home. But for this special event, I break the rules.

I show up at Greg's office and am ushered into a conference room and seated at a round table. Greg will be attending a meeting he thinks is in this room, so my back is to the door to forestall the surprise. I hear him before I see him, his deep voice resonating through the hallway, getting closer to the door.

And he is surprised, touched, really, that his staff pulled this off. He generally hates surprises, but he is as gracious as always. He kisses me, pats me, then wonders aloud about the wisdom of coming down to the city when I am in this delicate condition. His coworkers laugh and joke that I can only have the baby after the shower is over. Once the loot is in hand, it is safe to go into labor. One woman even says the frosting-laden cake is sure to do the trick. I guess a sugar overload is another of those old wives' tales guaranteed to work. But I have never put any stock in those things, and, plus, it is too early.

But that night, I get up at 11:30 to go to the bathroom and my water breaks all over the floor. I wait to see whether it really is the amniotic fluid or just extra pee. Once I am convinced that it is indeed the water, I go to wake Greg. He is groggy from the Tylenol PM he took at bedtime, and he is hard to rouse. When I say my water broke, he mutters, "You're kidding!"

My due date is over four weeks away, and my OB didn't once mention the chance of giving birth early, but I am not worried. I feel strangely calm and composed. I phone the doctor on call, fill him in, and am directed to come to the hospital within an hour. I then call my mom, who comes right over, even though it is after midnight. I leave a list detailing Emily's schedule and have her backpack and lunchbox ready for school, so mom can feel prepared.

And then we are off, setting out in the cold night to have this baby. We are giddy with fatigue and excitement. I do not feel any pain yet, so I can easily joke around. We hold hands all the way to the hospital and try out the names we have been contemplating. We are down to three names and plan to look at this little girl's face before we decide.

I am admitted through the emergency department and taken right up to a room. The maternity wing has changed since I had Emily—it seems homier and less clinical. My room looks like a hotel suite, except for all the monitors and baby warmer. I put on a gown and stuff more paper towels in my underwear since my water continues to trickle out. Greg won't sit down, even though there is a chair just for him.

Within short order, the doctor comes in to check me. When the water breaks, the medical team wants the woman to deliver within twenty-four hours to prevent possible infection, so I need to be checked frequently for progress. The doctor's fingers seem to be probing unnecessarily hard inside my body, like he is searching for something. I tell him it hurts, and he apologizes, saying, "I'm not sure what I'm feeling." He orders an ultrasound, and we are left waiting nervously.

It takes 1 minute with the ultrasound to see that this little girl is breech—her bottom is down and her head and arms are up. She is literally folded up inside me. There is no way she is coming out except through a C-section. I accept the doctor's verdict without blinking. It seems petty to quibble and, frankly, I feel so blessed to be having a "normal" child that I don't care how they get her out.

Things are slow on the maternity ward tonight, so my C-section can be performed right away. I am in the operating room before I know it, getting an IV and being draped. Once I am prepped, they let Greg in. I can only see his eyes above the surgical mask, so I stare at their blueness as the doctor makes the incision. I am a little loopy from the epidural and Demerol, and I get really emotional. I can't stop thanking Greg for everything—for marrying me, for staying married to me, for taking the leap of faith to have this next child. At the moment of the birth, I see only Greg.

Our second baby girl is born at 3:38 a.m., and she looks perfect. She is little, smaller than Emily was, but she has the same sweet cheeks. The nurses have trouble straightening her out because she was folded up for so long in utero. I can see from the operating table that her body is like a briefcase repeatedly snapping shut.

Lauren Elizabeth comes into the world in her own way, on her own timetable. Time passes before I can hold her, but I know right away that what my mom said is true: My heart is definitely big enough for this new little girl.

# CHAPTER 45

The difference between having a disabled child and one who is "typically developing" is like night and day. No one needs to tell us this because we find out all on our own. From the get-go, Lauren is way easier across the board. She checks out physically, no problems, no anomalies. After a brief jaundice scare that amounts to nothing, all we have to do is bring her home and watch her grow. We only have one doctor, the pediatrician—no team of specialists and no surgeries.

The calm manner in which the newborn phase unfolds is almost jarring to my senses. I guess I am primed for disaster after our experiences with Emily, so I just can't believe this is the way it is. Feed the baby and put the baby down for a nap. Run errands, sing to the baby, and put the baby down for a nap. No crises and no incessant crying. Greg and I look at Lauren for hours, wondering when the other shoe is going to drop, when this wonderful stage will come to a screeching halt. But there is no other shoe, and after some time we stop looking for one.

Lauren sleeps through the night at ten weeks, nurses like a champ, and hardly ever cries. She is a great napper and an enthusiastic smiler. I can actually get out the developmental milestone charts and look at them without falling apart. Lauren hits all of the milestones right on target, like she perused the book before me, so pretty soon I stop looking at the book altogether.

I am in love all over again, but I feel like I have to keep it under wraps. I feel guilty for loving Lauren right off the bat when it took me so long with Emily. Greg reassures me that Emily was hard to love at first—she was so difficult, and we were so focused on just helping her survive. He tells me not to feel bad, but I am besieged with guilt anyway. I don't want Emily to feel less love than Lauren or feel that she is unlovable because she is not perfect. If anything, I hug Emily more now that Lauren is here.

While I simply revel in what Lauren can do, so easily and so quickly, there is another dimension as well. I am surprised to find that having a "normal" child makes me respect and admire Emily so much more. Watching Lauren transfer a chewy toy from one hand to the other, or cross over her body at midline to retrieve a dropped toy, brings me right back to when I worked with Emily for hours on something so simple. At six months old, Lauren is easily more in command of her body than Emily was at two years old. I see Emily's struggles now for what they truly were—a massive effort to get her body to do something that was immensely hard to do.

My friend Sue, whose four-year-old daughter has multiple disabilities, has a baby girl three months after Lauren was born. We talk often about whether it is easier to have the child with special needs as your first child or later in the birth order, as if we ever had a choice. We can't decide, even though we ponder this question at length. Having Lauren has saved me. I am more patient with Emily, more of her advocate than ever. I see how the deck is stacked against her and how she perseveres. She becomes my little hero all over again.

This typically developing child is something to see. My nature is to worry, especially given my experience with Emily, but I start to relax in a way I never thought possible. As Lauren grows, sits, crawls, and then walks, I stop saying to myself every day, "She SEEMS fine." Instead, I change the refrain to, "She IS fine." I can feel myself changing as a mother, unclenching as it were, to reveal a softer side, a less compulsive side.

Emily is changing as well. At first parroting back to us in her bellowing voice, "BABY SISTER," now she says it directly to Lauren. Her speech is unintelligible, just jargoning, but it is Emily's way of acknowledging this new little person in her life. We have taught Emily to pat Lauren gently, and she does, hollering, "PAT PAT PAT!" The two girls never really interact, but Emily is definitely comfortable with someone else in her domain.

My self-esteem as a woman is changing, too. Bearing two children makes me feel powerful, invincible almost. But more than that, I feel redeemed that now I have a child who is not disabled. I have felt like a failure for years, for having an imperfect child, for not being able to fix her, for not being able to make life easier for her. I am ashamed that I have made Emily's deficiencies into my own, have aligned her imperfections with my worth as a person, but that is what I have done. Now I have a chance to set it right, to make it all up to Emily, and to give my all to these two little girls, my family.

# CHAPTER 46

Emily starts first grade at a new school. Because we moved, we are in a new district, so it is a big change all around. The "home" school, or the closest elementary school to us, doesn't offer the extensive services that Emily needs. But another one, still fairly close by, does. We have lucked out in another major way: The Primary Academic Life Skills teacher is county-renowned for her expertise with special needs children. This woman, Ms. Julia, will be Emily's teacher for first and second grades.

Academic Life Skills (ALS) is a program for kids just like Emily—those with cerebral palsy, spina bifida, Down syndrome, autism, or, in our case, a chromosomal syndrome. The program recognizes the severe delays these children have, yet promotes close adherence to the regular curriculum as much as the students can manage and tolerate. The focus of the ALS program, just like its name indicates, is a blend of the critical academic tenets and "life skills" that most disabled children will need to survive in the world.

ALS is a self-contained classroom within a regular elementary school, similar in many ways to the preschool and kindergarten models that Emily experienced. The primary difference is that ALS is an official program all the way through high school, a track that, if Emily follows it, will provide the structure and consistency under which she thrives. In special education lexicon, she will be based in the ALS room for periods of time during the day, but in "gen ed" (general education) for periods as well. The schedule is an ever-flexible blend of inclusion and "pull-out" time, varying with the class lesson and Emily's tolerance level on any given day.

Without ever formally discussing it, Greg and I seem to have developed a philosophy of education pertaining to Emily. I state this philosophy every time I meet a new teacher, and it goes something like this: We don't care what "label" is given to Emily (mentally retarded, developmentally delayed, disabled) as long as she receives the services she needs and is entitled to. In fact, we have learned that the more involved the child is labeled in school, the more help he or she receives. Therefore, we have no problem watching all the teachers and therapists check many boxes next to Emily's name. She is still our Emily, no matter what the words say, and if she gets a multitude of services because of the words attributed to her, so be it.

It doesn't sound novel or revolutionary, but in a way, our first little philosophy is fairly different from that of other parents. Through the moms' group grapevine, I hear of numerous parents going to the mat, fighting NOT to have their child affiliated with a label, such as "autism spectrum" or "severely developmentally delayed." I totally understand this philosophy, although I don't subscribe to it. It hurts, in a physical, someone-punched-me-in-the-stomach way, to think of my own child next to words outlining deficiencies and abnormality. But Greg and I choose to bite the bullet and be realistic about Emily. We imagine a look of relief on the teachers' and administrators' faces when we let this nugget fly.

The second part to our theory of Emily's education is that the general curriculum, as a mechanism for learning, is mainly irrelevant as it applies to Emily. Sure, there are the basics we want her to learn, like reading and functional math skills. But as for the rest, when looking at the scope of Emily's life, we are doubtful how much science and social studies she will need. Algebra? Calculus? Irrelevant for her. This is not to say we have no expectations for Emily, but rather that we are pragmatic about what she needs. One day, hopefully, she can lead a life of some independence.

So in all the endless meetings regarding Emily's education, of which there have been five prior to first grade, we take the road less traveled: We totally acknowledge Emily's syndrome as prohibiting her from learning in a typical fashion. She learns more slowly, needs much repetition, and may not learn some things at all. Her ability to think abstractly may never emerge. Given these facts, we encourage the teachers to focus less on the "given" curriculum and more on the basics Emily will need to function as a person on her own.

Again, a collective sigh of relief accompanies our proclamations. We are the parents who care completely about their child, are devoted to her entirely, and have been engaged with a team of experts practically from Day One to make Emily the best little girl she can be. But we are no fools; we know the obstacles, the hurdles, we have seen them up close and personal. We do not want Emily to struggle more than she has to. Sometimes it is hard enough for her just to get through the day.

With this mindset, I breeze into Emily's new elementary school at the start of the year. I have Lauren in tow, so I make it a quick, boilerplate announcement: Label Emily with whatever works to get a bunch of services, and don't push the "gen ed" curriculum unless you are sure Emily can handle it. The new teachers are receptive right off the bat. From the nods around the table, it looks like the ALS team is on our wavelength already.

Ms. Julia is olive-skinned and tall, with a head of lustrous black hair. Unlike Emily's previous teachers, Julia may be as old as me. She is definitely out of her twenties and seasoned. Hers is one of the names in the county that moms with special needs kids just know. She "gets it," understands instinctively how to reach children with special needs. She is smart, kind, firm, organized, and loving. She is a friend to us and to Emily from the first day.

Ms. Julia has four children in her ALS classroom. An adult is assigned to each child at all times, so the supervision is excellent. According to the schedule posted on the blackboard, the class will be kept hopping with a revolving door of activities, "work time," and time out of the room for either inclusion or therapies. The school day follows an ambitious schedule, but it is one I know Emily craves. She needs structured time to keep herself focused. Otherwise, there are likely to be tantrums and tears.

There are a few new things this year, this first "real" year of elementary school. Emily has been promoted to a higher technology assistive communication device. Her old "talker" is simply too basic for her now. Ms. Julia has a new model, the upgrade, on deck to show me when I preview the school and classroom in late August. The new model looks more like a large Blackberry, but way heavier. The screen is a touch screen equipped with voice-over. If Emily wants to issue a greeting to an adult or peer, she finds the page for social greetings, locates "Hello, my name is Emily," and presses that screen. A techno-woman provides the voice, and voila! Emily speaks!

Julia warns me that this model is significantly different from what Emily currently uses. She anticipates a long break-in period, as do I. Emily takes a long time to adapt to new things, from clothes to food, and this change may be a battle. But we are moving forward, up the ranks in both school and the equipment Emily will use, and that is all good.

# CHAPTER 47

The second big change for Emily as she enters first grade is a major change for me as well—she boards a school bus every day at the end of our driveway. The school bus signals the end of the Mommy transport that has characterized the last six years of Emily's life. For the first time, I watch someone else take responsibility for getting Emily where she needs to be. This provides a good opportunity for me to relinquish some of the control I try to wield over Emily and her entire world. Letting go of the vise-like control is a hard thing to do, but necessary.

The bus is bona fide, too, I discover with glee. I thought maybe the "special bus" of my childhood (Midwestern slang called it the Retard Bus) might be transplanted here in Maryland for Emily. The regular yellow bus rounds the corner into our cul-de-sac, a delight to see. The brakes squeal as the driver maneuvers the circle, then pulls to a stop and opens the door. Emily is laden down with a princess backpack filled with opening-day papers and a lunchbox, but she walks pretty steadily to the door as I accompany her with Lauren in an umbrella stroller.

Stepping onto a school bus is a rite of passage for anyone, and I am as proud as can be. There goes my Emily, perched so big in her seat (specially outfitted with straps for all the kids with motor issues). Her round cheeks press against the window, and she gives me a wide dolphin grin as I wave goodbye. My camera catches the occasion, and I practically squeal. I call Greg right away on the cell phone, choking back sobs. He wonders why I am crying and I can't really say. My tears are the bittersweet variety—I am happy and sad, both.

Of course, I can't give up control entirely, not on this first day, for sure. Lauren and I jump into the car and tear out of the neighborhood, following the school bus on its route. I am pleased to see that the driver is safe and the trip to school passes without incident. I drive all the way to the school, watch Emily get off the bus, greet her waiting teachers, and then I turn around. Compulsive, worrywart, whatever— I need to see for myself that she's safe. I can take a deep breath now and let her begin the first phase of breaking away from me.

This bus thing is all good. I am off the hook for driving detail, and this gives me another hour in the day. I have Lauren home all to myself, a luxury I am not sure how to relish properly. At this age, about seven months, Emily was a full-time, hands-on job. Ferrying her around to therapies, doctor's appointments, and errands was about all the life we had. But now I have a second chance to really enjoy this phase.

Always a woman with a plan, I decide to sign Lauren up for Infant-Toddler music classes. This class is the kind of thing I couldn't do with Emily not only because we didn't have time, but also because she really couldn't join in activities with other kids. To attend a class and not have the pain of comparison as my constant companion will be a refreshing change.

So every Tuesday, we cut short morning nap-time and head out to a local dance studio to shake rattles, pound on drums, and sing kiddie songs with 10 other infants. The time is silly, babies lolling all over the carpet in various states of drooling and moving, but it is freeing, too. I am always worried that all the seriousness of being Emily's mom means I have left that part of me behind. But it surfaces here as I tickle and giggle and sing with my second daughter. I am having the experience I missed with Emily, and it feels fantastic. The load that I carry on my shoulders day after day begins to lighten as I, literally, learn to lighten up as well.

The class lasts for ten weeks with an option to renew for another session. I strike up a conversation with one of the moms as we debate the upcoming winter and whether music class will be possible. The woman's name is Kathy, and I have been watching her and her son lately. I have room in my life for another friend, so I invite her over for a play date the next week.

My tolerance for most people is small probably because I like to be alone and I value my time. This said, I like to talk and love having women friends. So, I am ultra-picky and super-loyal. My instinct about Kathy pans out perfectly. I have hand-picked a woman who is much like me. We take to each other instantly, sharing stories over pasta salad and cookies. One of my barometers of friendship is the reaction people have to Emily. When I tell Kathy of Emily and her syndrome, her limitations, she doesn't flinch or blink. It turns out that she worked for Special Olympics for years and counts many disabled people as friends.

So my days, after Emily boards the bus, follow an appealing routine of playing with Lauren, going on walks, visiting the mall, and having friends over. Mine is the stay-at-home life I felt gypped out of with Emily. I feel guilty once in a while for delighting in Lauren and our days together, but I figure I earned them. I paid my dues, and then some, these past few years.

Although this time with Lauren is glorious, it also feels like a hiatus of sorts, the calm before a storm. A niggling feeling quivers right on the periphery, an uneasy feeling of doom lurking that I can't quite shake. I try to banish it, try to distract myself, yet it hovers like a virus. Greg thinks I am crazy, tells me to enjoy this time to the fullest. I begin to wonder whether my feeling is a portent of events to come or perhaps I have just become so hardened that I have lost my capacity to feel pure joy anymore.

We notice one day that Emily is pulling at the corners of her eyes as she watches TV. She stands about two feet away from the screen, squinting and pulling, stretching her eyes into a slit. A traditional eye exam is out of the question because Emily can't say with any accuracy or intelligibility what she sees. At the next moms' dinner, I ask around and, sure enough, there is an eye specialist who deals with the disabled.

Emily has quite a list of specialists: cardiologist, nephrologist, gastroenterologist, geneticist, so why not add another. I take Emily to see this developmental ophthalmologist on a Tuesday after school. Dr. Kotlicky is mild mannered and unfazed by Emily's stomping, yowling self in the exam room. Luckily, I have a video in our travel bag, so with a signal from the doctor, I pop it in the machine at the far end of the room, wrestle Emily onto my lap, and hope for the best.

As Emily gets older, she gets stronger, not just physically, but in her temperament as well. Simply put, she doesn't like to be messed with. She will not tolerate a Band-aid, a haircut (or any hair doo-dads, for that matter), let alone a comprehensive eye exam. But with the right props, as I am learning, it is doable, if not pleasant. I always have a repertoire of songs, an arsenal of snacks, a veritable bag of tricks, so to speak.

This eye doctor is gentle and quick. Even with the video on and my incessant commentary in Emily's ear, she squirms and starts to fight, so he only does the essentials. I am fascinated by how much he can tell about her eyes without her input. He holds a variety of magnifying glass instruments to the front and side of her eyes and studies the structure of her retina and cornea. The verdict is clear: Emily is farsighted and will need glasses, full time.

I am skeptical about how she is going to fare wearing glasses, but Ms. Julia tells me they have a protocol at school to wean children into new things, from glasses to wheelchairs. I am all set to send the new glasses in to school in a Care Bears case, tucked neatly into her backpack. But before I do that, I decide to be brave and attempt the maiden voyage here at home. I kneel down, facing Emily, and explain that these are her new, exciting glasses. She will wear glasses just like Mommy and Grandma, and she will be able to see so much better. I don't know if Emily grasps what I am saying, but she lets me fit the frames to her face and tuck the earpiece comfortably next to her head. She swings her head from side to side, looks out across the room, and emits a squeal.

From this day forward, Emily wears glasses with no fuss. It is obvious she sees better with them. I question how long she must have needed them before we noticed anything. The vigilance we must maintain as parents of a nonverbal child continues. Just when I think my eagle-eye is honed to perfection, another thing crops up.

Now when Lauren and I wave bye-bye to Emily on the bus every morning, her bespectacled face peers out the murky bus window. Greg and I jokingly say that Emily now looks like cousin Oliver from "The Brady Bunch." With her cherubic cheeks, bowl-cut hair, and now the glasses, we are actually not far off. She looks like a goofy little genius child, and when she gives us a wide grin, we can't keep from laughing.

# CHAPTER 48

My sister Maureen visits over the Christmas holidays when Emily is seven years old and Lauren is nine months old. She watches Emily tear wrapping paper into long strips, a fine motor activity she has perfected at school. Suddenly, Maureen says, "What's with Emily's feet?" I swing my head around, expecting to see blood or some sort of wound. What I do see is almost as surprising.

Greg and I bathe Emily every night, we dress her, put her shoes on (and take them off) several times a day. Yet we have somehow failed to notice our own daughter's feet. She walks around the kitchen, then back to the family room, pacing in her rhythmic way, so she really gives us a chance to observe now.

To put it bluntly, her feet are malformed. The arches seem to be on the outside of her feet, and where the arches should be, the tendons are completely flat. Her ankle bones are caving in toward the floor. Looking higher up her legs, I can see the outline of her legs even though she wears long pants. Her knees are turning in, buckling almost, and her hips are tilted in toward her body instead of in straight alignment. The lower half of her body is simply growing crooked.

I wonder when this happened and how we missed it. Emily has had a series of growth spurts lately, eating everything in sight, even motioning for seconds, necessitating a new wardrobe halfway through the school year. A thorough once-over of Emily's naked

body might have given us a clue earlier than this. Whenever I look
at Emily without clothes, I make it just to the roadmap of scars on
her chest before I busy myself with toweling her off, dressing, and
brushing teeth. I haven't noticed this because I haven't been looking, simple as that.

We see Dr. Khurana the next day and she agrees immediately
that something is going on. I don't feel quite as negligent when
the doctor declares that she was not aware of this problem until
I pointed it out. She gives me the name and phone number of a
physiatrist and an orthotist in a nearby town, and here we go—off
to more specialists.

Welcome to the land of orthotics, those ugly devices worn in
the shoe, sometimes up to the ankle, occasionally all the way up
the leg. Their job is to realign and straighten the feet and legs to
make them more functional. They are the equivalent of braces for
the legs and are custom-fitted for each patient. Orthotics cannot
just be ordered from a store. The protocol is that a physiatrist must
diagnose a problem and prescribe orthotics. Then an orthotist
casts, molds, and custom-fits the orthotics on the feet. The process
is labor-intensive, with multiple steps. From diagnosis to wearing of the orthotic device can take several months. For us, it takes
exactly three months, from Christmas time until mid-March.

Emily is easy to diagnose. At yet another Baltimore hospital,
this one an outpatient site for Ambulatory Surgery, we meet with
a physiatrist. I have never heard of a physiatrist before, but after
a quick look through a medical journal, I find that he or she is an
expert on the study of how the body parts work together, specifically the muscles, ligaments, tendons, and bones. If anything is out
of alignment or causing pain, a physiatrist is the one to see.

Dr. Potter wants Emily's entire medical history from me, and I
offer it while Emily flips through every book in the exam room.
The doctor is impressed with the comprehensive list I keep in
my purse. The list is a small packet, a chronological rundown of
every hospitalization, every surgery, and every medication that
Emily has ever had. This list saves me a lot of time and jogs my

memory when I fill out forms and answer questions. The doctor pages through my list and wants to make a copy. I am pleased to be deemed organized in this manner, when most of the time I feel scattered and unsure.

For the physical exam, the doctor has Emily disrobe to her underpants. She looks so small, vulnerable, and chalky white as she lies on the table. The doctor turns her this way and that, pulling her legs, and measuring her from hip to knee, knee to ankle. He spends a long time manipulating her feet. They look almost boneless, like a piece of whitefish, in the doctor's large hands.

Before he issues his diagnosis or approves the making of orthotics, though, she needs the "walk" test. With a quick glance down the hallway to make sure the coast is clear, he asks Emily to walk from one end of the hallway to the other. He points to a macrame wall hanging with a giraffe on it and says, "Walk to the giraffe, Emily."

Still in her underpants, Emily obliges. She is all white skin and bone, her vertebrae visible knob by bony knob. She lurches down the hall in her customary awkward way, and I am shocked to see the mechanics of her body, startlingly revealed by her nakedness. From the waistband of her pink flowered underpants on down, her body twists in, like a doll whose parts have not been realigned after a day of play. Her knees literally knock together, and her right foot drags so badly that it appears she is sweeping the floor with it. I am amazed she can walk at all.

So now we know why Emily looks clumsy, why she lurches and careens about, instead of moving smoothly—why, at seven years old, she cannot run well. Her body will not allow it. The chromosomal syndrome has robbed Emily of a normal heart, stomach, and kidneys; has slowed her development to a crawl; has rendered her nonverbal; and now is claiming her outsides as well. All her deformities used to be hidden within, away from plain sight, but with this new discovery, she will be marked outside as well. It does not seem fair.

Back in the doctor's exam room, he verifies the necessity of orthotics and refers me to an orthotist nearby. I learn that without a referral from a physiatrist such as this one, the price of orthotics generally runs above $1,000 per pair and is usually not covered by insurance. I also learn that Emily's "gait," the specific way she moves and the physiology of her muscles and joints, contains similar elements to cerebral palsy. I am taken aback by this word, although we have heard it before in conjunction with Emily's condition. After a moment of thought, I am actually not so surprised. Emily's syndrome is so rare—it is "like" a lot of things. She just doesn't fit nicely into any one slot. That is what makes her so unique.

Two weeks later, we meet with the orthotist for the first of three grueling appointments. Emily is not good at waiting and hates to sit still, so she acts like a real bear for the duration. First, the orthotist, "Dr. Dave" to us, measures her foot and then begins to cast it. He uses a plaster mix to coat strips of gauze, wrapping the gauze around Emily's foot to about midcalf. The mixture is sticky and cold, and Emily hates it. She squirms and wails, pulling her foot away, trying to hit the doctor and me, until I sit my own body across her legs so that she is immobile. The mold takes about five minutes to set up, and then it can be cut with scissors and removed from her leg.

Once the first mold is completed, we take a break and Emily signs, "all done." I explain that she has one foot left to go, and she looks panicked. The doctor leaves to replenish his supplies, giving me a pamphlet on his way out. The brochure is full of designs—turns out that custom-made orthotics can be affixed with kid-friendly artwork to make them more stylish. I guess the idea is to hide how hideous they look. There are boat and football orthotics for boys, ballerinas, butterflies, and sunflowers for girls. I show them to Emily, asking her, "Which one, Emily? Point to your favorite." But she doesn't seem to care, and I can't really blame her. A big clomping boot-shoe will still be ugly no matter what design she picks.

The left foot goes more smoothly than the first, either because Emily is worn out or because I pull out all the stops. I use a technique of Greg's, singing favorite songs right in Emily's ear, and it seems to calm her. Before long, there are two plaster molds, dried and hardened, propped in a chair like ghost feet. Even the casts look crooked and turned in. The orthotist tells me that the orthotic devices will be formed of rigid plastic and will be worn inside regular shoes, bought one size larger to accommodate the device. They will be uncomfortable at first, so he advises a gradual schedule of wearing so her legs don't get too tired and her feet don't blister.

It takes three more weeks to turn the casts into the bona fide orthotics, and then we go back for a fitting. Dr Dave goes back and forth from the exam room to his workshop in the back of the office, making adjustments. Padding needs to be added for comfort and to prevent abrasions. Occasionally the plastic shell needs to be melted to mold more precisely to the foot. The doctor is not kidding about uncomfortable. It takes both of us to force the orthotics onto Emily's feet and then cram them into her shoes. She fights us every step of the way, but once we have them on, we set her upright and watch her walk. She stomps around the waiting room, wobbly at first, curious about the added weight to her lower extremities, but walking nonetheless. Her cooperation is a victory in itself.

Even to my untrained eye, it is a miracle of modern medicine. Emily is straighter from stem to stern. Gone is the in toeing, sweeping walk, replaced by a more solid, steady gait. Her knees don't touch together and her shoes point forward, instead of toward each other, as she walks. The doctor explains that every six months to a year she will need to be fitted for a new pair as her feet grow and as her body grows and changes. I blanch at the thought of repeat appointments, dreading the repetition of this anxiety on Emily and, truthfully, on me as well.

Driving home with Emily that day, all decked out in her new butterfly orthotics, I am struck with how different Emily looks than she did just a year ago. With the Fearless Fly farsighted magnifying glasses on, and now her orthotics, she appears disabled, rather than just acting disabled. Greg and I have always thought it ironic that Emily looks so normal. Especially as a little baby, no one could ever tell. But now, there is no question.

I chastise myself for being so superficial. After all, what really matters is that all the major repairs to Emily—her heart, kidney, and abdominal surgeries—have left her healthy. The glasses and the orthotics are just tweaking, really, a fix for less serious issues. But somehow bearing scars on the outside seems like another cruelty that Emily should not have to endure.

# CHAPTER 49

I am used to being in crisis alert mode, ready at any time for another trip to the hospital, another diagnosis, or another thing wrong with our first daughter. I have lived that way for years, like a caffeine addict, always on an adrenaline high. But now, without my even being aware of it, the dust has settled a bit, and I am not constantly afraid. Life seems comparatively smooth sailing as far as the eye can see. I would like to think enough shoes have dropped so that we are probably out of the woods. Long stretches of time can go by where we just live, and I have come to relax into that as much as I can.

There is still that edge, though. Occasionally I feel rattled and nervous with some sort of intuition. I am not ready to sound the all-clear signal and get on with as "normal" a life as we can have. The last time I checked my "Emily list," the chronicling of all her surgeries, meds, and doctor visits, I came away disquieted. There hasn't been anything major for a long time. It is almost too good to be true.

Lauren celebrates her first birthday by walking back and forth in the family room, tumbling down and then getting up quickly. She is full of laughs, and her sparkly personality is infectious. She has been an easy baby. Our life seems calm, predictable, one day pretty much like the other. I feel thankful in a benign way for the gulps of untroubled air I swallow these days.

One day in April, I put Lauren down for a nap and set about tidying up the house. The phone rings and I blithely pick it up. The principal at Emily's school tells me Emily had a big seizure in the classroom and is en route to the hospital in an ambulance. She asks how soon I can get there. I tell her I am on my way. I grab Lauren's sleeping body from her crib, buckle her hastily into her car seat, throw my purse into the car, and speed down the road. My mom is out of town, and I cannot impose on a friend at this late notice to take Lauren, so I have to swing this by myself.

I call Greg on my cell phone while I drive, telling him what I know, which is not much. What I am thinking is, seizure? How can Emily have a seizure? She doesn't have seizures. I am panicky, jittery, and worried out of my mind. Greg says he will get there as soon as he can. He tells me to stay calm, that it will be all right, but I am not feeling so sure.

There is no telling how I make it to the hospital without getting into an accident. I feel so rattled it is a wonder I can drive at all. Somehow we get there, pulling into a parking spot right near the ambulance bay. I pull Lauren out of her seat, stabilize her on one hip, and then drape my purse and diaper bag over the opposite shoulder. I stumble as I run to the emergency room, trying to balance the bouncing baby and the two bags banging against my thigh.

I announce Emily's name to the ER clerk and am taken immediately to the pediatric wing of the emergency department. The hallway is a series of curtained-off rooms located around a central desk. I am shown into the first room on the right, which contains a bed, a chair, a small steel sink, and a TV, but no Emily. One of the nurses stops by to say the ambulance is on its way. I actually got here first.

Despite all of Emily's medical crises and hospitalizations, I haven't been back to the county hospital for Emily since she was being treated for jaundice right after her birth. It seems like a lifetime ago. I can't sit down, so I pace around the room and then out into the hall, still with Lauren on my hip, waiting for some news.

Lauren is getting heavy, but I can't put her down or she will run with wild toddler abandon all over the hospital.

Suddenly the slight beeping, whirring sounds at the central desk are punctuated by a gust of wind and the grating of the automatic doors opening at the end of the unit. I run out of the room to see Emily being wheeled in on a stretcher. She is so small on the white mattress, completely unconscious and covered with vomit. Her face is paler than I have ever seen it, and her eyelids are distinctly blue. Her hair is damp and matted with sweat, and her groin is covered with urine. Her limbs are splayed out at unnatural angles, and an IV line has been attached to her right hand. She looks seriously unwell.

The paramedic who brought Emily in is maybe nineteen years old, all loose-boned, farm boy stock with a square jaw and a spray of pimples across his forehead. He gives the nurses and doctor on call the rundown. "Seven-year-old female, MR, grand mal seizure at school, convulsive for 5 minutes, voided bladder and bowels, vomited once on site and once again en route, unresponsive, pulse thready and racing, blood pressure elevated, temperature normal."

I take this all in, wondering what MR stands for. Then, of course, I understand. The doctors need to know that Emily is mentally retarded because that will affect their evaluation of her. For a moment, I feel such pity for my child, unarmed and vulnerable on the gurney. I hate that this has happened to her, hate that she suffers yet again.

The teenage paramedic gathers his clipboard and duffle bag of supplies. Before departing, he gives Emily a long look of concern. He puts a hand on her shoulder, bites his lower lip, and pats her gently. I want to hug him for showing such humanity and kindness to my child.

While Emily is cleaned up and monitors are attached, the school principal comes in. School policy states that if a student suffers an emergency at school, an administrator must accompany the student to the hospital and stay until a parent arrives. I am thankful that this woman was in the ambulance with Emily, holding her hand. She tells me what she knows of the "incident," as she calls it, and urges me to call Ms. Julia to get the whole story.

Apparently, Emily was at recess within the room, just a five-minute break between work sessions, when one of the aides noticed her color was pale and she was staring into space. They called her name, asked her if she was feeling okay, with no response. Then she fell to the floor, convulsing and twitching. Before the ambulance arrived, she convulsed for five minutes until her body stilled and she fell unconscious. In the process of the seizure, she wet her pants, soiled herself, and began to throw up. I learn later that news of Emily's seizure spread like wildfire throughout the school, and teachers actually abandoned their classes, running down the hall to see if they could help.

The vision of this episode is deeply troubling to me. I am terrified, just riveted with fear. I wonder what caused the seizure, if she will come out of it unscathed, if she will have more. I know next to nothing about seizures, but I do recall two things: Many of the women in the moms' group have children with seizure disorders, and the majority of children with chromosomal syndromes similar to Emily's suffer with some degree of epilepsy. So, this condition is part of the special needs landscape that we thought we had somehow avoided, at least until now.

Once Emily is stabilized, it is a waiting game to get her labs back, testing for all manner of things in her blood and urine. Emily gradually wakes up, coming around in a disoriented, grumpy haze. She pulls the tape holding her IV line and fiddles with the sticky leads on her chest. I try to hold her gently, sing to her, but she is having none of it. She is uncomfortable, naked, cold, and scared. I did not think to grab spare clothes in my rush out of the house, so Emily is under a harsh hospital-issue blanket with nothing else.

Greg arrives after two hours in a rush and a panic. He is eager to be filled in, but there is not much to tell. He takes Lauren from me, and I hunt down a doctor. This is a county hospital, very general in nature, so I suspect we will be sent home and referred elsewhere for a more intense workup. Once I find the doctor, all he can say is that Emily's seizure was not caused by dehydration and was not cardiac related. He tells us to visit our pediatrician right away and make an appointment with a neurologist as soon as possible. We can take Emily home tonight as long as she stays stable.

Greg and I take turns that night checking on Emily as she sleeps. Every hour, we nudge each other awake, trudge into her room, and place our hands on her chest to check for even breathing. Time warps back to the early days, those newborn nights when her existence seemed so fragile. The old demon Fear is back, coursing through our veins as we confront this latest obstacle.

# CHAPTER 50

The word *seizure* connotes the most awful images: thrashing, bucking, writhing movements, stiffened limbs, tongue biting, urinating, and loss of control. True, this is indeed what many seizures look like. But with the onset of Emily's seizure disorder, I learn that this is also a stereotypical and often erroneous picture of a seizure.

I am aggressive in my pursuit of a neurologist, and I will not take an appointment even a week out. I am on the phone right away, stating our situation, attesting to the emergency circumstances. We have an appointment with a pediatric neurologist at Sinai Hospital, our old stomping ground, by the next day. Emily's anesthesiologist, gastroenterologist, nephrologist, and abdominal surgeon are all here, so it is familiar territory. There is something calming in the fact that, even although this seizure thing is new, at least the car can practically drive itself to the hospital and we definitely know our way around. It adds a touch of certainty to this fearful experience.

Another specialist, another doctor to trust with our daughter. The pediatric neurologist is older, has black hair flecked with grey, and is serious in a tender way, with a Mike Wallace demeanor. He takes an extensive history from me while Greg keeps Emily satisfied with books and snacks. Dr. Gratz has never worked with a patient who has Partial Trisomy 13 before, but that is nothing new.

We have never had a doctor who has. However, this doctor treats special needs children all the time; in fact, most of his patient load consists of disabled children, so we are in the right hands.

Dr. Gratz explains that seizures are essentially "brainstorms," or faulty firing of the neurons in the brain. In other words, when the brain misfires, a seizure occurs. Seizures fit several patterns. They can occupy most of the brain (generalized seizures) or only part of the brain (partial). In addition, they can be simple or complex depending on the degree of consciousness maintained by the seizure patient. A full-out, drop-down, thrashing seizure, where the person is rendered unconscious, is known as a grand mal or Complex Generalized seizure. A less devastating type, petit mal, falls into the simple, partial category. This is the kind of seizure you would want to have, if you could pick only one.

Then there are "absence" seizures, and as soon as the doctor describes these, I know without a shadow of a doubt that I have seen this before. Emily has been having minor seizures, while awake, and I didn't even know it. I think back to all the times Emily "spaces out," stares into the distance for a while and then blinks and is back. That is an absence seizure. So too are the times when she seems greatly fatigued, lies down, licks her lips, rubs parts of her clothing, and looks a bit pale and nauseated. It lasts a few minutes and then she rallies and hops right up. I have written all this off to a tired child who happens to have multiple disabilities, never once suspecting a deeper problem.

The doctor concurs with me, agreeing that it certainly sounds as if Emily has been having small seizures for a long time. But what about the episode at school? An EEG administered in the hospital is the only way to find out precisely what is happening. With no words to tell us, Emily can't even explain how she feels, if she senses an "aura" coming on prior to an episode. The EEG will give us a map of her brain so we can see for ourselves.

I am concerned about this test—not just for the trauma of the brief hospital stay required, but of the experience as well. For an effective EEG, the patient must be completely still for at least thirty minutes, even an hour, so the machine can catch an adequate sampling of brain waves. Emily is not likely to be still for even two minutes unless she is asleep. I think of our favorite anesthesiologist, based just feet away in another wing of this hospital, and decide to visit an old friend.

Dr. Zuckerberg is pleased to see me and astounded by Emily. The last time he saw her was six years ago, as a baby swathed in gauze. She was his first (and only) patient with Partial Trisomy 13, and he had no idea how well she would fare. Now she is a walking, emoting, enthusiastic little girl with spunk to spare. He is sorry to hear about her seizure event and reassures me he can help. With a little string pulling, he is able to arrange a sedated EEG for the next day. I am well aware that this is outside the usual protocol, that most patients have to wait weeks for such an appointment. Having a unique medical mystery of a child sometimes pays off.

The next day, I return with Emily and my mom to the hospital at 6:00 a.m. Emily is not allowed to eat or drink anything, so it is a task keeping her happy. After morning rounds, they are ready for her. Dr. Zuckerberg, chipper as always in his lopsided yarmulke, prattles away to the nurse about Emily as a baby. He pats her proprietarily, calling her "My little Emmie," and tries to soothe her. Emily is naturally feisty and is getting the gist that we are not here for fun. The doctor lowers the mask onto Emily's puffy cheeks, and within seconds she is out cold. We are invited to pass the time in the waiting room, and a nurse promises to retrieve us when the procedure is over.

Once ensconced in a chair, gripping a magazine I know I won't read, I begin to sob. The pain is just too much, back here where we started, all those years ago. The same medicinal smells and constant beeping of monitors are unnerving. Pieces of my heart shred again, seeing Emily flattened out in a bed, unaware. Mom knows I just need to get it all out, to cry like I couldn't back then, so she holds me until the tears subside.

After an hour, we can go back to Emily's bed. The test is complete, the neurologist will "read" the results a bit later, so all we

need to do is get Emily to wake up and take her home. That is easier said than done. Emily is like a cranky baby when she becomes
alert, fussing and whining. She swats at anyone nearby, practically
growling. I give her some time, keeping back a safe distance, but
talking nonstop, telling her I know she feels lousy, assuring her we
are all done now.

Finally we are able to get her clothes on with some semblance of
cooperation. Getting all the tape off her hands and trying to brush
the conductive glue from her hair is another matter. Emily launches
herself off the bed, arms flailing. In the process, she hits herself in
the mouth and something white goes flying. When I see the big gap
in Emily's mouth, I realize her first baby tooth has "fallen" out.

The tooth has been dangling by a thread for a week, and now
it is airborne in the hospital room. My mom scoops it up, and I
attend to Emily's bleeding gums. It adds insult to injury having a
bloody rag wedged in her mouth on top of everything else. Emily
is in a rage now, desperate to be gone. We wheel her out to the car
in a wheelchair and tote her wailing self home.

Dr. Gratz calls later that afternoon. Emily has an unequivo-
cal seizure disorder (this is new terminology; in previous years,
the word *epilepsy* was exclusively used). The EEG showed seizure
activity in the temporal lobe of her brain. She has a Complex Partial seizure disorder, a term we find ironically amusing because
Emily is nothing if not complex, and of course the "partial" seems
apropos because of her syndrome, *Partial* Trisomy 13. It seems fitting, almost: Nothing is simple about this child, nor is anything
complete.

This new development of the seizure disorder is difficult to see as
simply another thing to deal with, but with a few days perspective,
Greg and I decide to maintain a cavalier attitude about it all, if we
can. The neurologist starts Emily on a low dose of anticonvulsive
medication right away, telling us we will likely have to try many
different "meds" before we find one that is the right fit and dosage
for Emily. I know from the moms' group grapevine that this will
be a dicey, trial-and-error process until we get it just right.

But we are staggeringly lucky right off the bat. For once, things are easier than we predict. Emily takes her medicine well, twice a day, and the side effects are minor, mostly sleepiness. With help from the elementary school, I track Emily's seizure activity every day by writing down any staring episodes and overt seizures. Once I know how to spot them, I can pepper a page full of episodes, sometimes many in one day. But as we gradually increase the medication amount, upping it ever so slightly over three days, I notice a drastic decrease, then an almost total cessation in the seizures. Emily's system, quirky as it is, seems to accept this medication well.

Part of our morning and nighttime routine now is to give Emily her meds. The medicine is a precursor to breakfast and so automatic that we barely notice doing it at all. I know from all my research that "breakthrough" seizures can occur, especially with a change in Emily's weight or extreme tiredness or stress. So I am not naive enough to think we will never see a seizure again, but I count our lucky stars that we have all come through this latest adventure relatively unscathed.

# CHAPTER 51

One night, I am nursing Lauren right before bedtime, sitting comfortably in the oatmeal-colored easy chair tucked in the corner of our bedroom. Lauren pulls her lips off my nipple with a wet, smacking sound, grins up at me, and says, "Hi!"

I am speechless with wonder at my baby girl who has found her voice. She says "mama," "dada," "edda' (for Emily), and now, apparently, "hi!" I can already imagine having conversations with this little person, something I am unable to do with Emily. Emily is vocal now, but not intelligible by any stretch of the imagination. The folks at school can get the gist of what she tries to impart with her bellows and chants, but for the general population, no way. Emily has a seventy-five-word "vocabulary" of words or phrases that she can approximate, but, in truth, it mostly sounds like gibberish. It pains me deeply that I have never once heard "Mommy" from my older girl.

I decide that because Lauren can now walk and talk, I should stop nursing her. I put in the recommended year of breastfeeding, and now we are done. I throw away all my nursing bras and relish the new found freedom of not sharing my body with a toddler. A few weeks later, I notice the tell-tale twinge of ovulation deep in my right side. Being back to normal will be a good thing.

The super-size box of Tampax I buy for the period I feel sure is soon to arrive sits on the shelf, waiting. It's not until I reach for a spare tube of toothpaste one morning that I see the box, its green and blue stripes mocking me.

I race downstairs to consult the calendar. I stopped nursing in March, now it is early May, and no period. No cause for alarm. But the days tick by and I feel laid out with exhaustion, cranky, with a subterranean queasiness lurking in my innards. My breasts, so recently deflated to their usual size, take on a fullness that I recognize all too well.

I wait until Greg heads off on a business trip to take a pregnancy test. I am nervous and do not want an audience. Sure enough, I am pregnant, decisively so. I lay a hand lightly on my belly, rubbing gently back and forth. "Hello, baby," I say.

I am not sure how I feel about having another child. Lauren is only fourteen months old, a baby yet herself. I am tickled nonetheless, joyful with this unexpected blessing. I do the calculations in my head, figuring on a January baby. I am getting excited despite my misgivings, and I can't wait to tell Greg.

I decide to wait until Greg returns home from his trip, rather than spoil the surprise on the phone. This news is too special for a phone call anyway. I pick Greg up from the airport and he is sick, nose streaming and eyes bleary. He has a sinus infection, made worse by the air quality on the plane.

At home, he heads for bed as I put Lauren down for a nap. Emily is at school, so the house is quiet. I crawl in bed next to Greg, and I study his sleepy face. I snuggle down within his arms and am quickly asleep. I wake with a start, get up to go to the bathroom, and come back to find Greg waking up. He wants to talk about his trip, but he stops himself at the look on my face.

I am smiling in that way that you do when you are bursting with a secret. My lips just won't stay downturned, and are in fact dancing all over my face.

"We're going to have another baby," I tell Greg, searching his face for the first hint of his reaction. He gathers me in his arms, squeezes tightly, pulls back, and smiles.

"I'm so glad," he says, and I am so relieved I almost weep. Despite being exhausted and ill, Greg musters enthusiasm and is a surprisingly good sport. His ability to roll with the punches is one of the qualities I love most about him.

I settle into Pregnancy Mode, reducing my daily runs to vigorous walks and eating cheese by the pound. Pregnancy is harder this time because I have two children to care for and no leisure to take a nap when the fatigue hits. But I never feel too awful, and the early weeks pass in a flash.

Greg paints the spare bedroom yellow, and I put up a floral border. This room will be Lauren's Big Girl room so the baby can have the crib and the nursery. We head out to a local furniture store and settle on a dark wood sleigh bed with matching dresser and desk. It seems like Lauren doesn't get to be the baby of the family for too long.

My OB hears the heartbeat on her Doppler device right at ten weeks, says the early ultrasound looks fine, and sets me up with the genetic testing, just like we did with Lauren. I will get a CVS again at thirteen weeks. It feels like a formality, and one that I am eager to get through so I can relax and enjoy the rest of the pregnancy. The end of the first trimester is just around the corner, and that looks like a good omen.

Greg and I trek up to the Center for Advanced Fetal Care, where the genetic counselor, still reed-thin Amanda, jokes with us that we have been busy since our last visit. She reiterates that genetic testing is optional, but certainly recommended in cases like ours, where we have a child with a severe syndrome. We know what the CVS entails, so Amanda dispenses with explaining the drill, and we chit-chat about how Emily is doing and what Lauren is like.

The heady mood dissolves when I am getting the ultrasound. The high-tech machinery can pick up details with minute precision, and it is amazing and nerve- wracking at the same time. The job of the tech is to check everything, and she is thorough, scanning up, down, around, many times. I am fascinated by how much I can see of the baby, how it is squirming and wiggling, the size of a circus peanut doing flips.

It is a feeling more than anything said. The tech, an ebullient blonde woman whom we have had before, stops her banter and becomes focused, eerily so. She sees something, but won't say what. Greg and I clench hands, unsure what to do. Her job is not to interpret what she sees, merely to mark it for the doctor. All I can see is a cute little baby, dancing in my belly.

The ultrasound over, I stay on the table, waiting for the doctor to come in with a catheter to begin the CVS. It seems like forever until he emerges, pushing through the privacy curtain that cordons off the room. He looks preoccupied, almost gruff. He mumbles behind his beard, but I catch enough.

"There's a question of a cleft," he says, "so we'll expedite these test results."

My heart is hammering in my chest and I can't swallow. The doctor's meaning eclipses his few words. The cleft to which he refers is a separation in the bones of the face involving sometimes just the lips, sometimes the entire palate. They must see that on the scan, even this early in my pregnancy. A cleft can exist on its own, absent any other problem, a relatively minor birth defect. Not a pretty one, but ultimately operable, with good results.

The subtext, of course, is that many times a cleft exists as part of a syndrome. Emily happens not to have a cleft, but many children with syndromes similar to hers do. Midline defects such as a cleft are very common, almost a marker.

I press the doctor, urging him to give us answers, specifics.

"What's the chance that the baby has JUST a cleft, with no other involvement?" I choke out. The doctor is loath to play this betting game, but he knows I am pleading.

"It's about 50-50," he allows, turning to face his instruments. What I will remember later is that at no point in our brief conversation did he look me in the eye.

The perpetual optimist, I summon up some chirpiness for the CVS, admiring again the active little form on the screen, the seeming perfection of this baby. I certainly can't see a thing wrong. I ask the tech to scan the face again, slowly, and still, nothing. If there is a gaping hole there, I simply can't see it.

The CVS takes a matter of minutes, and then I wait a few moments before getting up. I am shaky and rattled, but determined not to faint. The genetic counselor stops in before we leave to tell us that, because our results are being expedited, she will call two times with news. The first call will tell us whether the baby has Down Syndrome or Trisomy 18. These are the biggies, the most common, and the easiest to test for. It will take a few days longer for the diagnostitians in the lab to highlight all the bands of the chromosomes, looking for more uncommon abnormalities.

We ride home in silence, worry creasing our foreheads, yet still holding hands. I am already adjusting my reality, thinking a child with a cleft is not so bad, really. This is not the worst thing that could happen.

We are greeted at home by Wendy, who is watching Lauren. She can always be counted on for a positive spin, and she comes through again. She takes my hands in hers and tells me that we don't know anything at all definite yet. We can do nothing but wait and not a thing will be gained by worrying. She is right, I know, but I can't help it. Within minutes of her departure, I am all over the Web, looking for answers.

What I find is a combination of reassurance and fear. Some sites mention that facial structure cannot be accurately studied until a fetus is at least sixteen weeks. At less than 14 weeks, maybe it is too early to see anything, too ambiguous.

Then some sites offer pictures of all the ways a cleft can present, picture after picture of infants with gaping, malformed faces. I wonder how I would feel about holding, feeding, and loving a child who looks so destroyed.

When Mom comes over later, I hand her the ultrasound pictures we brought home from the hospital. She scans one, then the other, remarking that she really can't see anything at all and it is best just to wait.

So we wait.

# CHAPTER 52

The CVS is on a Wednesday in late July. By that Friday, the phone rings and it is Amanda with the preliminary results. I shut myself in the pantry because the girls are both loud on this summer afternoon. The baby does not have Down Syndrome or Trisomy 18, she tells me. I make her repeat that once, twice.

"We're not in the clear," she says, sounding tentative, "but it's a good sign."

I try the same tactic with her as I did with the doctor. I need facts or statistics here.

"If the baby does not have these, the most common syndromes by far, isn't it highly unlikely that the baby has a much more rare syndrome?" I query.

Amanda hedges and says that is not necessarily true. Because neither Greg nor I have been tested, it is unclear what our actual problem is and how likely it is to occur. She would be remiss to pin a percentage on this pregnancy without more information.

Still, I am buoyed. My capacity to find the good even in an iffy situation is a tactic I use to keep on an even keel, and it is working now. Before I hang up with Amanda, she tells me she can give me the gender of the child. I agree, yes, let me know what it is and maybe that will help me clear my head.

"It's a little girl," she says, and I can hear the bubble in her voice as she gives me this, this beacon of hope, this little sister.

I emerge from the pantry and look at Emily, at Lauren. Emily is motoring around with a book, turning pages as she walks, muttering to herself. Lauren is occupied with a musical toy, banging happily away. This is as calm as things get around here, as close to domestic bliss as we come. I can see another little girl in their midst, a shadowy mirage of a girl, tinier, with less hair. She is part of us already.

The more I absorb this first set of results, the more hopeful I become. The news is good, and I want to share it. I load the girls into the car and drive off to Kathy's house. I leave the car running, dash up to her door, and barge in, yelling, "So far, so good!!" Kathy is pleased as can be, embracing me warmly.

Then we drive to the video store to get something to occupy the girls while I make dinner. In the parking lot, I just happen to spy Wendy's car. Again I am out the door, yelling, including another friend in what I hope is a proclamation of joy. When Greg gets home that night, he is cautiously optimistic, trying to temper my enthusiasm with realism. He reminds me all the results aren't in yet. But he can't help but show a little anticipation, floating a few possible girl names past me as we fall asleep that night.

The family vacation, back in full swing this summer, is on the Eastern Shore, a mere two-hour drive for us. I decide to go early with Lauren, and then Greg will drive out later in the week with Emily so she won't have to miss too much summer school. I arrive at the family compound, a warren of rooms in a rehabbed Victorian home on the water. I am in a giddy mood. Surrounded by family, I want to be full of good news. So, I push away any doubts and maintain a buoyant manner, working the baby-to-be into conversations, letting my tummy protrude as an outward sign of good tidings.

The bubble bursts the next Tuesday afternoon. I am walking on the treadmill while Lauren is napping, striding along at a fast clip. The phone rings and I have never heard Greg, calling from work, sound so subdued, so controlled. His voice, his lovely voice, is shattered.

"The baby has what Emily has," he tells me. I can hear him gulp on the other end.

"Are you sure?" I reply, thinking what a sick joke, unbelievable in its cruelty. Then Greg says, yes, he just heard from Amanda, it is true. I fall apart.

The phone is on the floor, I must have thrown it, but I don't feel myself doing that. I am lying on the carpet in the basement, screaming, "NO NO NO NO NO NO NO!!!!!" I don't know what to do with my rage, my sadness, my grief. I can't stop screaming. I hit myself in the stomach, cursing this baby who made me love her. I pull my hair, and I scratch the skin on my arms with my nails until I bleed.

I pick up the phone and Greg is still there, has heard my tirade, and is scared. He implores me to calm down, reminds me that Lauren is upstairs sleeping, that Emily will be home from school later, and that I have got to pull myself together. I wipe my face with a washcloth and pace from one end of the basement to the other, the sweat from my workout mingling with my tears. I am a mess, but I try to think, really think.

But there is nothing to consider, really. No way are we going to have this baby.

# CHAPTER 53

The decision to terminate the pregnancy is an instantaneous one, with no second-guessing, but it comes with an unspeakable amount of anguish. From the minute I know this baby is afflicted with the same syndrome as Emily, I recognize that I can't bring another child into this world, knowing what she will face. The fact is, Emily has done remarkably well despite all her issues, but there is no guarantee that another child would be so lucky, so strong.

A selfish motive lurks here as well. I am no hero, just the opposite. I know my limits, and having two children with special needs is more than I can face. Having Emily, sweet as she is, has profoundly scarred me, Greg, and our family as a whole. I just can't fathom doing it again. I won't.

Greg is obviously relieved when I calm down enough to tell him that I want to end this pregnancy as soon as possible. He was frightened that my tendency toward optimism might overshadow the obvious. But I can be a realist, and this is black and white, clear as day. This baby, if she makes it at all, will struggle mightily to live, to thrive, to grow, and to learn, just like Emily. And judging from the ultrasound, she may have more overt signs of the syndrome to boot.

Greg talks sense, completely supporting me. "It's all bad, Judith," he says, "but we can choose to have the pain right now and get it over with. The other alternative is to delay the pain until much later, and that's unacceptable."

Greg's pragmatic spin helps to settle me, and I segue into business mode with ease. As of this moment, the baby is dead to me. I break all ties, divorce myself from her; I become an automaton. The baby, if I think of her at all, takes on the shape of a malignant tumor that must be removed. This approach is cold, but it is the only way I can cope right now.

I put a call in to the hospital where I had the CVS. Amanda gets back to me immediately, and I tell her our decision. Much to my chagrin, this isn't going to be immediate or easy. Amanda explains that if I want the "procedure" to be done in a hospital setting, with general anesthesia, it will cost about $5,000, none of which our insurance will pay.

The other option is to go to the hospital clinic, where terminations are carried out under twilight sleep, and the cost is much lower. The down side to this is the emotional factor. Patients in the clinic are not genetic cases. They are couples who, by and large, are carrying normal babies. Amanda knows as well as we do that to face people who are terminating a normal pregnancy might be more than we can abide. Maybe a normal baby is a burden to some—I can certainly imagine cases where that is so—but to me it feels like a gift that is a sin to throw away.

As we hash out the dilemma, Amanda says maybe she can pull a few strings. If we can get the first appointment of the day, we can be whisked into the clinic before running into any other clients. That way we can protect our privacy and our grief. I agree to this plan and wait as Amanda gets us on the schedule.

Even with all of Amanda's string-pulling, it will be a week before I can get an appointment at the clinic. I don't want to think about all the babies scheduled to die in that time, including mine. Until next Tuesday, I have to walk around with a live baby inside me, wiggling, kicking, oblivious to her fate. The wait is cruel and wrenching, but there is nothing I can do. I am at the mercy of the hospital schedule.

I am petrified to tell people about the baby, about the termination. It is a real judge of character to present this to someone. Everyone I know has already passed the Emily litmus test, but there is no telling how they will react to this latest news. This subject is more volatile, more inflammatory.

To my vast relief, everyone in my life rallies around. The outpouring of love, support, and understanding is amazing. I feel guilty having doubted anyone's ability to handle this information. I have a safety net I didn't know was there until I really needed it.

My mom is the first one to come over, leaving work in a rush as soon as I tell her about the baby. She comes in the front door to find me lying on the living room couch, curled in a ball. She holds me, strokes my hair, and tells me something I will never forget.

"Some people are meant to be in our lives for a long time," she says," and some only stay a little while. Maybe you were meant to know and to love this little girl for only fourteen weeks. That's all you'll have with her, but during that time you did love her, you nourished her, and it's an act of love to set her free."

I can see my face reflected in Mom's glasses, and I see the pain in her eyes. It occurs to me as she speaks that this journey with Emily, and now with this baby, has affected her as well. Watching her daughter struggle so must be catastrophic.

Wendy comes over shortly after Mom, sitting quietly with me, crying with me. When I tell her we are not having the baby, she says, "Of course you aren't," with such matter-of-factness, such understanding. I begin to feel that I won't be maligned for making this decision after all.

So they come in droves, first Kathy, then Sue with sandwiches and flowers, then Heather, all bearing love and tears. The outpouring is a true testament to the small circle of friends I have formed over the years. When the going gets tough, they are right here. My friends demonstrate not a hint of judgment, just sadness.

On the phone to my parents and siblings, I am numb. I write out a script in my head and deliver it, deadpan.

"The genetic test came back, the baby has the same syndrome

as Emily, we're not going to have the baby," I say, heavy as lead.

My dad and stepmother, the most conservative of the bunch, surprise me. They are devastated, of course, but also full of wisdom and support. My father speaks of my marriage.

"If you have another disabled child, Jude, your marriage, your relationship, would suffer greatly. You're allowed to think of that, and of yourself." Dad and I are used to simple banter, so this seems like uncharted territory. This conversation is the first real adult one I have had with my father. His approval brings me joy in this time of ruin.

My brother Daniel, who lives in Maine, listens as I talk, occasionally saying, "Oh, Jude." As the conversation draws to a close, he says he will see me tomorrow. I wonder what he is talking about. He says he is leaving work right now and will drive straight through until he arrives. I can't believe it.

But this is what he does, dropping everything, flying down the interstate for ten hours to be with me. My baby brother, whom I see maybe once a year, pulls out all the stops. He camps out on the sofa-bed in the basement and helps with the girls all week while I try to pretend I am not pregnant, not about to kill my child.

When Daniel has to leave at the end of the week, I watch him as he finishes packing. Somehow, without my noticing it, Daniel has become a man, and what he has done for me this week proves it. Just his presence, the distraction of another adult to make the days go by, has helped immensely. His gentle nature with the girls and his unwavering acceptance of Emily make me proud to be his sister.

Nights are the hardest, when the visitors leave and the girls are in bed. I make a pact with myself not to touch my body, which is swelling unbidden with the pregnancy soon to be ended. But I can feel the subtle shift in my weight as I move under the covers, as Greg curls around me. When I shower, I dribble soapy water from my washcloth over my belly so I won't have to touch it. I force my eyes away from my midsection as I dress, and I avoid putting my hands on my hips. I am mentally excising the center of my body.

And that is what this feels like. If Emily and her complications left a big hole in my heart, this baby is tearing away at my guts. I wonder if I will ever be whole again.

# CHAPTER 54

The day before my abortion, Greg and I go to the hospital for the pre-op drill. I don't know what to expect, but I certainly know that it is more complex to terminate a fourteen-week baby than one at six weeks. A fully formed fetus presents many more difficulties than a collection of blood and tissue. The procedure requires two appointments in a row.

Amanda greets us there at 1:00 p.m. and ushers us into the clinic through a side door. I am weighed, and blood is taken. Then we are escorted into a tiny exam room to wait for the doctor. Dr. Fox is a youngish woman with glasses and a calm, professional manner. I wonder what brought her to this career of terminating pregnancies all day long. She explains that I will have a D & E (Dilation and Extraction), which is the procedure for a second-trimester abortion. As she mentions "withdrawal of the pregnancy material" and "suctioning the remains," I stop listening. My ears roar, and the room tilts.

The doctor notices that I am pale. Good thing there is a bed right here, so I can lie down and get my bearings. When I feel better, the doctor shows me the laminaria, thin, wood-like pieces that she will insert into my cervix to begin dilation. The laminaria remind me of oboe reeds or popsicle sticks. With my feet in the stirrups and my knees separated, Dr. Fox probes into my vagina, locating the mouth of my cervix with her gloved fingers. Then she begins the insertion of the laminaria.

If I thought I was faint before, that was nothing. The assault to my body, just by putting in the almost-translucent sticks, is monumental. I feel turned inside-out, nauseated, like I am being reamed by a broomstick. Greg's palm is serrated with tattoos of my fingernails where I clutch him, but he doesn't flinch. He just looks at my face.

The doctor finishes quickly, murmuring an apology for how much it hurt. She explains that I will feel crampy all night and can take Tylenol and Percoset for the pain. Once I am upright and sitting back in a chair next to her desk, the doctor writes me two prescriptions: one for the Percoset and the other for Plan B. It takes me a minute to understand Plan B is the morning-after pill. She has been briefed on our history--knows that this baby was wanted, but can never be. In essence, she is telling us not to get pregnant again, that the risks are too great. And if we do, here is our way out.

I stuff the prescriptions in my purse, stand up, and leave the clinic without looking left or right. Greg hurries to catch up with me, calling to me to take it easy, slow down. I am in a tailspin, reeling from the day. I didn't know I wanted another baby, but I guess I did, because the pain of losing this one, and knowing we will never have another, is a vise lock around my heart.

August 3rd is like the ten days before it in the Baltimore-Washington corridor: hot and humid. The swampy air and hum of mosquitoes is the familiar backdrop to everything that summer. Greg and I arrive at the clinic that morning after a restless night. I was crampy, all right, feeling minor contractions all night, unable to sleep. I just want to get this over with now. This last week waiting for the end has killed something in my spirit, and I am ready to move on.

Even at 6:00 a.m., we are not the only patients at the clinic. Despite technically being the first appointment, I realize that we are just one of the many "first" appointments that day. The clinic is an assembly line, many couples already lined up for their abortions at the crack of dawn. I try not to look at anyone else, to give people their privacy and their dignity, but I can't help it. The three couples I see are young, very young, maybe in their teens. They have an inner-city look to them, poor and unwashed. We are old enough to be their parents.

We wait five minutes, if that, before a nurse scurries into the waiting room and nabs us discreetly. She has been prepped by Amanda, knows we are coming in, and is giving us preferential treatment. I feel humbly grateful to Amanda, whose behind-the-scenes machinations have given me a modicum of solace. We are the Couple Who Has Suffered Enough, so we go to the front of the line.

A warren of rooms flanks the surgical hallway. Each has three reclining seats in them, separated by flimsy curtains. The nurse leads us into one of these rooms, thankfully uninhabited and quiet. I am to remove my clothes and jewelry here, sit in the chair closest to the window, and await my IV. I guess on a busy day, all three chairs in here would be occupied by women, anticipating their abortions. The thought makes me feel vile and sick.

I am shaking as I pull on the white, overwashed hospital gown. Greg helps me tie the back with the short sashes. I hand him my wedding rings, my earrings. Then I stand in front of Greg as he sits in a metal folding chair. I take his hand and place it on my swollen abdomen. I can feel him resisting, trying to pull back, but I am strong. I ask him, please, help me say goodbye to our daughter. He looks up at me with such exquisite pain. My hand is over his, over our baby. I say "I love you" to this little girl and to Greg.

A different nurse comes to take me to the operating room. Greg has to stay behind until the procedure is over. I have never felt lonelier as I walk down the tiled hallway, away from this man who has shared all this loss with me.

The operating room is cold, draped in white, and filled with the silvery glint of the instruments and machines. I am taken back to the time, almost exactly 7 years ago, when I brought Emily's inert baby body into a room similar to this. The day of her heart surgery looms large in my memory. It was the time when my baby's heart was fixed, yet something in me lay broken.

I am guided to the table and placed on it. The nurse begins to administer the twilight sleep through the IV, and just before I lose consciousness, I wonder why I have water in my ears. But it is not water. I cry so hard that the tears pool in my ears. The nurse wipes my face with a tissue and then calmly holds my hand.

I wake up in the recovery room, the same room where I got the IV. I am disoriented, giddy, wondering when the procedure is going to start. When Greg tells me it is all over, I am relieved and disbelieving. I don't remember a thing. For once in my life, I can totally understand why people take drugs. Oblivion is a wonderful thing.

When we arrive home, my mom and Maureen greet us at the door. I am so droopy I can barely make it up the stairs. Mom sits on the edge of the bed, stroking my hair. The click of her rings on her fingers is a sound I remember from bedtime as a child. She tells me that Emily and Lauren were good girls all day and then urges me to sleep.

Sleep I do, until the next day. I am spotting a bit, but otherwise I feel fine. After showering and putting Emily on the bus, I turn to Greg and ask him to dig me a small hole out in the backyard. I think he knows what I want it for, but he doesn't ask. Mom thinks I should plant a flowering tree to honor the baby, but I can't do that. That is too much of a reminder. I can do something, however.

I gather up the positive pregnancy stick, the ultrasound picture of the baby, a pair of infant-sized pink socks, and sympathy cards from friends that I can't keep, but don't want to throw away, either. I put all these things into an envelope, seal it, and press it into the hole, patting dirt on top to pack it in. I touch my fingers to my lips and touch the spot on the ground. I name her Sara.

# CHAPTER 55

The euphemism I start to use is, "When we lost our baby." That phrase is easier to say than anything else, and it takes the blame off me. I never once second guess our decision, but I feel like a baby-killer just the same. I am too hard on myself, Greg says, we gave this baby a gift. Still, if I say I lost her, it doesn't hurt so much.

I can feel the self-destructive demons circling, like crocodiles in the moat. I feel like punishing myself. My old stand-bys, starvation and obsessive exercise, are right there waiting for me, my ways of coping when life goes awry. But I'm just too tired. My body has been through enough, and I'm done with hurting it.

Without making a conscious decision, I reach out instead of pulling in. I call my friends as often as possible, talking, laughing, and catching up. At least one night a week, a girlfriend will swing by to take me out for supper, to go on a walk. I assuage my pain with connections and joy, and it works.

I agree to run the Metric Marathon with Wendy, as long as we take it slow. I haven't been running at all recently, and I don't want to get an injury. The race is in early October, the weekend that Emily turns eight, giving me less than two months to train. I go into this race with a completely different attitude. I will be happy to finish, happy to run outside for two hours with my friend. I am so out of shape that my thighs hurt for hours after every training run.

The race is local, traversing the hills of our town, sixteen miles of up and down. The course is challenging, but the cool weather and frequent water stops help. Wendy is in prime form, a spring in her step and energy to spare. I struggle to keep up with her, and the miles tick by.

At Mile Fourteen, I feel I can't go on. My legs feel like cement blocks, my chest is heaving, and I am fatigued beyond belief. I tell Wendy I am going to walk, just go ahead without me.

"Oh no, you don't," she says, motioning me on. "You can run two miles in your sleep!"

This saying is our funny little mantra to help us through the rough patches, initiated during the marathon training days. Those days all seem so far away now. Suddenly, I hit a wall of memories, Emily, Lauren, the baby, the struggles in my marriage. I cry and run at the same time. I try to tell Wendy I am really okay, that if I can get through all of that stuff, I can certainly run two lousy miles.

I dig deep for some strength and find just enough on reserve to get to the finish line. My finish time is my slowest ever but my proudest running moment. Greg, Emily, and Lauren are at the finish line, cheering me on. My little family looks so happy on this autumn day. I join them on the sidelines to usher more runners in.

There are other things that help me heal this fall. I decide I am ready to send Emily's profile into a rare chromosome support network. I have spent years perusing all the brochures that come my way, reading the life stories of the children and families afflicted with chromosomal syndromes. The profiles serve not only to tell the stories, but also to connect families whose children share the same diagnosis.

I pick *Unique*, a magazine out of the U.K. This magazine is a well-funded, extremely professional source for information and connections. I receive the magazine four times a year and have always wanted to include my little Emily in its pages. Now suddenly I am ready.

I write a 500-word article about Emily's life so far, include a picture, and submit it for publication. The article is accepted right away and published in the winter issue. Writing the piece is cathartic and freeing. A piece of my hard shell cracks off after I put Emily "out there," and some of the pain begins to drip away.

I don't really expect any feedback from the article, and I doubt severely whether I will hear from any other parents. After all, Emily's condition is 1 of only 50 documented cases worldwide. The chances of any other child sharing the same genetic mistake, an identical match on the human genome, is so remote as to be almost impossible.

One day I check my e-mail and, to my surprise, find I have mail from a woman in Canada. She read Emily's profile in *Unique*, saw her karyotype (published right above the article), and compared it to that of her son. It turns out that, although not identical, her six-month-old son, Benjamin, has Partial Trisomy 13, just like Emily. His karyotype is not an exact copy of Emily's, but it is pretty close. In Emily's entire life, this is the closest I have come to anything like a "match."

The woman's name is Soo, and she is in the raw stage right after diagnosis. I don't know where she gets the strength and wherewithal to get connected with a support group, let alone write an e-mail. I read her words, her plea, with admiration and curiosity.

Soo's son reminds me a lot of Emily back in those dark days. She tells me he has a heart condition, kidney issues, and great trouble feeding. Developmentally, he is already lagging. Soo is devastated, but determined to do the best for her son. She implores me, as the mother of an older child with the syndrome, to tell her what is down the road. I read between the lines that she craves some good news, some hope that her son will grow out of his syndrome, will be "normal."

Knowing my words will pain her deeply, I try to be brutally honest. I struggle to find a way to soften the blow. It takes me two days to respond, and I choose my words carefully, running my message past Greg before sending it.

I tell her that, on a daily basis, it is easier now than when Emily was an infant, now that the surgeries are over, the major milestones have been met, and she is in school. I also tell her that having Lauren is a balm, a curative for some of the pain.

But I also tell her that not a day goes by that I don't wish for Emily to be normal, that I don't wish life easier for her and for our family. Having Emily has been the single most devastating event of my life, defining me, challenging my marriage, and almost breaking me.

Then I reach out to this stranger in another country in a way I have not reached out to anyone before. Let me be your friend, I write to her. Let me help you now in these early days with your son. Please don't struggle alone as I did, burying your grief beneath a false smile of courage. I will read what you write, I will understand anything you say, and I will never judge you.

With this message, a dialogue begins and a friendship blossoms. We write each other weekly, sometimes tapering off to monthly missives. We provide updates on our children, send pictures, and wish each other luck with doctor's appointments, therapies, and surgeries. Knowing she is not the only one whose son has this syndrome is a help to Soo and a watershed for me.

For once, I am the mentor, the guide in this uphill struggle with a child's disabilities. I am no expert, not by a long shot, but I have made the rounds, and I can share what I know. Across the miles, I reach out my hand, and we hold on for all we are worth.

# CHAPTER 56

I am still the walking wounded that fall, trying not to think about the baby, trying to heal. It takes a concerted effort to be cheerful, upbeat. Having small children around doesn't allow much opportunity for self-pity, and I am thankful for the little distractions and childish moments that propel the days forward. Time passes like water, running through my fingers.

Emily's notebook comes home from school that November with a note from the principal. A family lives in the school district whose youngest daughter has just been diagnosed with a similar syndrome (the principal is not sure of the details). Is it okay for this family to contact me? I say sure, provide my phone number, and forget all about it.

A few weeks later, I get a call from Donna. She is rambling, sounds upset, but I get the gist. Her daughter, Sophia, is ten months old and has full Trisomy 13. Her entire 13th chromosome is duplicated, which makes it much more severe than Emily's syndrome. But her condition is on the same chromosome, so we are linked in that way. Donna is on her last nerve; she has two older kids needing attention and now a very sick child. She invites me to her home for a visit.

Donna asks expressly to see Emily, so we three girls make the trip out into the country to Donna's house. After a couple of wrong turns, I locate the house, a brown, barn-like structure with a modern, triangular flair to it. Donna runs out to greet me, beaming. I am not sure what to expect from this visit, but I sense that Donna is looking for some answers. I just hope I meet her expectations.

Emily, Lauren, and I go into the house, which is under extensive renovation. The house is going to be fabulous when it is done, but the construction has been at a standstill since Sophia's birth. I set Emily up with some books to page through and get out snacks for both girls. I hope they will stay occupied while I try to talk with Donna.

A moment passes before I see Sophia. She is on the dining room table, of all places, lying face up on a white fleece blanket. At ten months old, she is the size of a two-month-old, maybe ten pounds, if that. She has no head control, can't do anything but lie down. Donna says she has a heart condition, has seizures, and is deaf.

She is a cute little thing, with jet-black hair and a sweet face. I ask to hold her. I pick her up gingerly, cradling her head in the crook of my elbow. She looks around, not exactly at me, but she cranes to see what is going on. Her skin is soft, and she smells like a recent bath. Her breathing is labored, and Donna mentions nebulizer treatments and a slew of medications. Her chest is rattling with every breath. I know two things for certain: This is the saddest baby I have ever seen, and this little girl is not long for this world.

Donna watches Emily careening around her house with a wistful look on her face. She knows, too, then. Her baby may grow a bit more, but will never flourish like Emily. Sophia's health is too compromised, her condition too delicate for survival. I wonder if Emily's robust health and abilities, limited as they are, are an affront to Donna.

Our conversation takes an interesting turn as we broach the common topic of when our children were diagnosed. It turns out that Donna and her husband knew at eighteen weeks gestation that Sophia had this condition. This could be a version of me, then, if I had chosen to continue the pregnancy with our little girl. I would have the baby here, but not for long. I would witness the suffering, the torment, the slow death.

As starkly as if it is written in bas-relief, I see the future of this little girl, of her mother. The future is one I will not share, chose not to embrace. The specter of my own hurt little girl hovers over the room. I clear myself of all guilt, all recrimination. I have been dragging around a load that is suddenly and finally lifted.

I tell Greg that night in bed that it took the physical manifestation of the fate we escaped to convince me, once and for all, that we did the right thing. The visit with Sophia seems heaven-sent, a lesson in what might have been.

I am not surprised to get a card in the mail a month later. The embossed missive is a notice of Sophia's death by pneumonia. She was eleven months old.

# CHAPTER 57

Emily is eight years old, suddenly. Her ankles are sticking out of pants that fit two months ago, the "high waters" marking a rapid growth spurt. She is up to my breastbone now, I barely have to squat to look her in the eye, and she is wickedly strong. Her body is all knobby elbows and knees, arms akimbo, and feet stomping as she perambulates around a room.

Greg and I joke about a future career in grape crushing at a vineyard; her stomps are that emphatic. The jokes are a weak attempt to mask our fear: The disparity between Emily and her same-age peers is alarming. We knew this would happen eventually, yet we are wholly unprepared for it now.

Emily is in her second year with Ms. Julia, and we feel thrilled to have this favorite teacher back. It seems there will always be "issues" beyond the obvious academic ones to tackle with Emily, and who better to guide us down that road than this wonderful instructor.

The school schedule, with every minute accounted for, is just up Emily's alley. The day is broken down into increments of fifteen minutes, and Emily knows what is coming next. She consults her personal schedule, Velcroed to a board at the front of the room, and begins to flap her hands when the next event is near. She has a time slot for each class, each break, lunching in the cafeteria, and even toileting. The regimentation keeps her organized and on task.

I try to duplicate this sense of order at home, to some degree. Greg fights this idea, hates to make definite plans for the weekends in particular, because he gets so little free time at his job. But I insist, noting how much better Emily behaves when she has a list of events.

I use the PECS pictures, our old standbys from preschool. Each laminated card has an event on it, like "playground" or "carousel." I line the cards up on the counter, a few for the morning routine, then a slew of fresh cards after lunch. Lauren even gets into the swing of this, consulting the lineup to see what is next. I am pleased to see that within days of implementing a home schedule, Emily is less disjointed, plays better, and is in a cheerier mood.

I am not ashamed to ask the teachers for ideas whenever I have a problem or a question from home. These professionals have saved us numerous times in the past, and their fresh perspective often yields positive results.

Right now I am mystified by a facial quirk Emily has. Just about the same time her seizures began, Emily started making what we call THE FACE. The look is a grimace of sorts, an open-mouthed rictus that lasts anywhere from ten to thirty seconds. Emily tilts her head back, turns slightly to the right, and opens her mouth as far as it can go, the biggest yawn a person can make. I try saying, "Close your mouth, Emily," with no effect. I try clamping her mouth shut using my hands on her head and chin like a vise. Still nothing. Like a crocodile going in for the kill, Emily stretches wide and holds it.

The look is ugly on such a cute little face, and it pains me to witness it. I begin keeping track of when it occurs, and a pattern of sorts presents itself. THE FACE is often worse at the end of the day, when Emily is tired, and also when she is agitated. She makes THE FACE on a regular basis when she pages through books and magazines, a pause as she turns pages. She holds her breath for the length of the expression and then exhales with a loud gasp. It is not pleasant to watch.

I don't know whether it is a tic, a muscular issue, or a deliberate ploy for attention, but I wish it would stop. Only the disabled do things like this, a bizarre aberration. My little girl, who can stop traffic with her cornsilk hair and boisterous laugh, is now causing passersby to stop in their tracks when she does this imitation of a human flytrap.

So I muster up the troops at school for their input.

"What is this ugly face she's making, and how do I help her to stop?" I plead, but there are no easy answers. The occupational therapist posits that Emily is getting a sense of oral feedback from the grimace, a deep pressure feeling that is stimulating for her. She challenges me to try THE FACE myself at home, to see what it feels like. I do, gaping my mouth open as wide as I can and holding my breath simultaneously. My head rushes a bit, my eyes water, my jaw aches. Not a position I would make voluntarily.

But I see the OT's point. Emily has always been hyposensitive, or undersensitive, to oral stimulation. This hyposensitivity is the reason she struggles to talk, why she fills her mouth with food before chewing. She craves input and has found a way to create her own sensation. On an intellectual level, it is easy to understand, but when confronted by THE FACE in all its glory, an explanation is really moot.

I ask the staff to help me figure out ways to decrease the gesture, and they agree. We come up with a protocol, a series of reminders to Emily throughout the day. Ms. Julia also mentions that a slight tickle to the underside of Emily's chin sometimes has the desired effect. I feel shallow for allowing this facial expression to take such high priority, but the crew at school understands. Part of Emily's education, academics aside, is in socialization and normalization. She needs to learn how to fit in with and relate to others. A reduction in THE FACE will certainly help with that.

So we plug onward, two steps forward, one step back. THE FACE recedes for a day or two, maybe a week, but then it is back with a vengeance. I check books out at the library about stimulation and sensitivity, pertaining mostly to autistic children. The books verify what we already know. THE FACE is a subconscious effort on Emily's part to feel something, to get a sensation she craves. It must calm her somehow, must lend a quiet moment to the hectic landscape of her life.

After six months, THE FACE hardly fazes us at all. Only in the company of people new to Emily do I find myself explaining it. Like a birthmark or bad haircut, we witness THE FACE every day and can see past it now. We laugh about how Emily is the perfect dental patient; the dentist will surely be able to see her tonsils at this rate. The irony is that when we do go to the dentist, Emily clamps her mouth tight and won't open for anything.

Then we are confronted with alarming sleep issues. Our champ of a sleeper, logging a solid eleven hours a night from age four months on, is hell on wheels now at night. Down at 7:30 or 8:00 p.m., asleep like she has been pole-axed in battle, the bedtime routine is undisturbed and unchanged. But beginning at three in the morning, Emily kicks the walls of her room, bellows, and bangs on the door. She never falls back asleep or grows quiet.

We are flummoxed. I call the pediatrician to set up an appointment. Meanwhile, Greg moves Emily's bed to the middle of the room. She is foiled by that for one night, then gets creative, standing by the side of the bed, donkey kicking the wall while gripping the mattress. Greg and I are bouncing out of our bed all night, taking turns putting Emily back to bed, telling her to quiet down and go back to sleep.

Emily checks out fine at the doctor's. Nothing overt explains these night wakings, no ear infection, urinary tract infection, or fever. Her heart, lungs, and abdomen all get a complete workup, with a clean bill of health. The doctor suggests Benadryl or Melatonin, which may help her sleep. She can't prescribe a heavy-duty sedative given Emily's heart condition and epilepsy.

The Benadryl is a disaster, rendering Emily hyper for hours. I find Melatonin at a health food store, give her the maximum dose, and hope for the best. This herbal elixir has no effect, other than perhaps a shorter time falling asleep than normal, which does us no good. I am at my wits end and exhausted like the newborn days.

Greg and I start growling at each other in the night, keeping score as to who has gone in to tend to Emily more. Truth be told, the kicking is so loud that we are both awake, no matter who gets out of bed. Greg tries lying next to Emily, calming her with songs, willing her to fall asleep. But this has the opposite effect, getting her so excited to be with Daddy that she is unmanageable.

Once in awhile, I decide to give up the fight, go in and get Emily, and take her down to the basement with me so Lauren and Greg can sleep. I hop on the treadmill while Emily watches a video. But one day, I emerge sweaty from my workout, look at the clock, and declare, Enough is Enough. By 5:00 a.m., I have already run six miles. This is not the answer. Watching videos is a reward for Emily and a big mistake.

I tell Greg I don't care if she is awake, we can't make her sleep, but we need to find a way to make her quiet so the rest of us have a chance at a restful night. Greg goes to Target, gets three inflatable air mattresses, queen-sized, and positions them around Emily's room. He pushes her bed against the wall, framed by the mattresses, boxing her into a cocoon of rubber. Her lovely pink room becomes a padded cell, not at all pretty, but we are desperate.

That night, no audible kicking. A miracle has occurred, and we are elated. We can still hear her bellowing, but we have made a definite improvement. We tell Emily we will come in to get her at 6:00 a.m., but no earlier. I post signs around her room, written with a black indelible marker on slips of pink paper and accompanied by my own weak drawings. They are simple reminders to be quiet, stop kicking, and wait until 6:00 to get up.

Emily can tell time, or at least identify the numbers, so we put a digital clock in her room, perched on the bookshelf. We turn it face down at bedtime, hoping she won't be too stimulated by its presence. When Emily awakens in the wee hours, she turns the clock face up and watches the minutes tick by on the red face, glowing in the darkness. Some nights, she counts every minute, out loud, for three hours until we come in. We buy white noise machines for Lauren and Emily and run a fan in our room, trying to block out as much as possible. We put a child-safety doorknob on Emily's door so she can't get out. At least we know she is safe, albeit still loud.

The sleep troubles, THE FACE, whatever is causing these new developments in Emily, it is yet another lesson. Lest we get too complacent or think we know everything there is to know about this child, along comes a new wrinkle. Life with Emily is never boring.

# CHAPTER 58

Despite the ongoing struggles with Emily's behavior, the objectionable FACE grimace, her sleep problems, her health considerations, and all her special needs, she advances at a rate we never thought possible. She makes such great strides at school that Ms. Julia calls me in and invites me to observe.

I come to the elementary school for two hours on a Wednesday afternoon, leaving Lauren with my mom. Emily is so excited to see me that she bends her head down, flaps her arms, and squeals with glee. Her hug is tight and ferocious. I watch Emily during one segment of "circle time," where the teacher directs questions to the students and the students answer. Most of Emily's classmates are nonverbal, as she is. They all use various devices, sign language, or PECS to communicate.

Emily is able to tell Ms. Julia, using her communication device, the day of the week, the month, the weather, what clothes she is wearing, and what she had for lunch. After each correct response, the teacher and aides clap and cheer for Emily. It is no mystery why she loves school. I am amazed by Emily's enthusiasm and her clear intent. She does not just guess the right answers, nor is she being prompted. She really knows.

Then Ms. Julia lets me observe Emily's "work time," a segment of the day where Emily works on the curriculum or as much of the second-grade curriculum as she is able to tackle. This work is done on the computer, and Emily is a master. I have seen her do computer games at home, but I am clearly out of the loop about her prowess here. Emily is all over the computer, opening and closing windows, going from one site to another with ease. As I watch her, I am aghast. To have so underestimated my child's receptive language and innate ability seems criminal.

Emily boots up a story, guided by Ms. Julia. The short tale is about a man and a dog, perhaps twenty-five sentences long. As the sentences appear on the screen, one at a time, Emily seems to scan the words, then presses "next," prompting the following sentence to scroll across the screen. At the close of the story, a series of comprehension questions appears. Emily whizzes through the questions, pressing the answers from a field of three (multiple choice). Done, she turns to make eye contact with me and Ms. Julia.

All of a sudden, I am no longer in an elementary school classroom. I am in a geneticist's office, eight years ago, hearing the doomsday prophecy that Emily will "absolutely" never learn to read. I can actually hear the cadence of the doctor's voice and see his grave face as he tried to seal Emily's fate. He could not have been more wrong.

What I have just seen before me is ironclad evidence that Emily is reading, is smart, and can understand. Her capacity to learn is amazing. Ms. Julia even tells me Emily is reading close to grade level, a miracle again. Without being aware of it, I have been selling Emily short. She walks around with books all the time at home, loves to flip the pages, and enjoys video versions of those books, but at most we thought she had memorized the story lines from all the repetition.

Ms. Julia tells me that most special needs kids have more ability than is evident from an initial evaluation simply because the communication troubles get in the way. The trick is to figure out how to reach these kids, she says, which combination of teaching method and technology will break the ice.

Break the ice indeed. Emily is red hot and anxious to show me more. She proceeds to the next story in her lesson book, reading through the paragraph and then answering the questions, all correct on the first try. I can't wait to tell Greg and then call our families. It seems imperative to let everybody know what this little girl can do.

Before I leave that day, Ms. Julia asks my permission to sign Emily up for the MSA, the Maryland State Assessment. The assessment is an exam given statewide to students to test their proficiency with the curriculum. Normally, it is not required for special needs students because they are frequently quite far removed from the curriculum.

Ms. Julia feels Emily can manage the test, with the appropriate accommodations. She will need more time and, of course, access to a computer to plug in her answers. Emily's fine motor skills are so poor that she cannot even write her own name, let alone bubble in responses on a test sheet. I agree to let Emily take the test and think nothing more of it.

I get a call two months later from the school psychologist. She has the results of the MSA and would like me to come in for a meeting to discuss them. I feel panicked: has Emily done something wrong? But I am assured that it is a formality because the test, especially the first time administered, can be a bit confusing, and a face-to-face meeting is the best way to conduct a proper analysis of the results.

When I arrive at the school the next day, I am ushered into the conference room, a long anteroom off the central office. The whole team is there, to my surprise, all the therapists, aides, teachers, and even the general education teacher whom Emily sees for homeroom inclusion. A sea of faces and fidgety fingers surround the table. I wonder what on earth is going on.

Ms. Julia is here, right across from me. She is not looking at me, but she does slide a packet over to me. The document is fifteen pages, single-spaced, all about Emily. As the team gets settled in and introductions are reviewed, I glance at the packet suspiciously. Is Emily being expelled from second grade? I fear the worst.

But no. The psychologist is the spokeswoman at this meeting, and she begins as I continue flipping through the packet. It seems that, in addition to the MSA, the team threw in a psychological evaluation of Emily as well, namely the Woodcock Johnson Test of Achievement. The psychological evaluation is another device used to measure student performance and is especially calibrated for the disabled. So Emily has had a double whammy these last few weeks, tested nonstop. No wonder she has been so tired.

The testing methods are explained to me, sample questions are read, and I wonder what this is all leading to. Then I look at Ms. Julia. She hasn't been able to look at me because she has tears in her eyes. It turns out that Emily performed at or above grade level on the letter-word portion of the test, just below grade level on reading comprehension and academic knowledge, and on grade level for mathematical concepts.

With these scores, there is no way Emily fits the accepted criteria for mentally retarded. Her intelligence is simply too high. I can hear sniffing all around the table, not a dry eye in the room. The team is congratulating me, patting me on the back as they file out, as if I have anything at all to do with this. They look as happy as I feel and as proud.

In order to effectively test Emily, it has taken this long to accurately assess what she knows. And now it appears she knows a lot. Not being formally labeled mentally retarded is huge, a stellar shot in the arm for Emily and for us. But it doesn't change who she is, simply a little girl who gives it her all every day.

I need to see Emily before I leave the school. I catch up with her while she is in P.E. with her peers, the "regular" second grade. Emily's aide is with her, helping her hold a basketball, showing her the dribbling technique. All around her, the other kids swarm, models of grace and easy form, jumping, dunking basketballs, running forward and backward. All Emily can do is to lope slowly across the court. She can't throw with any accuracy, nor can she catch. But she is in there, in the thicket of kids, swaying, smiling, giving it a try.

# CHAPTER 59

Emily finishes second grade, Lauren is over two, and times are good. The summer meanders by, each day like the one before, hazy afternoons at the pool and long, firefly evenings on the deck. A peace has descended over the family, a sense of all disasters over.

I enroll Emily in a camp for special needs kids, run by a therapy group in the county. The staffers are all adults—professionals with experience in physical therapy, occupational therapy, and speech therapy. Finding a camp experience for Emily has been tough, at least one locally, and I am thrilled to discover this one.

Camp is held at an elementary school near our old neighborhood, so I am familiar with the grounds. Emily is excited to meet the staff and the counselors, an enthusiastic bunch of high school students. They are all decked out in green polos, pumped up to start the day. I direct Emily and Lauren down the hall, laden down with the camp supplies: bathing suit, sunscreen, spare clothes, and a sack lunch. The school is vacant except for the rooms requisitioned for the camp, and the halls echo with our steps.

This camp is regimented, like school, only not academic at all. The day features art time, snack time, swimming time, and then lunch. Regular fun for not-so-regular kids. I stow Emily's supplies in a locker and then lead her over to the art table to begin the day. She squeals and flaps, eager to begin. It looks like so much fun to

Lauren that I have trouble peeling her away. I tell her we will have fun time with Mommy while Emily has her days at camp.

But the honeymoon is short-lived. When we arrive after lunch to pick Emily up, Mia, the director, pulls me aside. It seems Emily's needs are more pronounced than those of the other kids, especially her lack of communication skills. Mia doesn't mince words. Emily was a struggle all day, trying to pinch the staffers in frustration and wetting her pants on several occasions. They have some ideas to help acclimate Emily, but in the meantime, I am asked to trim her fingernails, as she actually drew blood on one of the helpers.

I spend hours on the phone with Mia, hashing through a behavior plan similar to the one used at school. It does a bit of good, but not enough. The camp ends up being a mistake, just too much for Emily to handle. We slog through the rest of the camp, three weeks total, but it is a battle every day. When I receive the summer "therapy notes," mailed home soon after the camp ends, I am not surprised that we have been disinvited for subsequent years. It hurts to have Emily rejected, but I chalk it up to a learning experience. The only good that came out of the entire experience was a chance to spend some of the summer days with Lauren.

Lauren is the kind of kid commonly referred to as a "pistol" or a "hoot," and those are apt terms. She is a bundle of energy and verbal beyond belief. Greg and I joke that we wanted at least one child who could carry on a conversation with us, and boy does she ever. There is never a quiet moment with Lauren around. Like me, she has an independent spirit and a stubborn streak. She potty trained herself, deciding one day she was done with diapers and that was that.

The costume box is a huge hit at our house, filled to the brim with anything from princess attire to full cowboy regalia. Lauren delights in trying on different outfits to suit her various identities. Her penchant for pretend play is huge and thrilling to watch. Emily lacks the ability to play imaginative games, and the discrepancy between the two girls yawns widely as we see the layers of play Emily is missing.

By two and a half years old, Lauren can do so much more than Emily, at eight, ever has. The disparity is a double-edged sword, really. Watching Lauren is magical, each new stage a revelation. Her rapid-fire development, though, only highlights Emily's deficiencies. Watching the two girls growing away from each other this summer is bittersweet, Lauren soaring ahead and Emily struggling to maintain the status quo.

Although it is not marked on the calendar, it might as well be. August 3rd shines like a beacon, the macabre anniversary of the pregnancy we terminated one year ago. I start feeling edgy the week before as the date looms closer. I feel the need to do something, anything, to honor the day. Greg doesn't mention the day, may not even remember. He won't be keen for any sort of ceremony or remembrance.

I think about all my friends and family who rallied around, holding me up when I was falling down. I decide to buy the nicest notepaper I can find and tell them, for probably the first time, what they mean to me.

On a rainy afternoon, two days before the dreaded day, I sit with pen in hand. In this day and age of e-mail, I am out of practice with personal missives. I write for an hour, note after note, telling all the people in my life how extraordinary I found their love and support during that horrible time. It seems an insignificant contribution, but it helps me. Grief is lighter on my shoulders after I finish writing, and I feel cleansed.

The day arrives, dawning a cloying blanket of humidity. Emily's summer school is over, so I have both girls home all day. We get out all the puzzles, a favorite of Emily's, and we begin to put together a huge stack. For a moment, I step outside myself and rise above the scene. Two little girls are seated, side by side, engaged in a game. Emily sits awkwardly, her calves splayed behind her, head bent laboriously over the puzzles. Lauren chats amiably to herself, spinning the puzzle pieces, laughing.

Suddenly, a shadow settles next to the girls, but there is no cloud in the sky, no explanation for the hovering presence I feel. My heart feels it, though—another little girl, a filmy visage of a sister who will never be. I am not scared to feel her; in fact, I have been wondering when she would come to me. I know she will speak to me, I can feel it in my bones.

Her voice is light, tinkly, full of air and whisper. She says simply, "Thank you," before she vaporizes. The sun returns to the room, bathing Emily and Lauren in its blazing glare. They are oblivious, concentrating on their game, but I am transformed. I call Kathy right away, my friend who sees signs, believes in visions, and can tell me what this means.

Kathy says maybe the baby meant thank you for taking care of me, even for such a short time, perhaps thank you for letting me have a glimpse at your family. But in bed that night, it hits me. My little girl, whom I could not have, is absolving me. She is thanking me for doing the right thing, for sparing her the suffering and pain. I rise out of bed, walk downstairs, and put on my flip-flops. Quietly, I open the sliding glass door out to the deck and walk into the backyard, lit only by stars.

My impromptu burial site is still there, unmarked except by a smooth hollow at the base of the tree. I squat down and smell the loamy earth, the moss, the bark. I touch my fingers to the spot where my memories are buried and say a final goodbye.

# CHAPTER 60

Right before Christmas of 2005, I notice a burning sensation when I pee. I am convinced it is a urinary tract infection and head off to the doctor right away. I have newfound respect for Emily, who has had more urinary infections than I can count. I had no idea they hurt so much. The doctor prescribes a round of antibiotics, and I feel back to normal in days.

I guess everyone knows that antibiotics interfere with birth control, or they should. After all, the warning is printed right on the bottle for all to see. But I am not thinking about this at all, just busily packing for our cross-country trek to Indiana, the grueling ten hour car ride we have agreed to make this holiday season. I have lists all over the house: food, clothing, books, and toys. To ensure success on a trip with kids, I have a routine.

Another routine we have before a trip is a sort of joke between Greg and me. Whenever we have house guests or prepare to leave on a trip, we make love the night before, knowing we won't have a chance for a while. When we're done, we say, "See you next week!" or, perhaps, "See you next year," if we are traveling over the Christmas and New Year's holiday.

This time is no different. On the Thursday before Christmas, we roll away from each other, sweating, and say, "Thanks, see you back here in a week!" We sleep curled in each other's arms.

Back in Maryland after the holiday week, I go on a New Year's Day run with Wendy, an eight-miler that challenges me both with the length of the run and the cold weather. But the post-run fatigue doesn't subside, and I can't seem to recover. All week I feel under the weather, not right at all.

When I eat three pieces of cheddar cheese for breakfast one day, then ham and bean soup for lunch, I suddenly know. At no other time do I stockpile protein like this. On January 10, my period is one week late. I don't need a pregnancy test to tell me the rest.

Panicked does not begin to describe it. I berate myself, what a fool for not using backup birth control, for forgetting about anti-biotics. I decide not to tell Greg, half praying for a spontaneous miscarriage, and then feeling guilty for entertaining this thought. In nine years, I have had four pregnancies. Only one (Lauren) has been a positive outcome, in obstetrics parlance. I am thirty-eight years old, and the odds aren't in my favor. I can't decide what to do, so I do nothing.

The days go by, six weeks pregnant, seven weeks, eight weeks. My first appointment with the doctor is nerve wracking. I fear I will be scolded, but the doctor is pragmatic, businesslike. She sends me off for an ultrasound to determine whether the pregnancy is even viable, then we will go from there.

I can't believe Greg hasn't noticed anything, but he is at work so much, I can't expect him to. I am hiding the nausea and the weird foods. Even the fatigue is easy to explain, as we are both wiped out anyway. I am at the doctor's without Greg knowing. I can't seem to find the right time to let him in.

The ultrasound tech is Trish, a friend of my mom's. She helps me guide the transducer wand into my vagina, and there it is. The sac is clearly visible, the heart pulsing away. The squirmy little bean measures just right for the dates I have given. Trish hugs me, con-gratulates me, and wishes me the best. I find it ironic that the sonog-rapher knows I am in the family way before anyone in my family.

The next day, I deliver Lauren to her little preschool, where Wendy happens to be her teacher. Normally, we exchange a few pleasantries, plan our next run. But I have been evading her for weeks now, thinking up one excuse after another to postpone running. Today, I finally meet her gaze, all out of excuses. She must see the fearful look in my eyes. Later that day, I get an e-mail from her. She is coming right over, no ifs, ands, or buts.

While Lauren is napping, Wendy and I sit on my couch. I am bursting, so I blurt it all out, no finesse, a sloppy torrent of words, but finally I say it all. Wendy understands how fearful I am, holds my hands while I cry. She has had her own struggles with pregnancy, has just had a son with her new husband after a year of trying. She is no stranger to fear and wanting. When she was expecting and nervous every day, I used to tell her, "Every day is another day," and that is what she says to me now. This phrase is another one of those sayings that get us through.

As Wendy leaves, she advises me to tell Greg as soon as possible. Keeping a secret of this magnitude can be hurtful, even if I am scared out of my mind. I promise I will, just as soon as I find the right time.

# CHAPTER 61

Before I can tell Greg about the pregnancy, life intervenes again. Typical February weather closes in, with the trees bare, the morning light dull and wan, brittle winds whipping around the house. For once, Emily appears to be sleeping in. We eat breakfast at seven o'clock, and still she sleeps. Greg and I are thankful for the respite from the wall-kicking and the early rising, but the quiet is so out of character for her that we are mystified.

By eight o'clock, we are downright worried. Emily has been in bed over twelve hours. Something must be wrong. I run up to check on her, only to find her sleeping peacefully, not feverish. I suppress my worry, chalk her lethargy up to a busy week at school, and begin to putter around the house.

At ten o'clock, Greg and I decide to wake her. Emily is in a stupor, almost limp, hard to revive. We walk her down the hall to the bathroom, but before we can help her to urinate, she begins vomiting. I clean her up, wipe down the toilet and the floor, and return her to bed, where she falls back into a deep sleep.

I have Dr. Khurana paged and she returns my call immediately. By now, she knows that this family doesn't mess around. After hearing my story about the sleeping and the vomiting, she thinks maybe Emily has the flu and advises us to wait it out. She reminds me that Emily often does not get fevers when a typical child might.

Her physiology is so unusual that the standard symptoms of disease don't often apply.

During the early afternoon, the pediatrician calls back. She has spoken with her husband, who happens to be a neurologist. Both of the Khuranas now think that something more serious might be going on. We are advised to get to the emergency room as soon as possible.

My mom is out of town, so we will have to take Lauren with us. Taking a pre-schooler to the ER is not the best situation, but it will have to do. Emily is really dragging, fussing if we touch her the least bit, vomiting bile. She obviously feels awful.

We are triaged into a room in the ER and introduced to the doctor on call, a lovely woman with silky hair, a calm manner, and a name to match her mellifluous voice, Dr. Bell. She takes Emily's history, which I can rattle off in minutes. As always happens, Dr. Bell is intrigued by the rare syndrome Emily has, amazed by all the surgeries. We explain the sleepiness today, the vomiting, how uncharacteristic this is for Emily. As the nurses are hooking Emily up to an EKG, preparing to run some tests, Emily begins to have a seizure.

We have learned how to pinpoint a seizure coming on. Emily's lips go grey, she looks frightened and disoriented, and she frequently wets her pants. At times, her eyes might flit back and forth in the sockets. She becomes clingy, whimpers, and then falls asleep to recover. An entire episode, start to finish, lasts thirty seconds to two minutes. Her seizures are unremarkable as seizures go, fairly mild, but scary nonetheless.

In the hospital bed, Emily's head moves back and forth, she licks her lips, vomits. I tell her, "It's okay, baby, Mom and Dad are right here." I remark to the doctor that because Emily's has been sleeping and throwing up all day, we haven't given her the seizure meds. Maybe this small seizure is a "breakthrough" one, her body not sustaining the correct amount of anticonvulsant chemical.

Dr. Bell leaves us to check on the lab results. She is not out the door a minute before Emily begins seizing like I have never seen before. Her body is jumping on the bed, back arching and limbs flailing. I holler down the hall for the doctor as Greg takes Lauren out. The doctor comes running, calling a Code Blue. Emily's bed is whisked down the hall to another room, a bigger one equipped with more machines and supplies.

The seizure goes on and on, one convulsion after another. Emily turns blue from lack of oxygen so they need to intubate her. An intubation kit is wheeled in, and two doctors stabilize Emily's head while another tries to insert the breathing tube. One try, two tries, Emily's head is cranked back at an unnatural angle and they still can't get the tube in.

I mention that Emily has tracheomalasia—her airway is floppy, not rigid, another of her many anomalies, and the doctors regroup, try again. This time, they get it. A powerful drug, Dilantin, is administered through her IV to stop the convulsions. Pretty soon, Emily is finally still, and her color is returning thanks to the oxygen tube.

I can hear Lauren, now that the commotion has stopped for the time being. She is in the ER playroom, traumatized by what she has seen, crying out for me. I hand signal Greg over the nurses' station that I will switch places with him. So Greg takes up my post at the head of Emily's bed, holding her hand, while I head to the playroom to placate Lauren.

The playroom is an attempt to distract sick kids or their siblings. The effort works for Lauren, who is fascinated by a plastic wagon, balloons, and a kiddie table with fish swimming in the transparent top. But I am not as easily distractable, pacing to and fro across the multicolored carpet, making feeble attempts to play. I am wondering why Emily was so sleepy, why the onset of these seizures, what could be causing this.

My thoughts are interrupted by another call of Code Blue. I peer outside the playroom to see doctors scurrying back to Emily's room. I can't tell what is happening, but I can see Greg's head over the others periodically. He emerges after several minutes, crosses the hall, and tells me the doctors here are out of their league. Emily needs to be transported to Sinai Hospital, where her neurologist and several of our other specialists practice.

Greg agrees to ride up to Sinai in the ambulance with Emily while I take Lauren home for the night. I plan to find a sitter for the next day so I can relieve Greg in the morning. As we kiss goodbye, I can smell Greg's fear. I imagine him in the ambulance, hunched over Emily's limp body, their faces swathed in the red-blue glare of the flashing lights.

# CHAPTER 62

The next day, a Sunday, I drop Lauren off over at Kathy's, who has agreed to watch her for the day. I hightail it up to Sinai, exceeding the speed limit the whole way. The house last night was eerie without Greg and Emily. I moved over to Greg's side of the bed, put my head on his pillow, held on to Emily's security blanket, and yet still I did not sleep.

I know exactly where to find Emily—the Pediatric Intensive Care Unit, where she was all those years ago. It may be my imagination, but it seems as if she is in the exact same room. When I round the corner, I find Greg, decimated with fatigue, lying back in one of the vinyl chairs next to the bed. Emily is all wired up on the bed, wearing a hospital gown, completely inert. She is scary-still, and I put my hand on her chest to see whether she is breathing.

Greg explains that Emily has been breathing on her own and has had no more seizures. It would be hard to have a seizure now, he says, she is practically comatose on drugs. The plan is to keep her pretty well sedated until they can run more tests. They have ordered an X-ray, a CT scan, an MRI, as well as blood tests. Emily is the Mystery Lady on the PICU today, everyone scrambling to solve the case.

I am on the day shift so Greg can go home to rest. I have brought a stash of pretzels, crackers, juice, and books. I have been forgetting to eat properly and stay off my feet to stay healthy for this baby I'm carrying. In the relative privacy of the hospital room, I can assuage my growing nausea with the crackers. This is definitely not the time to tell Greg about the pregnancy, but I won't be able to hide it much longer.

The day passes with long stretches of solitude, punctuated by technicians who wheel Emily down for the various tests. I walk along with her, down into the bowels of the hospital, where all the radioactive machines are. At the last minute, I remember to leave the X-ray room, doing the little I can to protect the baby, although I know its fate is already determined.

I am glad for the enforced rest of the day, a camp-out, of sorts, with drugged Emily. She hasn't moved a muscle all day. With an adult diaper on, she resembles a giant baby, especially with her pudgy cheeks. No one on the floor acts like this is a crisis, so I try to adopt their attitude. The doctors will figure it out, and we will get it fixed.

And figure it out they do. Emily's neurologist stops in at the end of the day, carrying her CT scan. She has a sinus infection, a severe one. The seizures occurred because her system was so compromised by the infection, her brain went haywire. The CT scan shows her nasal passages and forehead just packed with infected mucus. Even my layman's eye can see the helmet of pain my daughter is sporting.

I think back over the last few weeks, when this infection must have been forming. To miss an illness this severe seems negligent, so I revisit Emily's health, her mood, to see where I slipped up. Yet there was no fever, no runny nose, no coughing. Emily is not able to tell us if she is in pain, so if she had a wicked sinus headache, we would never know it.

It is yet another lesson learned. The clues to illness in Emily are subtle and not textbook. She has never "presented" normally, either physically or symptomatically. My eagle eyes were remiss in not picking up this infection. I blame myself, and I resolve yet again to be more observant in the future.

Emily is given an IV antibiotic and a take-home prescription for twenty days. That ought to kill this bug for good. The anticonvulsant medication is slowly dialed back, and she begins to come around. Emily is not happy to be in the hospital, angry at all the wires, tape, and gauze. She occupies herself for half an hour trying to pick the IV board off her wrist while the discharge papers are written.

At home, Emily still has enough medication in her system that she can't walk. She is loopy and cranky, so we put her to bed. Greg and I are so tired we can hardly see straight. Lauren is content to take an early bath and read books in bed. As we are getting ready for bed ourselves, Greg approaches me.

"Anything you want to tell me?" he asks. I look up at him, at the suspicion in his eyes.

"Nooooo," I hedge, trying to squirm my way out of this. Greg places a sheet of paper from our insurance company on the bed. One glance tells me that it is the benefit statement for the ultrasound I had two weeks ago. Clear as day, it says, "maternity costs."

I've got some explaining to do.

# CHAPTER 63

The time has come to face the music. I have been hiding this pregnancy from my own husband, and I need to fess up. This feels like it might be an ugly scene, so I draw on all the reserves I have, sit up straight in bed, and turn to Greg.

"I'm pregnant," I say, "about eight weeks along. It happened over Christmas when I was on those antibiotics. I'm so sorry—I never meant for this to happen and I was wrong to keep it from you. I'm just so scared and I could never find the right time to tell you."

Greg looks at me, at the floor, back at me again. His face is ashen. The fact of this pregnancy, plus my deception, has revved up his fear mode. He was almost back to trusting me, and now my omissions seem like another betrayal. And he's right. By not confiding in him right at the get-go, I become untrustworthy. I wonder how to make this right.

"The ultrasound looked good," I tell him, searching for a positive spin. "The doctor says so far, so good. We just have to get the genetic testing in a month. Maybe this baby is a second chance."

Greg swallows audibly. He is rendered speechless, mute with disbelief. He crawls into bed with me and turns away. I don't know where things stand, but I am leery of Greg's silence, his obvious disapproval. It does feel better, though, to have broken the silence and revealed my secret.

The next day, I am just about to make an appointment for the genetic testing when I approach Greg in his study. I ask him what day works with his schedule. He looks up at me, weary and afraid.

"I can't go through this again," he says, "it just hurts too much. Please call and get this taken care of right away."

"What are you talking about?" I retort, unbelieving. "Are you telling me to get an abortion before we even know if this baby is okay?"

"Jude, what are the chances that we'll have a healthy, normal baby? Look what's already happened to us. I can't put this family through that again." Greg reminds me that the doctor who terminated the last pregnancy gave us Plan B, in case of an accident. Although it is too late to use that now, the message is clear: You guys are not supposed to get pregnant again. He feels like a fool for our carelessness.

"What about Lauren?" I respond. "We could have another child like Lauren, a perfect child with no disabilities."

"What are the real chances of that, Jude?" Greg repeats solemnly. He has always been the voice of reason, excellent in a crisis, but now his realism smacks of coldness to me. I can't stomach his flat affect, his certainty. In fact, I can't even stay in the room. I turn on my heel, go into the family room, and sit on the couch, shaking. The nausea roils inside, exacerbated by stress. My stomach pooches out ever so slightly as I sit, and I lay my hand protectively on it.

It is way too early to feel the baby kick, but I swear I feel a pulse right under my belly button, a thrumming. I lick my lips, stand, and adjust my shirt down tight over my belly to emphasize the bulge. I march back into the study.

"No," I say. "I won't. I will not get rid of this baby if there's even the slightest chance that it's okay. I could never live with myself."

I can feel my face flaming with defiance. I am not good with conflict. I always end up crying, but this once I am courageous. I hope I am not burning bridges with Greg. I need his support through this.

So I make the appointment for a Wednesday in March, my mom's 62nd birthday. She doesn't even know about the pregnancy yet. I guess if I am going ahead with this, I will need to let a few people know what is happening, first of all my mom.

Mom stops over later that week to visit with the girls. She has been traveling and has brought trinkets back. We are chatting, drinking tea, when I ask her to pray for Greg and me. She immediately looks stricken. Neither she nor I are the praying type, so for me to invoke that word means something serious is up. When I divulge to her that I am pregnant again, she does her best to look happy and sound hopeful, but I know she is worried sick.

I ask Mom if she would like to accompany me to the genetic testing, even though it is on her birthday. She says there is nowhere else she would rather be. When I tell Greg that night, he is relieved to be off the hook. He doesn't want to see even the shadowy ultrasound shape, can't fathom falling the slightest bit in love with this baby.

The other wagons circle around, my friends, other family members. It helps to know that many people are pulling for us, are putting us in their prayers, but it pains me to see their worried faces. I can't imagine how I will make it through the next month.

# CHAPTER 64

I am not above superstition, and I will take any sort of sign these days. I take to wearing a necklace Greg got me for my birthday. I won't take it off to shower or exercise, wearing it day and night. It becomes an amulet of faith. I make bargains with God, promising to be the model mother, wife, and citizen if this baby is okay. I will do volunteer work, feed the hungry, help the poor.

Every craving becomes a harbinger of good news. Despite my mom's warnings of a stomach ache, I polish off an entire can of sauerkraut, cold. I am into salsa, salad dressings, tomato soup, and cheese. I tell myself that only a healthy baby would demand such an eclectic fare. Every wave of nausea, the tiredness, and tingling breasts are all good news.

Kathy and her husband Frank come over for game night. They joke with me about all the chips and salsa I am able to put away, exclaiming that things must be moving along well if I can be such a robust eater.

But I know this is all smoke screen. The health of this baby was determined at conception, and nothing I do now makes a whit of difference. But my superstitions help me to feel in control, and I need that right now.

March 8th is the day of the testing. Mom comes over early, chats with the girls, and tells Greg I will be fine. She promises to take good care of me during the exam. Greg looks torn, knowing he should be the one to accompany me on this trip, but he just can't make himself do it.

Up in Baltimore, I know the drill, could find the Center for Advanced Fetal Care in my sleep. As we walk out of the parking garage, Mom turns to me and haltingly says that maybe I should think about scheduling a termination before we leave today, just in case. She doesn't mean to sound pessimistic, it is just that she would hate to see me wait such a long time, like I did a year and a half ago.

I know she is just being pragmatic, like Greg. But I am inflamed that now a second person close to me won't show me hope, won't entertain the best-case scenario instead of the worst. I guess when enough disaster happens, you stop looking for the good.

At the office, Mom and I sit side by side in matching grey chairs. I am careful to stay far away from the chairs Greg and I sat in the last time. More superstition. I fill out the requisite paperwork, noting this as my fifth pregnancy, with only two children to show for it.

We have to wait for while, so I play the people-watching game. You never know the private pain people suffer, I think. Some of these women, judging by their age, have been trying for years to achieve pregnancy. Others have severe health problems that render pregnancy high risk. And here I sit, apparently very fertile, but with a bum's luck having a typically developing child. Creating a family has never seemed so precious.

Finally, it's my turn. First comes the genetic counseling session, again with Amanda. I am so pleased to see her, I nearly cry. Having a familiar face in this medical environment is a blessing. Amanda dispenses with the long explanation of the procedure, just reminding me that I will get an ultrasound first, then the CVS. My muscles tighten, remembering the catheter probing deep inside, pinching.

The ultrasound room and the sonographer are both new to me this time. I take this as another good sign. The room is warm and dark, only the glow of the screen illuminating the tech's face. My mom, a sonographer herself, leans in during the whole ultrasound.

She feigns motherly interest, but I know she is looking at the baby clinically, really inspecting it. I watch her face for any flicker, any expression at all.

The techs are trained not to say anything. It is not their business. But I am too anxious for convention. I ask her, "Does everything look okay?" She knows my history, has seen my chart, so maybe out of pity, she tells me, "As far as I can tell, everything looks good."

Mom grips my hand hard and nods. The physical structure of this little jumping bean looks good to her trained eye, so that is one hurdle crossed. The real test is with the chromosomes, though, and those are all inside.

We move into the next room, and I am situated on a bed with stirrups. The doctor enters and he is the same man, the beard and gruff manner. Maybe I imagine it, but he seems disheartened, like this job of checking on babies is too much for him. Maybe it pains him to look at me, the woman who plays Russian Roulette with children.

He inserts the catheter, nabs a bit of the placental tissue, and is done, lickety split. Of the three CVS's I have had, this one is the fastest. The doctor invites me to look at the genetic material he has collected, and I say a silent prayer, practically stroking the microscope.

Mom and I head home, stopping for salads. I obsess about the test at our lunch table, turning the wallet-sized ultrasound pictures this way and that in my hands, searching for clues. I can see the whole baby, all the limbs, the oversized belly and head. I am numb from fatigue and from the day, but I can feel my heart turning over in my chest.

At home, I need to head upstairs to rest. Before I go up, I point to my purse. Greg wonders what I am gesturing about.

"Want to see a cute baby?" I ask. I need a way to make him see, to make this real to him. He knows he can't refuse. He pulls out the length of pictures and flattens them on the counter.

"Ohhh," he murmurs, bending down for a closer look. I have heard that, for a man, actually seeing a picture of the baby is the first realization that his wife is pregnant. Greg is not very good at hiding his emotion, although he tries. I can see his face working for composure, eyes darting from one baby image to another.

He is not cold, I realize. He is scared out of his wits. He has been burned time and time again. This man I love wants this baby more than he can say.

# CHAPTER 65

I experience deja vu, all over again. The waiting, the pacing, and the endless "what ifs" play in my head. Everyone I know perches on pins and needles to hear about this baby. We haven't told Emily or Lauren a thing. How to explain someone who might not be? How to tell Emily that imperfection is unacceptable?

On Friday, two days after the CVS, we get the first-tier results. They are negative for Trisomy 18 or 21, just as we expected. The real results are in the more meticulous screening for the rare disorders. That is where our trouble lies. Amanda again asks me if I want to know the gender of the baby, and this time I say no. I don't want to envision my child, if I can help it. Vagueness feels good right now.

Lauren turns three next week, so I busy myself going to the party store, buying up all the Wiggles plates, tablecloths, napkins, and party hats they have. I scrub the house, do all the laundry, and straighten shelves and closets. Every time the phone rings, I jump.

At the end of the next week, I take Emily to the local hospital for a follow-up CT scan to see whether she has kicked the sinus infection for good. We park in the lot and head toward the automatic doors. Walking with Emily is an adventure, as she veers and careens in a haphazard fashion. But holding her hand feels good, and I swing her arm as we walk. I look up at the fourth floor of the hospital, the maternity floor, where I had Emily and Lauren, and the hairs on my arm stand up. I know, suddenly and without a shadow of a doubt, that the next time I enter this hospital will be to deliver this baby. The certainty of this feeling shores me up for days, pushing away doubt and fear.

On Tuesday, nine working days after the CVS, we still wait to hear. I go in early to Lauren's preschool to help set up the room, in overdrive from adrenaline and anxiety. At thirteen weeks pregnant, I have started to feel better, but I definitely look pudgy. No one at the school, except for Wendy, knows the ordeal we are enduring. I try to maintain the facade of business as usual, but I am so distracted I can hardly think straight.

After I leave Lauren at the preschool, I have two hours until I need to return. This window of time is tough, just enough to run errands or have a quick workout, but not long enough to accomplish anything major. I usually fritter away the morning, organizing the house or buying groceries.

Today is different. Heather has invited me to her new townhouse just a few miles from my home. In her infinite wisdom, she knows I need a long walk and a long talk. We take a vigorous hike along the trails surrounding her neighborhood.

The day is gorgeous, springtime taunting before it is really here. We chug up and down the hills, next to woodland and small creeks. I have known Heather since 1994, really my oldest friend. She prattles on, filling the air and all the worries in my head with family news and gossip. My cell phone bangs against my leg in the pocket of my windbreaker, mocking me with its silence.

I pick up Lauren at preschool, and then it is home for a simple lunch before naptime. My legs are tired from the long morning walk, so I decide to lie down for a minute in my favorite red upholstered chair. As happens so often lately, I am asleep within seconds.

I am awoken by an odd jingling, and in my sleep stupor I think for a moment it is the microwave timer, maybe the doorbell. I jump up and feel a distinct head rush from rising so quickly. It is not the doorbell or the timer—it is my phone, lying on the kitchen desk, ringing incessantly. I know before I answer that it will be Amanda.

"It's good news, Judith," she says, unable to hide the smile in her voice. "The baby's chromosomes are all present and all normal."

"I can't believe it," I say. "Are you sure?" I feel like I am floating above my body, looking down from above at a woman in a sunroom, clutching her shirt, falling to her knees.

"Everything is perfect," Amanda reiterates. "Do you want to know the sex?"

"YES!" I screech, then, "I mean, yes, please."

"You're going to have a boy."

• • •

I call Greg at his office and tell him he is going to have a son, that the baby is fine. Greg is mute, then sniffling. He has hardly allowed himself to think about the pregnancy at all, much less the possibility of having a son. The family line will continue after all.

I burn up the phone lines all afternoon, holding Lauren on my hip most of the time. She is aware something is going on and is agitated, clingy. When Emily gets home from school, she motors around me with her books, calling my attention to certain pages or pictures. I can't wait to tell the girls about their brother on the way.

When I call Kathy, her phone clatters to the floor and I lose the connection. I wonder what is up. Five minutes later, she and her son come barreling up the driveway, parking crookedly. Kathy runs up the sidewalk, hair flying, purse bouncing by her side. Before she can ring the doorbell, I open the door for her.

Kathy can hardly stand, is hugging me, crying, pushing a wadded brown bag into my hands. She is beside herself with relief, expelling the emotion I have been repressing all these weeks. She is my mirror image, a puddle of joy. It is not until this moment, with my friend framed in the doorway, that I know it is going to happen. I am going to have a little boy.

Kathy points to the brown bag. It is crumpled, the neck mushed into a lump; an offering.

"Open it," she says. "I had a feeling, and I hope it is right."

I unroll the bag, peer inside, and laugh with a snort. The bag contains a kid-sized baseball mitt and a baseball. Kathy didn't just purchase this. She has been keeping it at her house, waiting.

"I had a feeling," she explains again between sniffs. "I just knew the baby was fine, and I knew it was a boy."

I touch the baseball, feel the slick smoothness of the mitt. My fingers rise to stroke the center of my necklace, worn now nonstop for two months. Superstition is foolish, I know, but it seems to be my new thing—hoping for another chance.

When Greg gets home from work, his eyes find mine over the swarm of the girls' greetings. I can see in his eyes how relieved he is. He squats down, circling his arms around Emily's waist on his right and Lauren's on the left.

"Guess who's coming this summer, girls?" he asks. They both look at him, eyes wide. "You're going to be big sisters," he continues. "You're going to have a baby brother!"

# CHAPTER 66

The pregnancy makes me large and ungainly right away. I become a grunter, rising from any position with a cacophony of moans. Greg tells me this will be a big baby and it better be, with all this discomfort. With all the test results now in, I am hoping to relax, but that is not in my nature. I will be thirty-nine when I deliver, making this a high-risk pregnancy, normal chromosomes or not. Every few weeks brings yet another bloodletting, urine test, or ultrasound. As each exam confirms the health of the baby, I can feel the taut wire surrounding my heart give way just a bit. But I won't be able to totally relax until I see this little guy with my own eyes. I pray for a mild summer and an easy delivery.

In late spring, my sister Rachel flies out from Illinois to help me with Emily. At Emily's last dental appointment, her dentist noticed a cavity in a molar. This is normally a small thing for a typical kid, but with Emily, it is going to be a struggle. Emily has never opened her mouth voluntarily; indeed, she clamps it shut and writhes away, bellowing "UH-UH." The open-mouthed FACE that we still can't seem to banish is nowhere in sight when we need it. So, dental exams are a trial, as would be a filling.

One of the many nice things about living in such a suburban/ urban area is the wealth of pediatric specialties. We have certainly sampled our share in the last nine years. Now we get to investigate the field of pediatric dentistry and, more specifically, dentistry for "challenging" patients. There is a center up in Baltimore that is renowned for this, so off we go.

Emily needs a filling, a thorough cleaning, and a little sealant on her teeth to make them less permeable to decay. She will need to be sedated for all of this because it will take several hours. Although not technically called a surgery, it involves anesthesia, which is always dicey. Rachel knows how nervous I am about the entire thing, and her presence is a godsend.

We arrive at the hospital at 6:00 a.m., with no breakfast for Emily. Rachel walks her around, distracting her, while I fill out the paperwork and talk to a myriad of doctors. Emily's lengthy medical history is fascinating to them all, my written summary of all her procedures getting passed from hand to hand. But she is not a chart or a medical mystery; she is my child, and I want to get this over with and move on.

Emily is given a syringe full of chloral hydrate, the same substance used to induce sleepiness prior to her heart surgery all those years ago. I can hardly reconcile the big, gangly, noisy girl on the bed with that tiny baby. The chloral hydrate takes a while to kick in, so we read the Dentist Book, one of many laminated "social stories" made by her teachers and aides. A social story is basically a tale, using a series of photos of real children (including Emily), to reduce fears about an event. We have social stories for Getting a Haircut, Wearing New Clothes, and My New School. We even got one for Lauren's arrival, entitled My Baby Sister.

The story lulls Emily, whose fingers flip pages in a decrescendo of movement. Within minutes, she is whisked away and we are left to wait. We take up seats in the hospital lobby, pick up ratty magazines, fidget. A long time has passed since Rachel and I were alone together, without kids.

Rachel did not have children when Emily came along, but now has two, a girl and a boy. Being mothers together has bonded us, made us closer than ever. Rachel frequently apologizes for not being more aware of my struggles with Emily, for being absent when Emily was an infant.

But I am not a grudge holder. If I have learned anything, it is that people do the best they can do. To expect more sets up a vicious cycle of disappointment. I take Rachel's hand, put it on my rounded belly, gesture to the hospital around us, and say, "You are with me now."

After three hours, the surgeon comes out and signals us over to a window. The light coming in illuminates a set of films, X-rays of Emily's mouth. According to the surgeon, when they got in there, they were stunned by what they found. Emily's molar was decayed to the root, and there were three additional cavities. So she needed surgery after all, the extraction of the molar.

I feel terrible, negligent for letting my daughter walk around with, literally, a rotten hole in her mouth. The dentist assures me that it is not my fault, or Greg's, for not brushing properly. Rather, Emily's hyposensitive mouth doesn't swallow saliva effectively, nor does she swish and clean out her mouth with her tongue. Food stuck in her teeth stays stuck. From now on, an electric toothbrush is a must.

A relief descends to have the surgery over. Rachel and I are led back to the recovery area, where Emily is blotto. Her mouth gapes open, with crusts of blood and toothpaste at the corners. I clasp her hand, knead the long fingers. Emily in repose does not relax me, however. Her slack form looks more dead than alive, and I am anxious to get her out of here. So, too, are the recovery nurses. As soon as Emily so much as blinks, they haul over a wheelchair and try to hoist her inert body in. Try as we might, we can't get her to sit upright. She slides down in the seat, her backbone gone to jelly.

The medical system rears up all over again, too anxious to move out one patient in preparation for the next. Not even in command of her own body, Emily is wheeled out to the waiting car and dumped into the back seat. I decide to set my chagrin aside and head home. For once, I am thankful for all my practice with post-surgical recovery. I know pretty much what to expect and can take this haste, and Emily's semiconscious body, somewhat in stride.

Sure enough, Emily comes to at home, vomits copiously, sleeps all night, and then bounces back to her regular self by the next day. The dental saga is an ordeal I am loath to repeat, so I set about buying new toothbrushes, one for downstairs and one for upstairs. I cross my fingers for no more cavities and no more surgeries. The next time I see the inside of a hospital, I hope, is when this baby makes his appearance.

# CHAPTER 67

Evan Gregory comes along on September 15th, almost precisely ten years after Emily was born. Evan is the name we picked all those years ago if Emily had been a boy. I nickname him "Evan from Heaven." He looks like a mixture of Greg and Emily, with my nose. There is a certain symmetry to a decade gone by between my first and last children. This little boy completes the family, completes me. With his birth, a calmness settles over me, a stillness that feels oddly right. I haven't been still in so long.

I am tired after the birth, a wrenching, raw sensation pervading my entire body. I can't get comfortable on the hospital bed, so I scootch off and perch on the chair in the corner. The nurse brings Evan in, checks our ID bands, and then lets me nurse him as I sit. He falls into the slack-jawed sleep of the newly born, and I put him back in the bassinet.

I have a photo album here at the hospital, a cheap plastic booklet with a few family pictures. They say babies respond best to the human face, so I thought I would show Evan his family. I talk to his swaddled body as I page through, explaining Daddy, Mommy, Emily, and Lauren. Through his sleepy haze, I hope he can hear my voice, my love. I stop at each picture, examining all the faces, tracing our similarities, the green and blue eyes of me and Greg, and of our children.

The picture of Emily is one taken of her years ago. It was one of those perfect days at the playground, when Emily was finally able to explore her newfound mobility. She spent the day marching around, asserting her independent self. In this picture, she is in a swing, throwing back her head with abandon, hair flying in the breeze. Her smile is a mile wide. I can almost hear her laughter.

I trace her face in the picture with my fingertip, then her red overalls, smiling myself at the memory of that day at the park. I can see shades of my own child self in Emily, the full face, the white hair. My oldest, the most similar in looks to me. I wonder now if my struggles with Emily were mostly just struggles with me.

Having a newborn again throws the routine at home out of whack for a time, but before long, we are up and running again, order established. I take a perverse glee in managing the juggling act that three kids present. We still get everything done, although not very quickly. Emily is oblivious to her brother for a time, then six months later, suddenly seems to realize he is here to stay.

"Baby Evan," she bellows, pointing to him, flapping with excitement. She won't hold him or touch him, but it is a start. Lauren is the little Mommy, helping to comfort Evan and doing little jobs for me. It is something to see, all their fair heads lined up on Emily's bed for story-time or in the car.

When Evan is about seven months old, I take Emily to a birthday party for a classmate of hers. Her friend, Parker, has autism, but his twin brother does not. The party is for both of the boys at a local bowling alley, and I am thrilled to go on this venture with Emily. Our together time has dwindled greatly since Evan's birth, and I find myself missing her.

On the way up to the bowling alley, I rub Emily's arm over in the passenger seat. She rifles through the CDs, pitches several onto my lap and gestures to one she wants. Emily is a music lover, for sure, and we sing loudly, laughing with each other. Emily's adult teeth have come in, and her mouth zig-zags with her crooked smile. She still has the pillowy cheeks of a baby and those smoky hazel eyes.

At the bowling alley, kids yell and balls thwack into pins. I worry that the stimulation will be too much for Emily, but she takes it in stride. She is the only girl at the entire party, having reached the age where childhood parties are segregated into boy—girl. Her friends from her Academic Life Skills class have their parents with them because they can't be left unattended, but the other "typically developing" classmates of the twin brother are all on their own. The bowling alley is a sea of fourth-grade boys with spiky hair and attitude.

Once all the kids' names have been entered into the computer scorekeeper, it is time to play. I wonder how Emily will fare here, what my role will be, and I sit back to let events unfold. There is pizza to munch on, French fries, and balloons galore. The lanes echo with a cacophony of preteen fun.

When Emily's turn rolls around, the boys yell for her and then pull her to her feet from the chair where she is stationed. A little blond-haired boy named Zack guides her over to the balls and selects one he thinks is light enough for her to carry. He escorts her to the lane and then helps her set the ball on a ramp contraption specially arranged for disabled players. Then he urges her to push the ball, his voice rising as he says, "C'mon Emily!"

Emily watches her ball roll down the lane, hands flapping, squealing. Her ball wobbles a bit, skirts the edge of the lane, and then lazily takes out four pins with a decisive clack. The boys clap and yell for Emily and then lead her back to the bay for her second turn.

A lump rises in my throat so big I almost choke. Emily is something to see, my lurching, spinning girl in the company of all these young boys, being helped, being cheered, being accepted. My dream has always been to watch this little girl joining with the others, more like them than different, more a part of things than alone.

# CHAPTER 68

Most of the time, Greg is on Emily bath duty. He has bathed her all her life, practically, and they have a routine of songs and clapping. She needs help getting in and out of the tub, and she is getting too big for me to lift, so I usually opt out of the ritual. It stands to reason that Greg is naturally perplexed one evening when I ask if I can do the bathing detail with Emily. I leave him downstairs with the two little ones and commence the night-night song to entice Emily upstairs.

I can't explain my sudden impulse to give Emily her bath. The chore is physically demanding, and I am wiped from nursing Evan all day and being with the kids. Still, I long for some more time with Emily, a real rarity these days.

Emily strips her clothes off, a new skill she performs with pride. She dumps the dirty clothes in the laundry and then walks down the hall to pee. Her eyes are glazed from a hard day at school, but she goes through all the motions without a hitch. Greg has her programmed, that's for sure. When I ask Emily if Mommy can give her a bath, she squeals and flaps.

Emily sits in the tub, much like a baby would. She likes to splash and blow bubbles, generally creating a ruckus during her brief time in the water. I soap up a washcloth and clean her, top to bottom. She is remarkably compliant for such a tired child. Even rinsing her hair is not a challenge, as she lets the warm water run down her face, blinking and darting her tongue out to catch the drips.

I help Emily out of the tub and then place her on the floor to towel her off. This is where she often loses it, pitches a fit, and just wants to be done. I sing a soft song, "Clementine," while I ruffle her hair. Her skin is patchy with dry flakes, so I rummage for some cream.

Emily lets me douse her with the lotion, a real miracle. I remember the deep pressure massage we did with her as a baby, the rhythmic circular motions that would relax her. I try to duplicate that feeling, rubbing lotion down her arms, her chest, and her legs.

When I rub her chest and her tummy, I become acutely aware of her heart surgery scar and the budding breasts on either side. The scar is white now, a tiny river meandering between the twin hills of her breasts. I know in Emily's womanhood, the shadows of her breasts will obliterate the scar.

I am struck suddenly, an almost physical blow, right there in the bathroom, with my love for this girl. I am not enfeebled or disabled by Emily. I realize that now. Just as she is not solely defined by her diagnosis, neither am I. I am enriched and made more compassionate for Emily's presence in my life.

As I pull Emily's nightshirt over her head, I kiss her lightly on the cheek and then run a chain of kisses down her scar. The skin is so tender and translucent I want to weep. Amazing how time has almost healed this scar completely, has almost healed me.

# EPILOGUE

One day when Emily is about three years old, we set off to go visit Greg at work. We make this trek about twice a year, for the adventure of the Metro ride as much as for the fun of seeing Daddy at work. I have packed quarters for parking and a small lunch. We are ready to go.

Emily is a good traveler, staying in the stroller while I wheel her through the Metro station and onto a southbound car. She snacks from a plastic tray attached to the stroller, a trail mix of Cheerios and raisins. I am in my shell, trying to deflect the stares that inevitably come our way when we are out and about.

By age three, people can definitely tell something is wrong with this child. Emily doesn't talk, using grunts or sign language to convey her needs to me. Plus, she is so little for her age and not walking yet. The signs are there, obvious. So, I use tunnel vision to shut out any observers, protecting myself, protecting her.

But on this trip, I can't ignore the lady across the aisle. She comes huffing onto the train one stop after us, shifting her considerable weight from side to side. She is a black lady, middle-aged, wearing an eggplant-colored ensemble. Her skirt is rucked up crookedly, and her hair, or maybe her wig, is unnaturally formed, unusually dense. She rummages through her purse, chuckling to herself, fiddling with her many bracelets. I can tell she is staring at us, and I studiously avoid her gaze. I think she might be crazy.

She gets off at Takoma Park, before us. As she maneuvers out the door, she passes me a slip of paper. I am alarmed at first, not wanting to get involved with her rantings or obsessions. But my curiosity gets the better of me, and when the doors close behind her, I allow myself a peek.

The paper wad is a receipt of some kind, maybe from a drugstore. It is smudged and crinkled. I am about to toss it away when I notice something has been written with a slanting hand on the back. I turn it over.

*"Know that You are One of God's Best, because He Gave You Her."*